IMAGES
of America

MADISON COUNTY

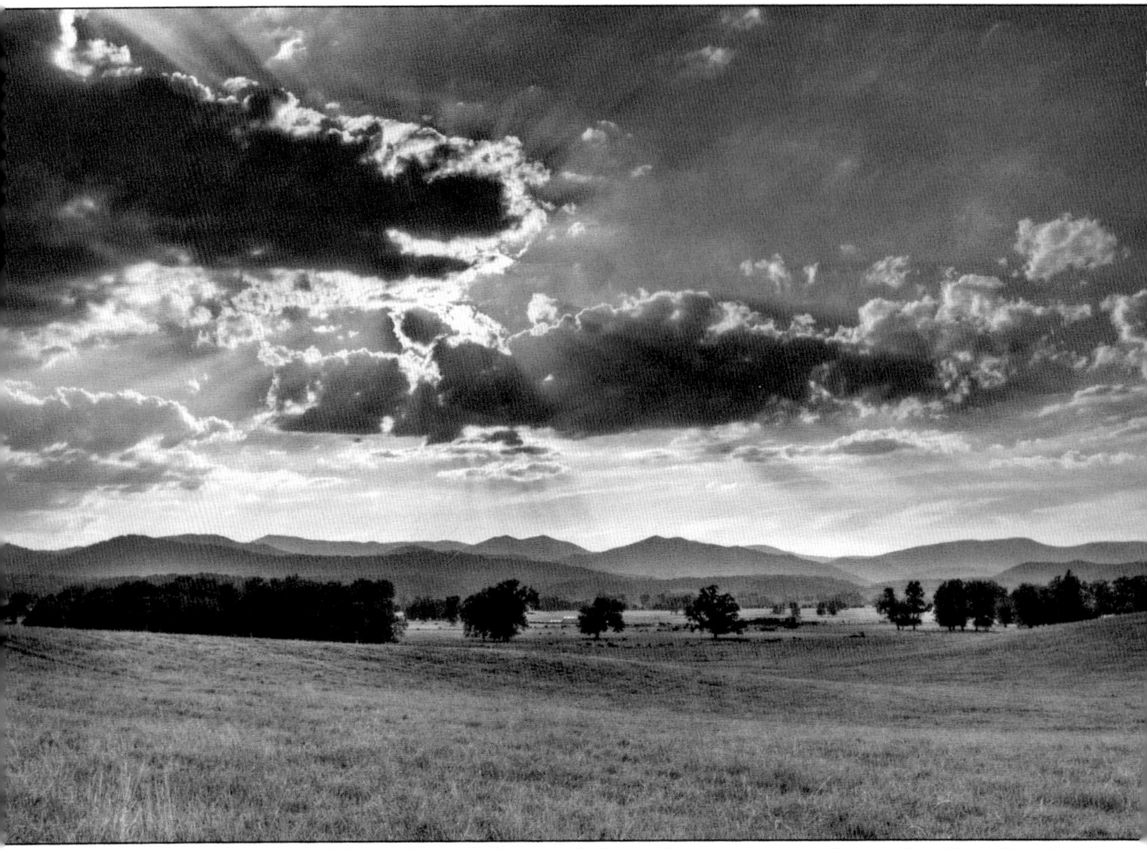

This photograph is of the Hebron Valley in Madison County. It is a rich, gently rolling farmland, shielded by the Blue Ridge Mountains, well-watered and well-warmed. Early settlers of Madison County started their farms here in the early 1700s. Native Americans used the resources of the valley 10,000 years ago. It is the heart of Madison. (Photograph by John Berry.)

ON THE COVER: Thanks to all of the good neighbors who brought their tractors to help with spring plowing on the Hume Lillard farm in Graves Mill, the job got done. Lillard spent time in the hospital in February 1953 and came home faced with the daunting task of preparing the ground and planting corn. Madison County neighbors are the best. (Ruth and Randall Lillard.)

IMAGES
of America

MADISON COUNTY

Trish Crowe and Doris Lackey with
the Madison County Historical Society

ARCADIA
PUBLISHING

ISBN 978-0-7385-8720-2

Published by Arcadia Publishing
Charleston, South Carolina

Printed in the United States of America

Library of Congress Control Number: 2010934563

For all general information, please contact Arcadia Publishing:
Telephone 843-853-2070
Fax 843-853-0044
E-mail sales@arcadiapublishing.com
For customer service and orders:
Toll-Free 1-888-313-2665

Visit us on the Internet at www.arcadiapublishing.com

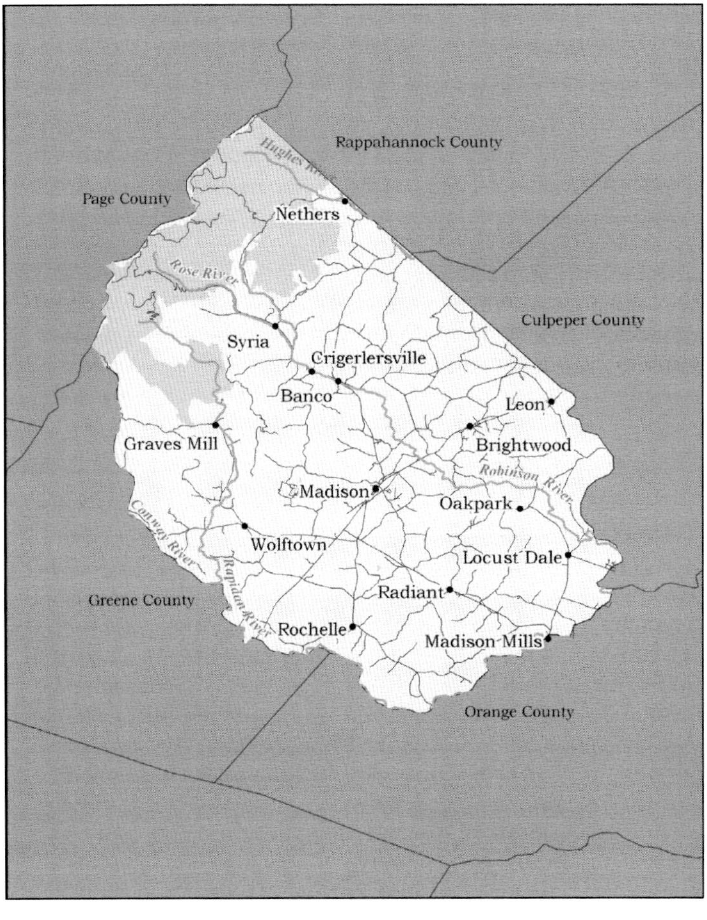

This map of Madison County is designed to show the major rivers that border or flow through the county and the location of the oldest villages and crossroads. The shaded area depicts the land encompassed by Shenandoah National Park. (Jessica Hardesty.)

Contents

Acknowledgments

Many people have made significant contributions to the creation of this book, contributions that are essential to its achievement. To the team that spent numerous hours researching, gathering photographs, scanning pictures, and managing the database, we are particularly grateful. Madison County Historical Society curator Beppy White contributed hours of writing and fact-checking, Mary Wright provided organizational and computing services, and Charles Moncrief designed the database used to store over 600 photographs. We are grateful for the work of Madison County historians Margaret Davis, Vee Dove Tull, Dewey Lillard, Harold Woodward, Doug Graves, and the late Claude Lindsay Yowell, who established the place and context from which to tell the Madison County story. We also appreciate the help of archaeologist Dr. Carole Nash and architectural historian Ann Miller, who told us about Madison's earliest times. To readers and editors Susan Pell and Eugene Ince, we offer much gratitude. The Madison County Historical Society, its board and members, gave us support and encouragement that is much appreciated. Finally to all those who allowed their personal reminiscences and photographs to be included in this book we say a heartfelt thank you. This is your book.

INTRODUCTION

The granite underlying the Blue Ridge Mountains that mark the western border of Madison County is about one billion years old. Human beings have been living among these mountains for 11,000–12,000 years, but the first European saw them only 350 years ago. Madison County as a political entity is just 218 years old. Its history, in terms of its mountains, is like the blink of an eye, but is interesting nevertheless. The purpose of this little book is to relate with many pictures and few words the story of Madison County and its people that has developed over the years. As one turns the pages, old friends and relatives may be seen, perhaps even oneself a bit younger.

Madison County's recorded history begins with John Lederer's late-17th century visit to western Virginia and Governor Spotswood's rollicking ride over the Blue Ridge with the Knights of the Golden Horseshoe in the early 1700s. Early Madison was populated by individuals and by communities of people bound together by cultural similarity who settled together throughout the county. The Germans of the Hebron Valley who were one of the first groups to settle in a community are an example. English settlers populated the southern, eastern, and western parts of the county. Some Scots-Irish and others chose the mountains and they and their descendents made a hard living there. All the people who settled in Madison County faced hardships in the early years but the lives of the mountain folk were particularly affected in the 20th century by the chestnut blight, the Great Depression, and the formation of Shenandoah National Park.

Once there were more than three billion American chestnut trees east of the Mississippi. One quarter of the trees covering the Appalachian Mountains were American chestnuts. In 1640, Spanish adventurer Hernando DeSoto recorded that the mountains were white with the bloom of chestnut blossoms. The trees' products of wood, bark, and nuts were important to the mountain settlers for their own use and as a money crop. A fungus, which was deadly to the American chestnut tree, was accidentally imported to North America around 1900 and by 1940 had destroyed almost all of the billions of mature trees.

The tragedy of the chestnut blight was compounded by the Great Depression of the 1930s. Falling prices for their produce hurt all farmers. Business activity declined. Jobs were lost and unemployed men looking for work were everywhere. Necessary supplies were frequently purchased by barter rather than with cash. Not only the mountain families but the whole county suffered during the Great Depression, as did the rest of the state and nation. But agriculture continued to be the county's economic bedrock, and businesses in Madison County continued to develop manufactured goods and provide services. Most of these remained local but some grew into large enterprises with statewide and even nationwide consumers.

Shenandoah National Park was established in 1935. Almost 200,000 acres of Virginia was ceded to the federal government by the Commonwealth of Virginia in an area about 80 miles long along the crest of the Blue Ridge. The western extremity of Madison County lies within the park. A number of mountain families lived in this area. The policy of the state government was to remove private occupants from park property. Poverty and hard times in the mountains encouraged some families to take the compensation the government offered and they left of their own accord. Some of the older people who wanted to stay were granted life tenancy. But the requirement to remove some mountain families forcibly caused much distress and is still a hard memory for some Madison County citizens.

Sunday mornings find a good many Madisonians on their way to church. The early hegemony of the Anglican Church as the official church inhibited the establishment of other denominations while Virginia remained a colony. After independence, the separation of church and state became a political issue that was settled by the first amendment to the Constitution of the United States. Freed of restraint, other denominations, particularly Baptist, developed rapidly in the county.

Education and the establishment of schools was a priority for the first settlers. The school set up by Hebron Lutheran Church in the 1740s was open to all children and lasted for almost 100 years. In the early 19th century, old field schools were built by communities, which also paid teachers' salaries. The state became responsible for public schools in 1870, but funding was scarce and private schools continued to grow. Locust Dale Academy, established in 1858, and Woodberry Forest School, established in 1889, were both private college-preparatory high schools.

There is great natural beauty in the mountains and rivers and forests and fields of Madison County and there is much natural wealth in the soil. However, the real worth of Madison County is in the people who have tended its forests, tilled its fields, loved its springtime, and weathered its storms. These Madison citizens are farmers, teachers, business people, politicians, soldiers, preachers—men and women of all races and religious persuasions, all of whom have made individual contributions to the quality of life in Madison County. Only a few are pictured in these pages. There are many more.

Madison County people have taken some part in all the wars that have been fought by American troops since the French and Indian War ended in 1756, but only two battles have actually been fought within the county. Union and Confederate cavalry forces clashed at Jack's Shop near Rochelle and again at James City near the border with Culpeper County in 1863. The county suffered heavily during the Civil War, as did the rest of Virginia and all of America as men were killed, died of wounds, or died from illness far from home. Casualties during later wars were fewer but no less tragic.

On May 1, 1793, Madison County became officially separated from Culpeper County. In June of the same year a two-acre lot was purchased in the central part of the county on which to build a courthouse. This area was called Madison Courthouse and it was the county seat. In the 19th century, Madison Courthouse was incorporated as the town of Madison and grew to become a thriving community of 500 people. Today the population of the town is only 215 people and the population of the county is nearly 14,000.

Madison County people think that controlled growth may be all right but they have watched with great concern as the pastures and woods of other Virginia counties have been transformed into rows of townhouses and acres of asphalt. Madison people treasure the farms and homes that are part of their county's history. While much may be said at election time about inviting industry into the county to increase the tax base, there is a very strong sentiment in favor of keeping the county rural and green, and keeping agriculture as its major enterprise.

One

Early History

Colonial Virginia was originally divided into eight shires that were later called counties. The land that eventually became Madison County was part of the areas of York and Northumberland Shires. Only Native Americans inhabited the western expanses of these shires in the foothills of the Blue Ridge Mountains. These tribes hunted and fished in the Piedmont area for more than 10,000 years.

A series of divisions created new counties from the old as western European expansion increased. Spotsylvania County was created in 1721. Orange County grew out of Spotsylvania County in 1734. Orange gave birth to Culpeper in 1748, and Madison was formed from Culpeper in 1792.

The explorer John Lederer, who crossed the Rappahannock and the Rapidan Rivers from the east in 1669–1670, may have been the first European to see Madison County's mountains. In his journal he described the area as "a hilly country with small rivers."

In 1716, Gov. Alexander Spottswood led a group of friends who called themselves the Knights of the Golden Horseshoe on an expedition that passed through much of what would become Madison County. They were looking for a pass through the Blue Ridge Mountains to the Shenandoah Valley.

Madison County did not exist as a political entity when the independence of the 13 colonies and their establishment as states took place. The Revolutionary War was fought before Madison County was partitioned from Culpeper County, but many men from the Madison area served in the Revolutionary forces.

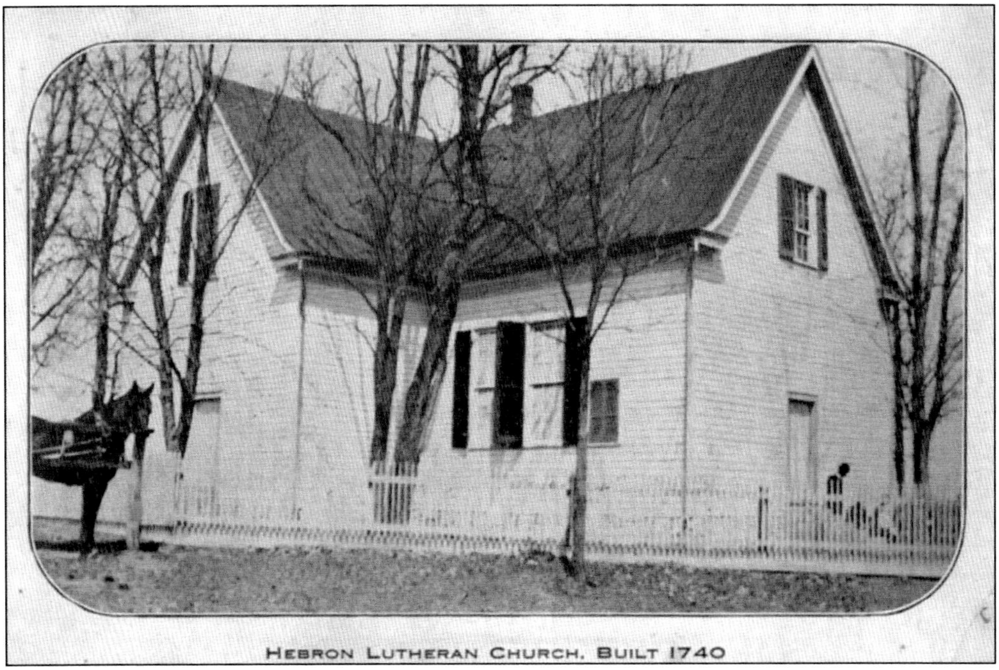

The Hebron Lutheran Church is the oldest Lutheran church in the United States in continuous use by Lutherans. A section of the original 1740s church is a part of the structure today. By 1748, a two-room community school built by the congregation was open to all children in the area. It may have been the first public school in Virginia. (Steve Grayson.)

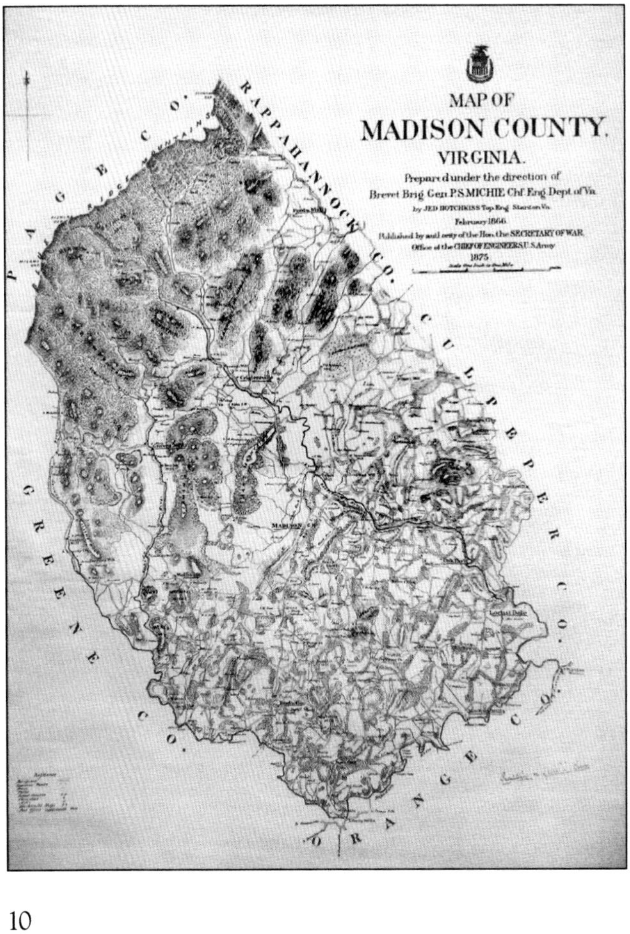

This map of Madison County was prepared in 1866 by topographical engineer Jed Hotchkiss of Staunton, Virginia. Hotchkiss served as a cartographer for the Confederacy during the Civil War and continued map-making after the war. This map is a part of the Hotchkiss collection on file at the Library of Congress. (Madison County Historical Society.)

This is the oldest known marked gravestone in Madison County. It reads "Here Lies the Body of Lucy Taliaferro, Died Nov. 4, 1729." The tombstone is in an old private graveyard on a farm near Rochelle in the southern part of Madison County. The Taliaferro name is an old name in Madison County but her connection to a family could not be found. (Madison County Historical Society.)

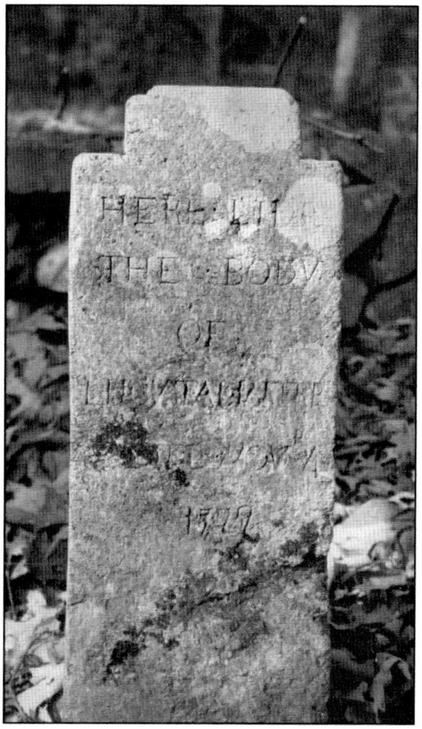

The Blue Ridge Turnpike, built around 1850, connected Gordonsville to New Market. It was a toll road built by a private company. The turnpike ran through the center of Madison County and crossed the Blue Ridge Mountains near Syria. It was along the Blue Ridge Turnpike that the Graves family established their first ordinary in the 1850s. (James and Rachel Graves.)

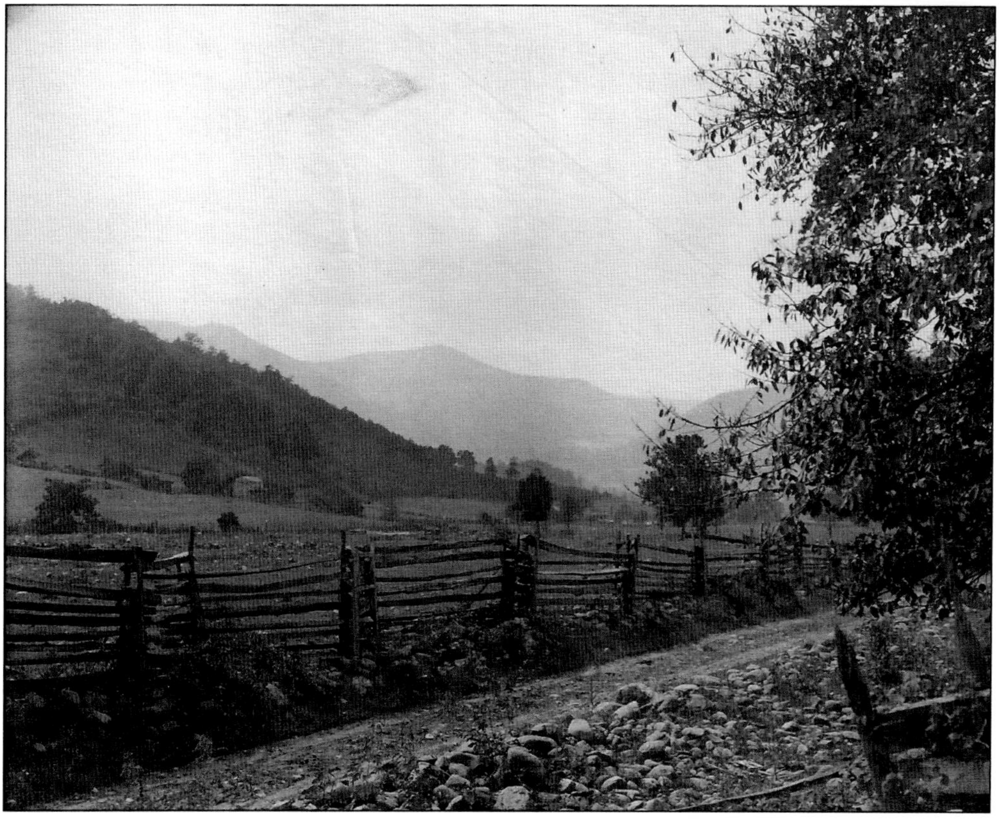

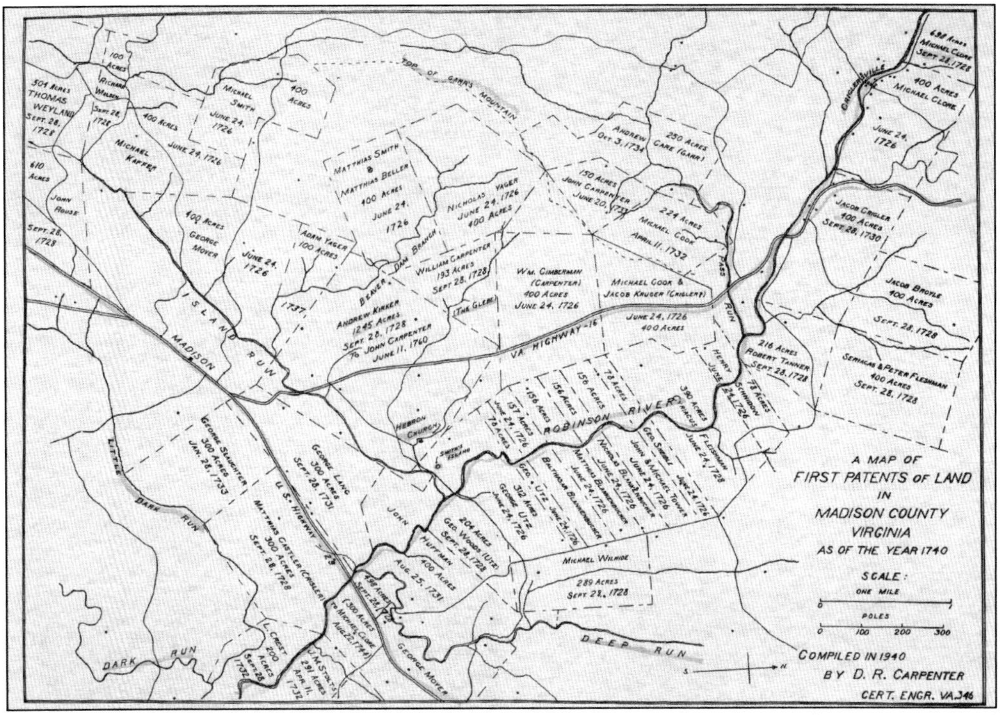

This map shows the location of the earliest land patents in Madison County that were acquired by German settlers. These land patents were in place by 1740, though some had been attained years earlier. They are primarily located in and around the Hebron Valley. The cartographer, who compiled the map in 1940, shows the location of the later town of Madison and Virginia Highway 16, which is now Route 231. (Cartographer Delmar R. Carpenter; courtesy of Madison County Library.)

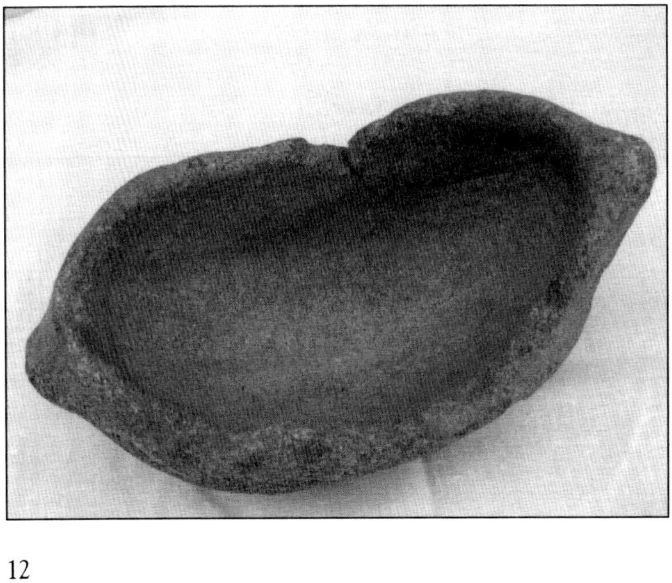

This approximately 4,000-year-old Native American bowl was found in a cave on Blakey Ridge in Madison County in the 1970s. It is made of steatite (soapstone), a stone that is found in the Virginia Piedmont area. Archaeologists have discovered many artifacts to substantiate significant movement by Native American tribes throughout the area as much as 10,000 years ago. (Madison County Historical Society.)

Two

Communities and Crossroads

Madison County was settled both by individuals seeking new land and new homes, and by small groups of people united by some characteristic held in common, like nationality, religion, or political belief. The German ironworkers indentured to Governor Spotswood were settled by him in Orange County in a place he named Germanna. When they were able, many left Germanna and moved into what would become Madison County, establishing a community of Germans living primarily along the Robinson River and White Oak Run.

At about this same time, a group of Quakers settled in the future Madison County. In 1726, William Rush, known to be a Quaker, patented 400 acres of land on what became Quaker Run near Criglersville.

English people from the predominately English Tidewater region of Virginia also moved into the Madison County area. In 1726, Joshua Fry was the first Englishman to patent land in Madison when he took possession of 1,000 acres in the area known as Locust Dale. It is not clear that Joshua Fry ever lived in the Madison area, but his son, Henry Fry, built a home on his father's land near Locust Dale, now called Meander.

Eventually other groups established themselves. More than two centuries later, the first Mennonites moved into Madison County. In the 1950s, five families moved to Madison County, establishing a community that has contributed significantly to the quality of life in the county.

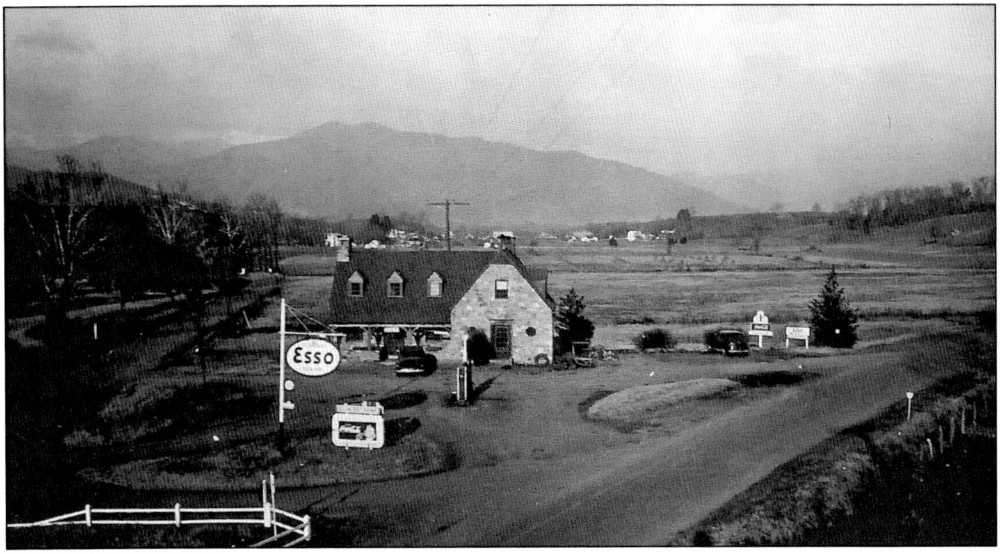

This view of the old Greystone Inn was taken in 1945. The Robinson River runs through this valley of rich farmland. The Coates family farm is seen in the background as well as the village of Criglersville. Doubletop Mountain appears to be guarding the valley below. Fork Mountain is also seen on the left. (Lillian Mitchell and Robert Finks.)

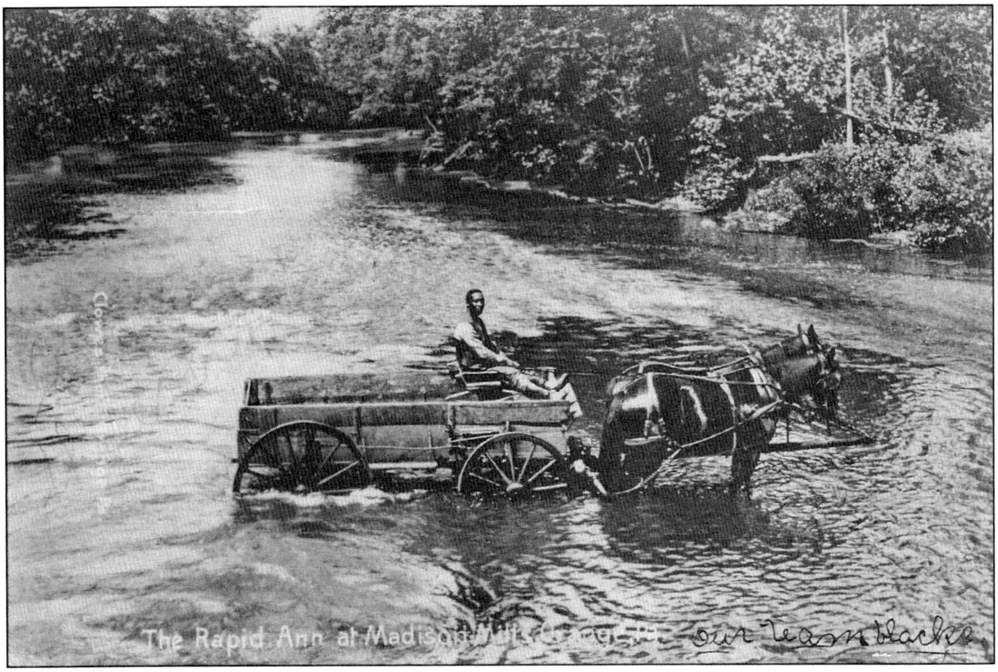

Bridges were scarce in Madison County in the late 1800s and early 1900s, but there were numerous fords across the rivers. Here a man stops to rest his team in the Rapidan (Rapid Ann) River near Madison Mills. His wagon is empty and it is believed that he had carried a load of goods to the town of Orange, unloaded there, and was returning home. (Steve Hoffman.)

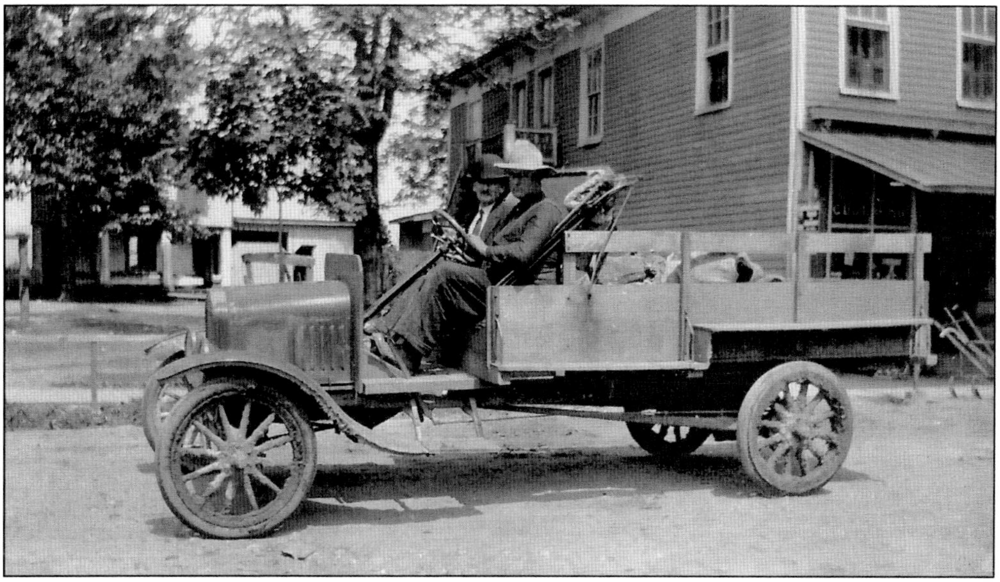

This is a mail truck on Main Street in front of Court Square. The old Banks Store (Gibbs and Estes) is in the background to the right. (Katherine Clore Craft.)

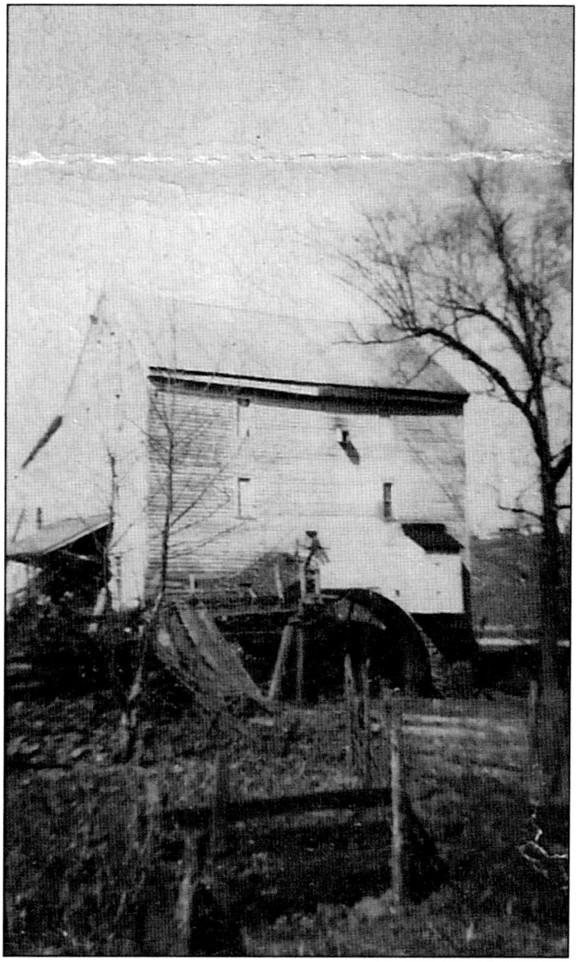

Repton Mill, near Old Pratts, is one of many mills in Madison County that served early settlers who brought their wheat and corn for grinding. Access to a mill was essential to every community. The first mill permit in Madison County was issued to James Madison Jr. on the Rapidan River in the area now known as Madison Mills. (Gertha Houston.)

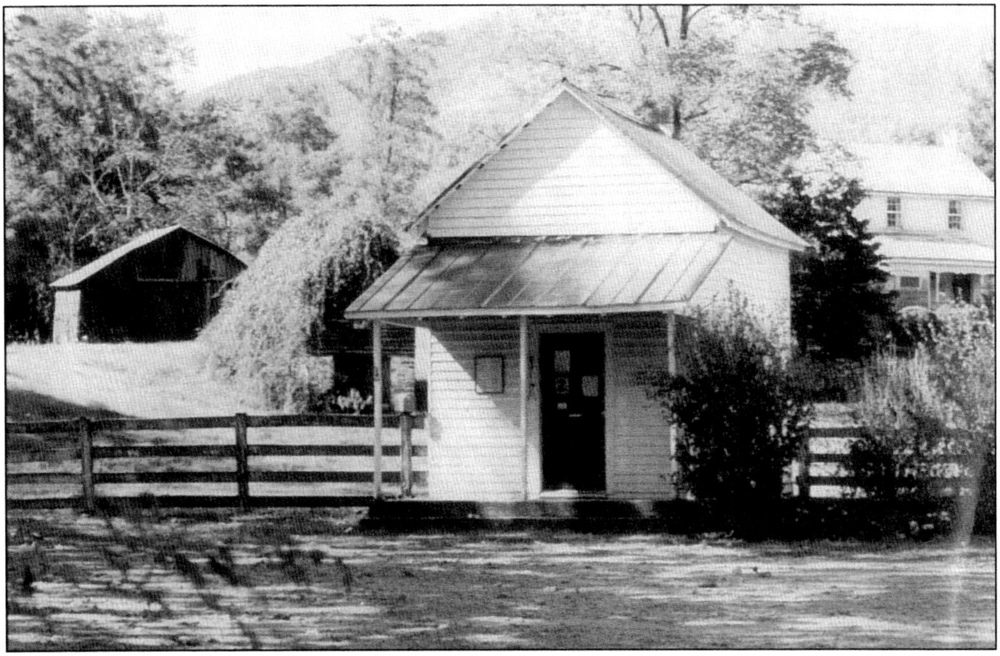

This was the Graves Mill Post Office until the flood of 1995 washed it away. It replaced the post office in the old Elmo Utz store in 1956. Dolly Seekford was the first postmistress in this building, which had been donated by the Bacon family of Graves Mill and moved to this location by Buck Hawkins and other men of the community. (Ruth and Randall Lillard.)

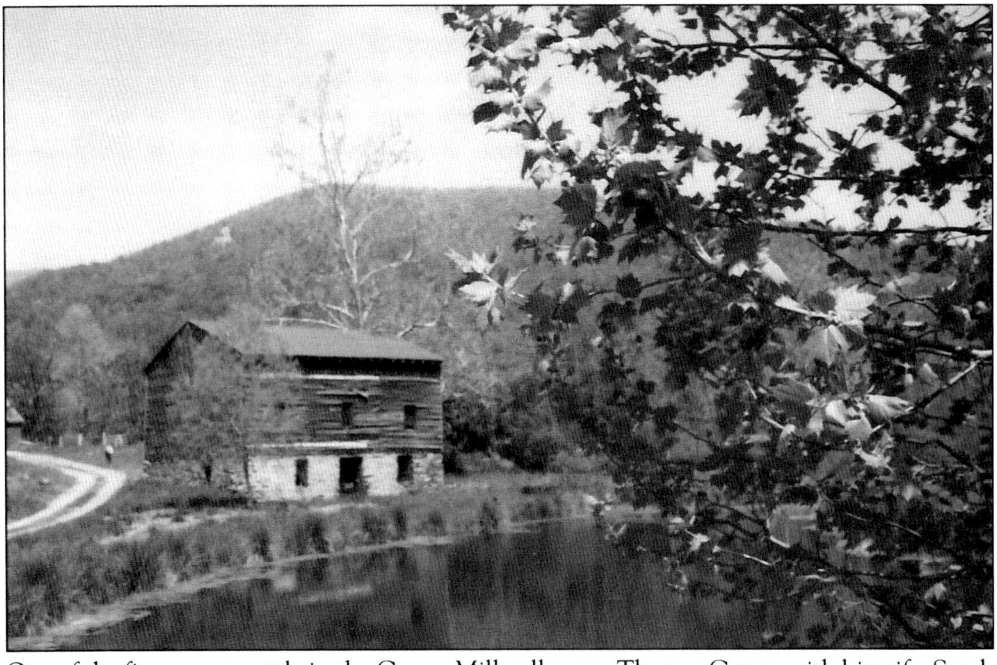

One of the first men to settle in the Graves Mill valley was Thomas Graves with his wife, Sarah Dulaney, in the 1750s. The Graves Mill area had fast-moving streams suitable for a mill. The Graves Mill Gristmill was built of wood and stone and served local families for 150 years. In the 1800s, flour was shipped to the deepwater port in Fredericksburg for export. (Shirley Estes.)

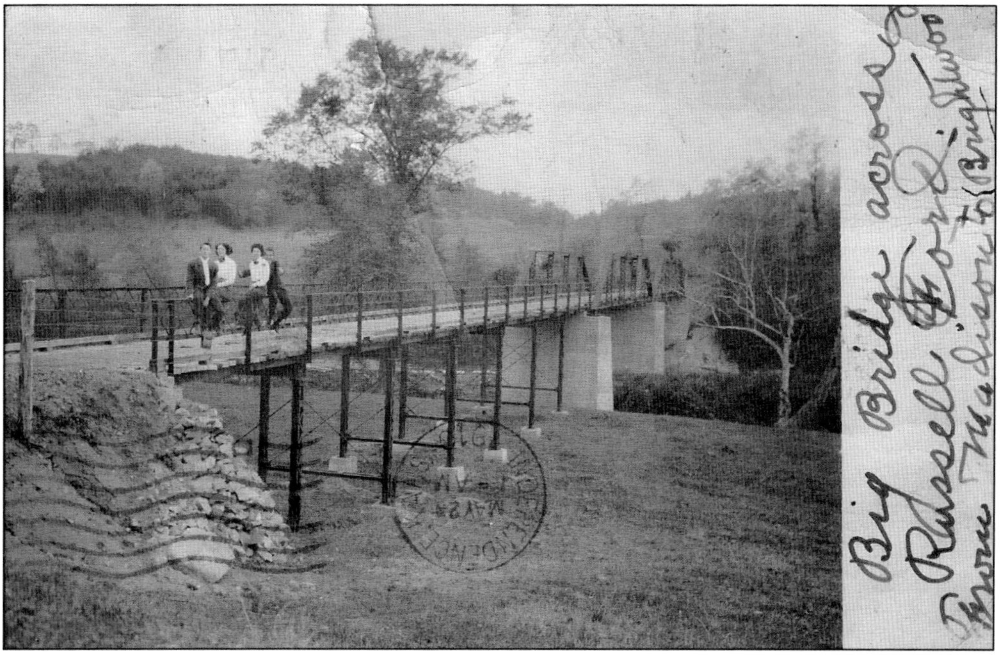

The bridge at Russell's Ford was important for county residents' transportation. It crossed the Robinson River on present-day Route 29 between Madison and Brightwood. This postcard is postmarked 1910. (Steve Hoffman.)

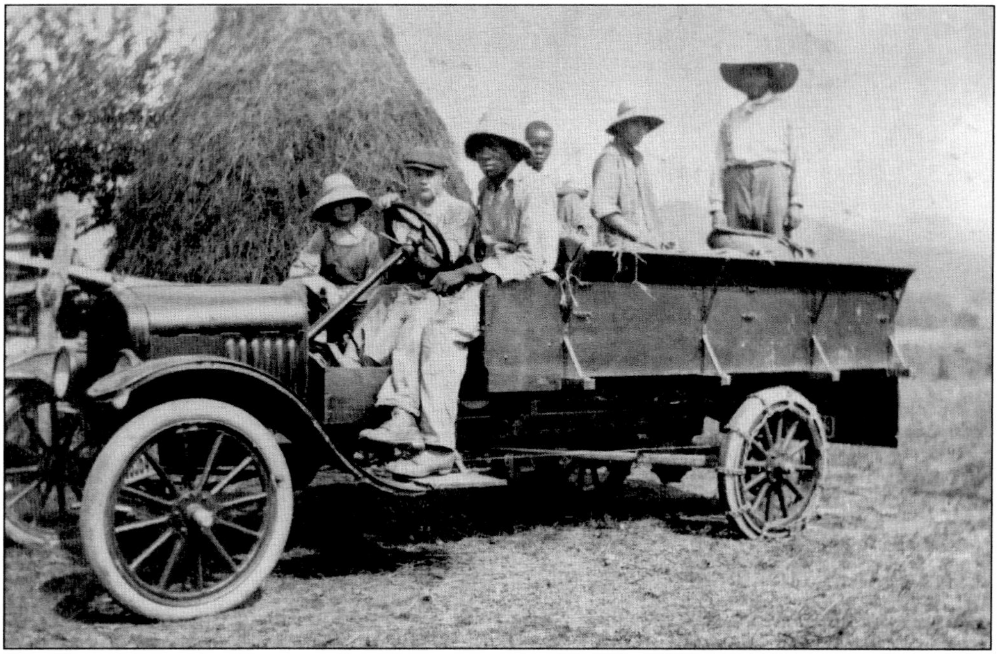

This 1919 Model T truck with solid rubber tires was purchased in Baltimore, Maryland, without a body. Two men drove it to Madison sitting on the gas tank, reported to be a very uncomfortable ride. At his shop in Old Pratts, James Beauregard Lacy later built the body. In the front seat, left to right, are Mildred Hood Daniel, Haywood Hood, and Eddie Lee Terrell. The riders in the back are unknown. (Ruth and Randall Lillard and Mary Hood.)

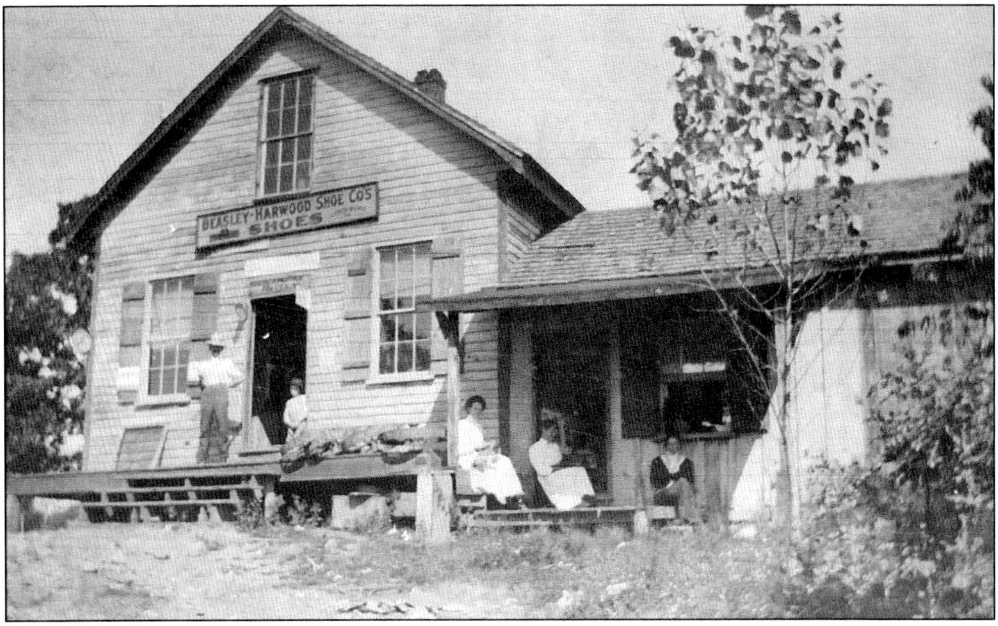

This postcard shows the Old Pratts store and post office There is a sign for the Beasley-Harwood Shoe Company above the door. Mada Gibbs ran a seamstress shop in the store and ladies of the community met there once a month to exchange seed bags, which they used for cloth to make clothes. Later the store became a general merchandise and millinery shop. (Steve Hoffman.)

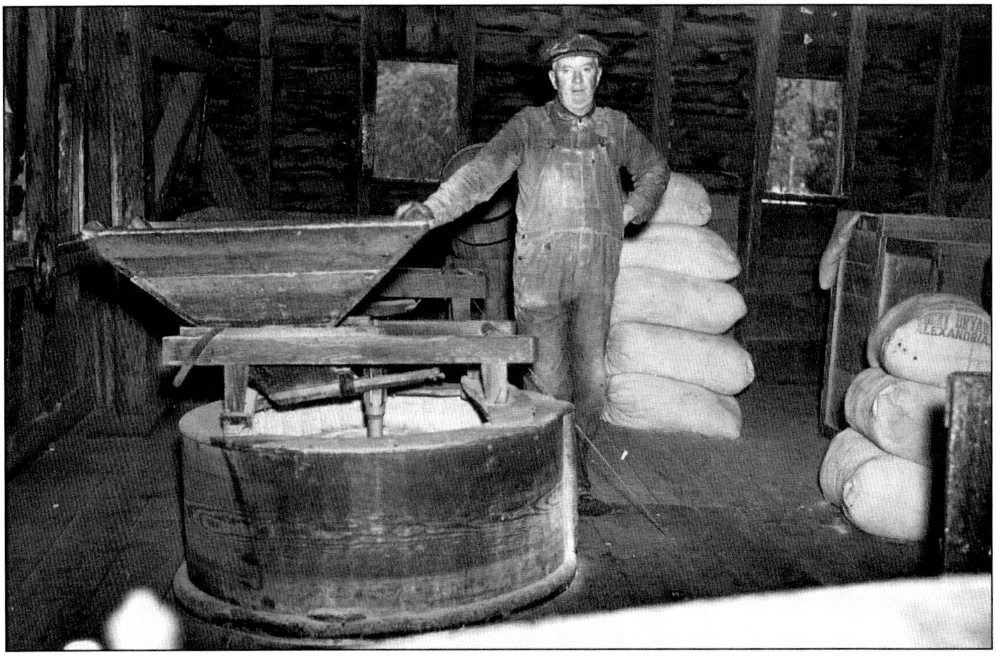

Capt. Benjamin Lillard, who served in the American Revolution, obtained a permit to build a mill on the Hughes River in northern Madison County in the 1790s. It was run by William C. Nethers (pictured here) and has retained that name. Corn was ground between two stones but it could not be ground too fast or it would get so hot it could not be held. (Photograph by Arthur Rothstein, courtesy of Madison County Historical Society.)

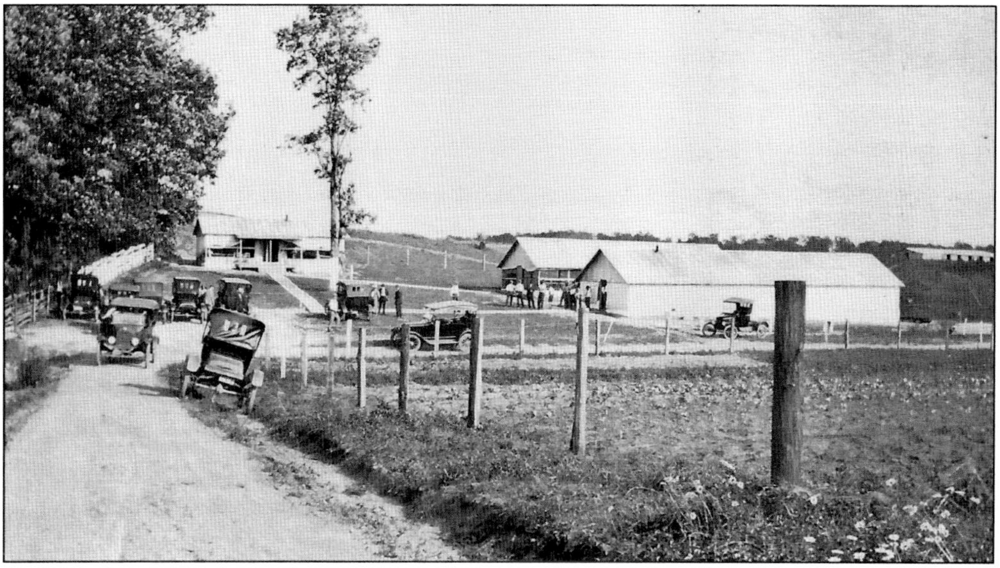

In the early to mid 1900s, there was a state-run convict camp on the Clore Farm (present-day Hoover Ridge) near Pratts. Convicts were used extensively for road construction, and camps were set up where they were needed. In 1925, the road was paved between Pratts and the town of Madison, with the roadbed being made of rock crushed by the state convict road gang. (Katherine Clore Craft.)

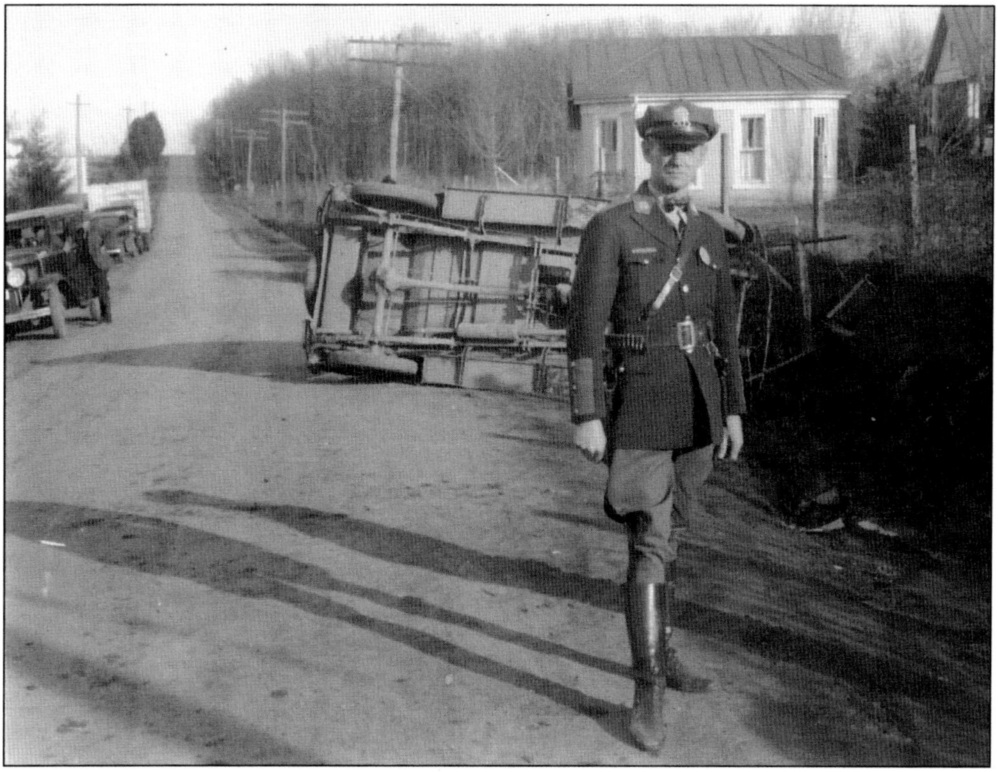

Herman Dulaney, the first Madison County state trooper, stands in front of a wrecked vehicle near Peola Mills. (Robert Dulaney.)

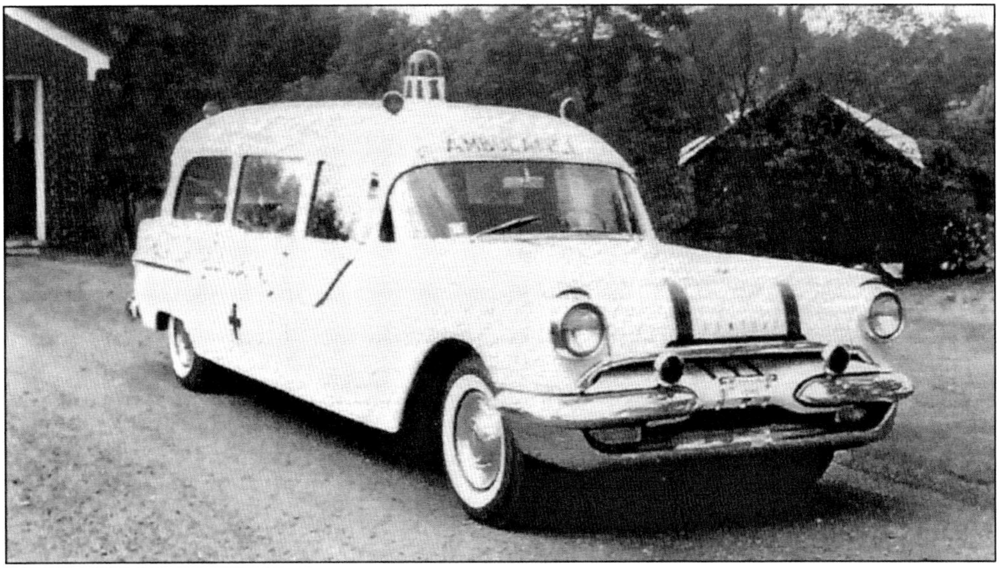

The Madison County Rescue Squad's first ambulance was a reconditioned hearse. The totally volunteer squad was formed in 1963 and two of its founding members, Paul Coates and Margie Lamar, are still active today. The rescue squad currently has a paid daytime staff but the night staff still consists of volunteers. Madisonians are proud of their rescue squad, which has won numerous state awards for its excellence. (Madison County Rescue Squad.)

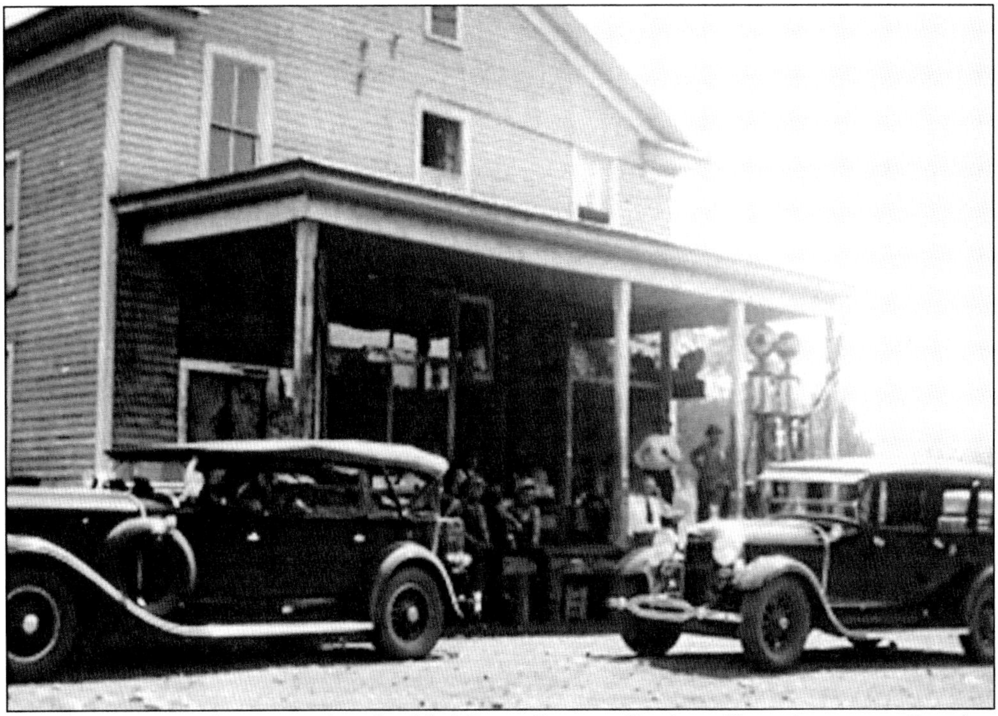

President Hoover often stopped at the McAllister Store in Criglersville on his way to Rapidan Camp. Before the road was finished to the camp, the Hoovers would leave their cars in Criglersville and ride horseback the rest of the way. The store held the post office, and Ray Berrey was a postmaster. (Madison County Historical Society.)

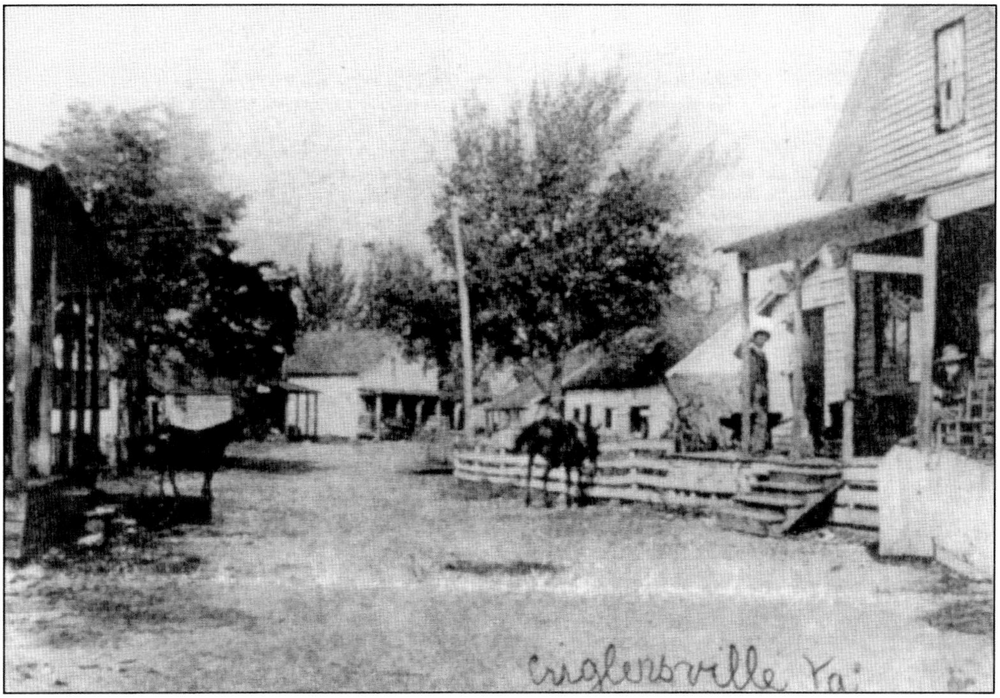

Criglersville is one of the oldest villages in Madison County. In the early 1900s it had a general store, a bank, a funeral home, and a doctor's office. Lewis Crigler began buying up land from 1810 through 1816 in this area. At his death in 1816, his land was divided up among his many children and the town of Criglersville was named. (Steve Hoffman.)

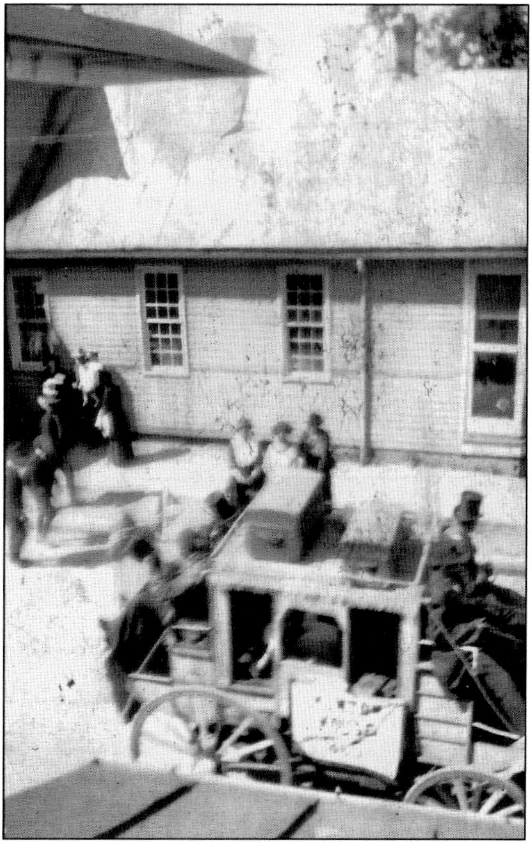

The stagecoach, which ran from Washington to Charlottesville, made regular stops in Madison. Here it is in back of the Hunton House Hotel with the summer kitchen in the background. It appears that this photograph was taken from the roof of the carriage house in the very early 1900s. (Vee Tull.)

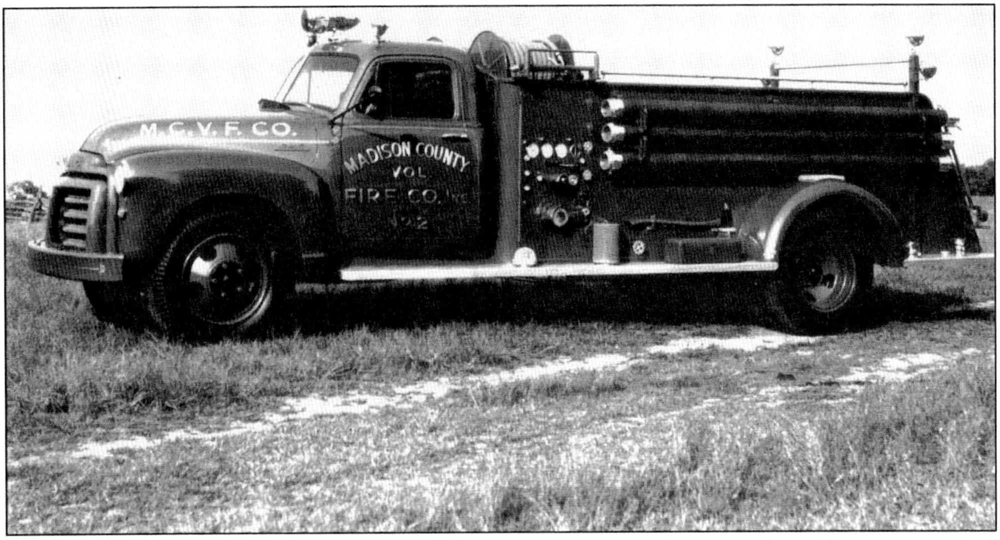

The Madison County Volunteer Fire Department, in existence for more than 60 years, is a vital component of the Madison community. Today the fire department has a new state-of-the-art building, and a variety of fire trucks populate the bays. The fire truck in this *c.* 1950 photograph was the department's second. (Madison County Fire Department.)

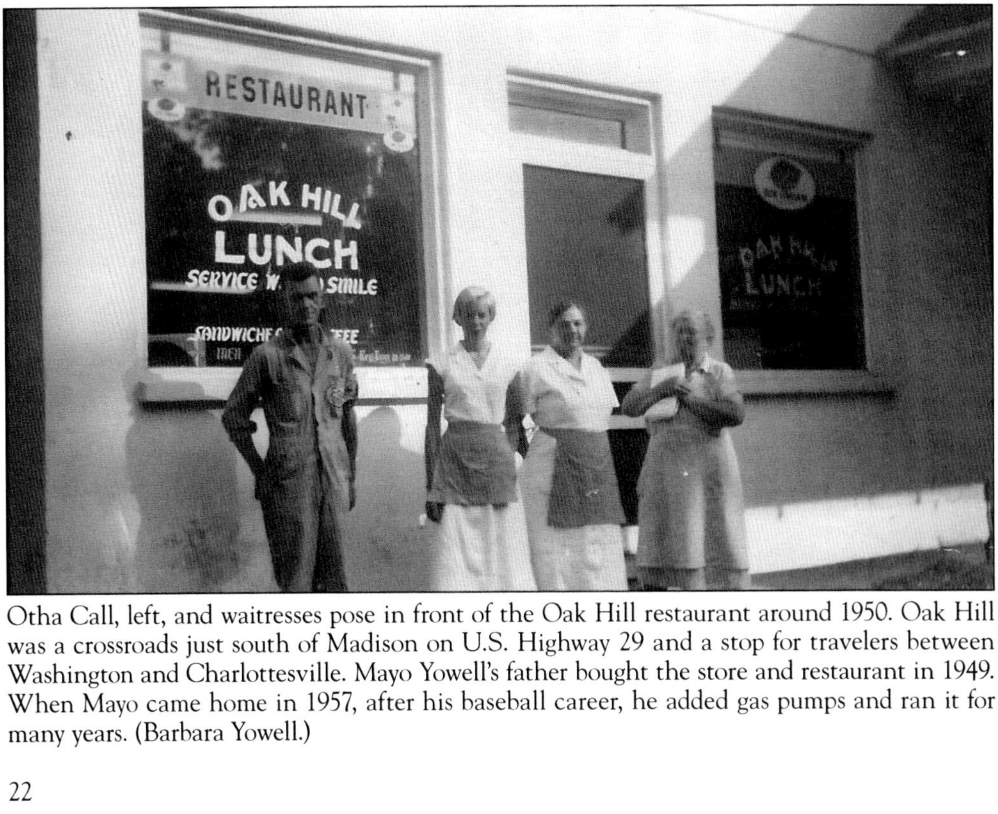

Otha Call, left, and waitresses pose in front of the Oak Hill restaurant around 1950. Oak Hill was a crossroads just south of Madison on U.S. Highway 29 and a stop for travelers between Washington and Charlottesville. Mayo Yowell's father bought the store and restaurant in 1949. When Mayo came home in 1957, after his baseball career, he added gas pumps and ran it for many years. (Barbara Yowell.)

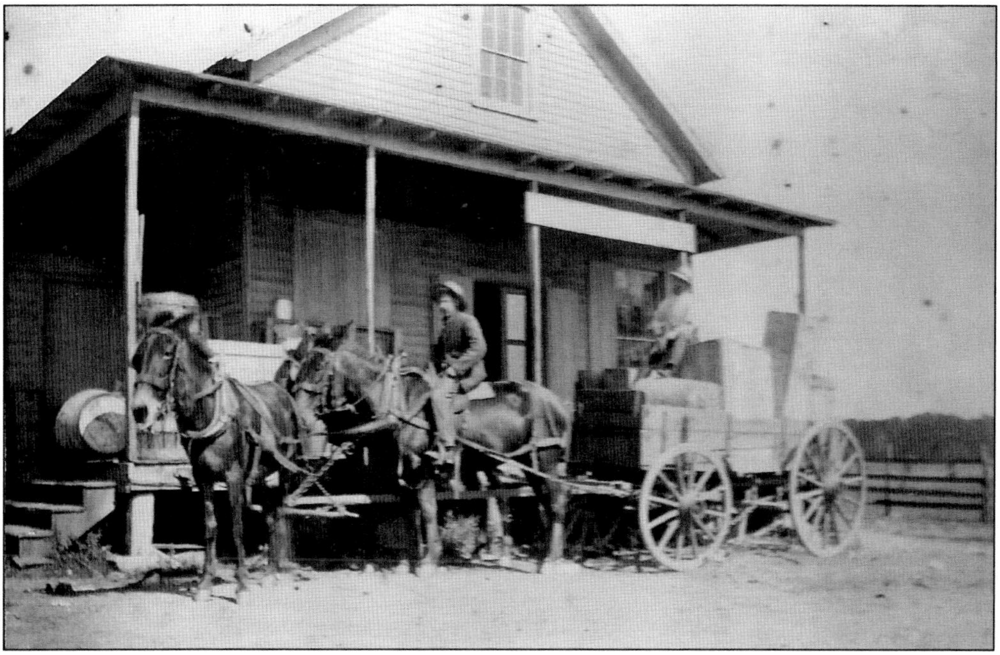

This photograph of a three-horse hitch and wagon in front of the old Lacy's Store in Oak Park was taken around 1900. The post office moved into this store in 1928; it subsequently burned in 1935. The store and post office were rebuilt on the same foundation and are still in operation today. (Courtesy of Max Lacy.)

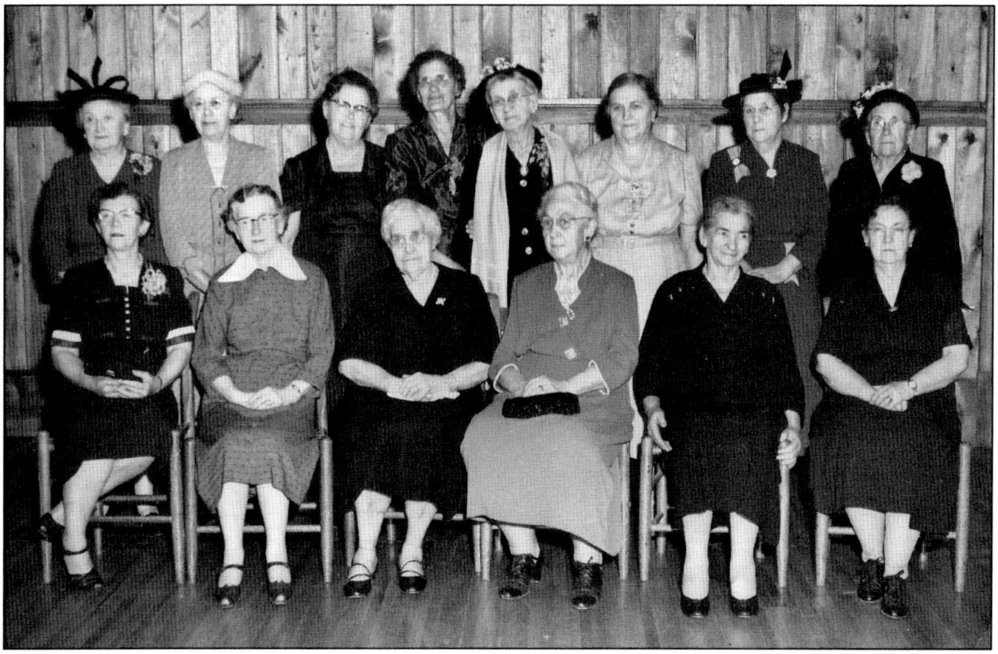

Homemakers and gardeners frequently participated in Home Demonstration Clubs, which were started in the 1950s. They were an opportunity for women to get together and enhance their homemaking skills as well as socialize with one another. In this picture are the charter members of Madison's club, which began in the 1950s. (Judith G. Mahanes.)

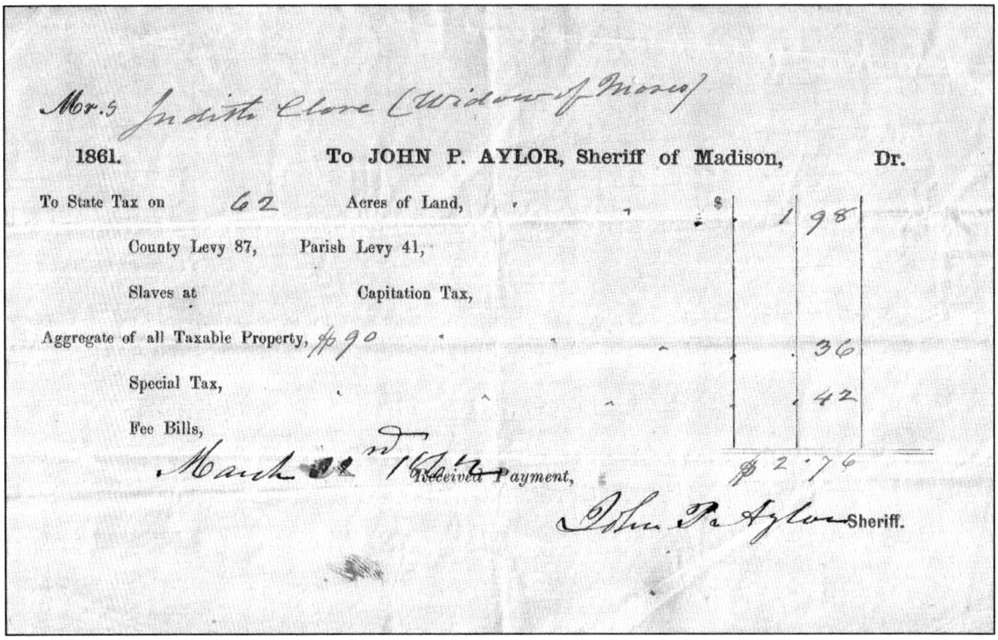
Mrs Judith Clore (Widow of Moses)

1861. To JOHN P. AYLOR, Sheriff of Madison, Dr.

To State Tax on 62 Acres of Land, $ 1 98

County Levy 87, Parish Levy 41,

Slaves at Capitation Tax,

Aggregate of all Taxable Property, $90 36

Special Tax, 42

Fee Bills,

March 2nd 1862 Received Payment, $2.76

John P. Aylor Sheriff.

This 1861 tax bill belonged to Judith Clore, widow of Moses Clore. She was known as "Typhoid Judith" because she went to visit relatives in Kentucky and returned with the typhoid virus. Although immune herself, an epidemic ensued in Madison County and hundreds of people died. (Harold Woodward.)

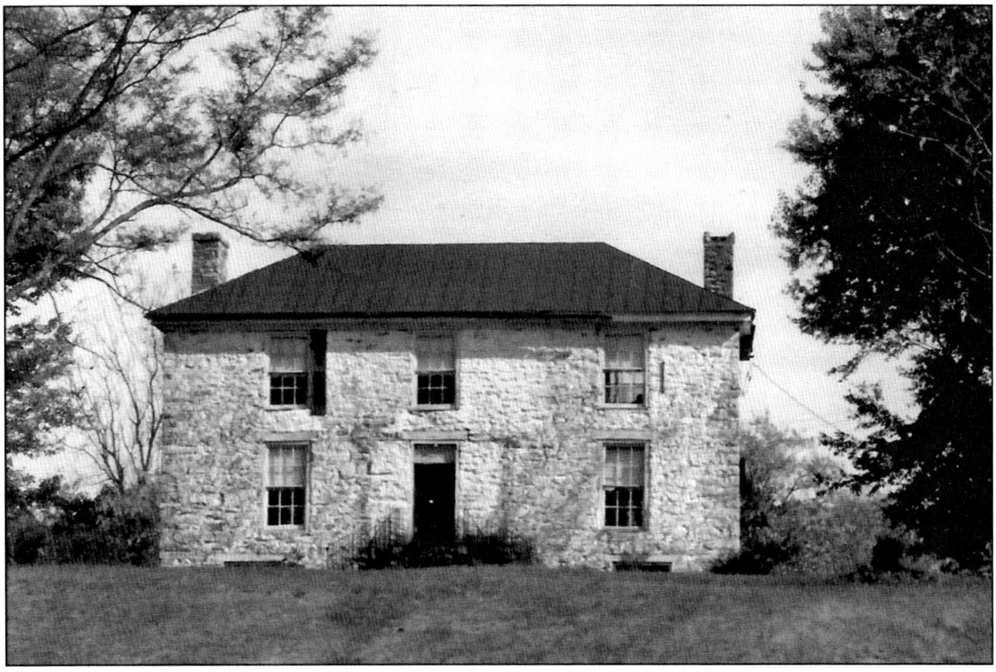

In 1868, Madison County bought this house with 265 acres near Banco and designated it the county poor farm. A manager lived in the fieldstone house and folks who could not support themselves lived in cabins on the farm and were cared for by the county. Those who were able worked on the farm. (Martha Cornwell.)

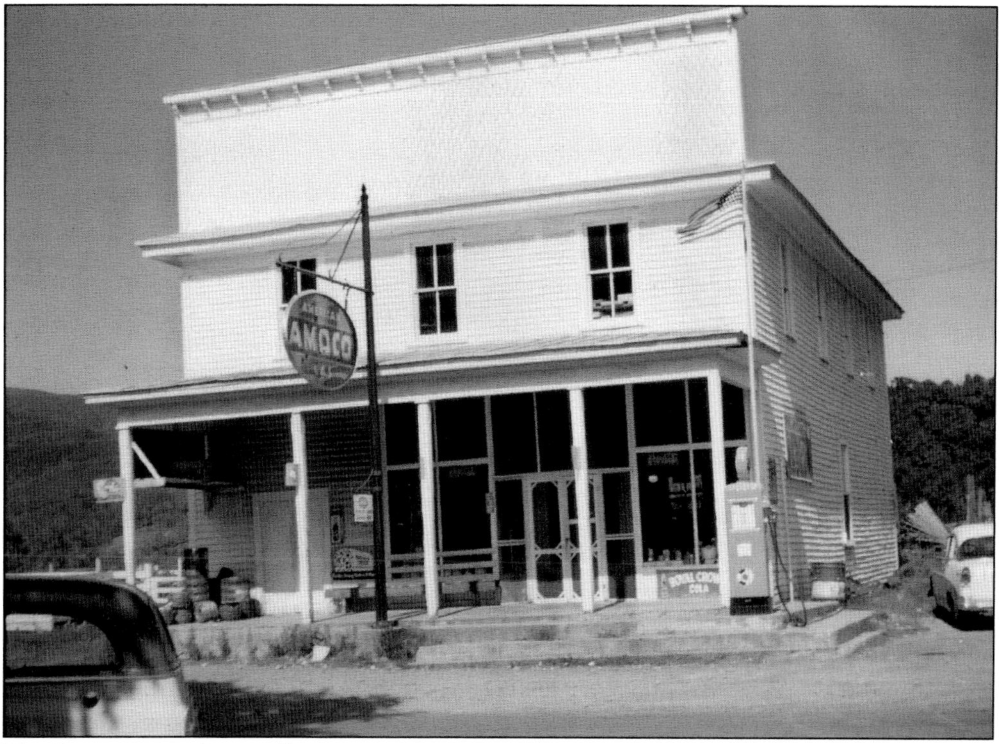

The Syria store and post office stands in the village of Syria near Graves Mountain Lodge. It serves both local residents and lodge guests. The first store burned to the ground in 1915 and was rebuilt (pictured above) only to burn again in 1969. The present store is built of cement block and stone. (Courtesy of James and Rachel Graves.)

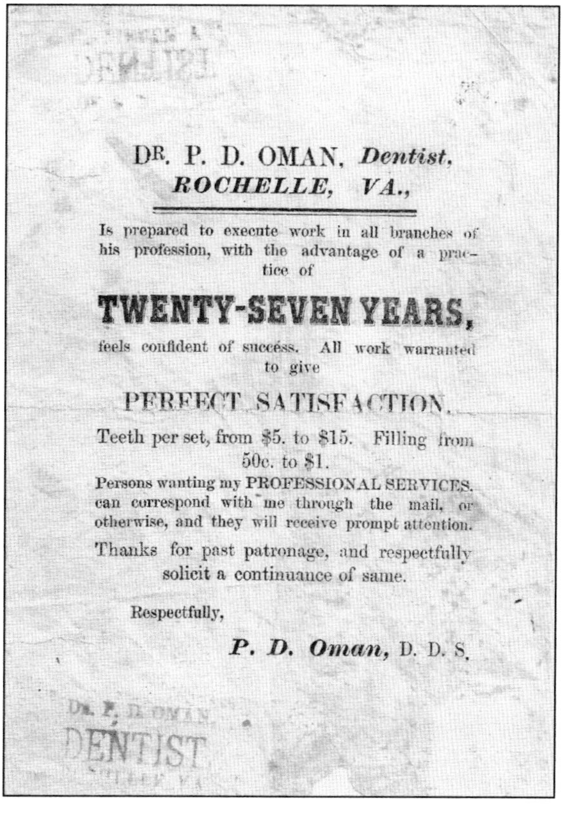

DR. P. D. OMAN, *Dentist,*
ROCHELLE, VA.,

Is prepared to execute work in all branches of his profession, with the advantage of a practice of

TWENTY-SEVEN YEARS,

feels confident of success. All work warranted to give

PERFECT SATISFACTION.

Teeth per set, from $5. to $15. Filling from 50c. to $1.

Persons wanting my PROFESSIONAL SERVICES can correspond with me through the mail, or otherwise, and they will receive prompt attention.

Thanks for past patronage, and respectfully solicit a continuance of same.

Respectfully,

P. D. Oman, D. D. S.

DENTIST

The village of Rochelle, at the crossroads of Route 231 and 621 between Old Pratts and Uno is believed to have been named by Huguenots who migrated from France and came to the Piedmont area of Virginia in the early 1700s. Rochelle's resident dentist, Dr. P. D. Oman, served the area in the late 1880s. (Harold Woodward.)

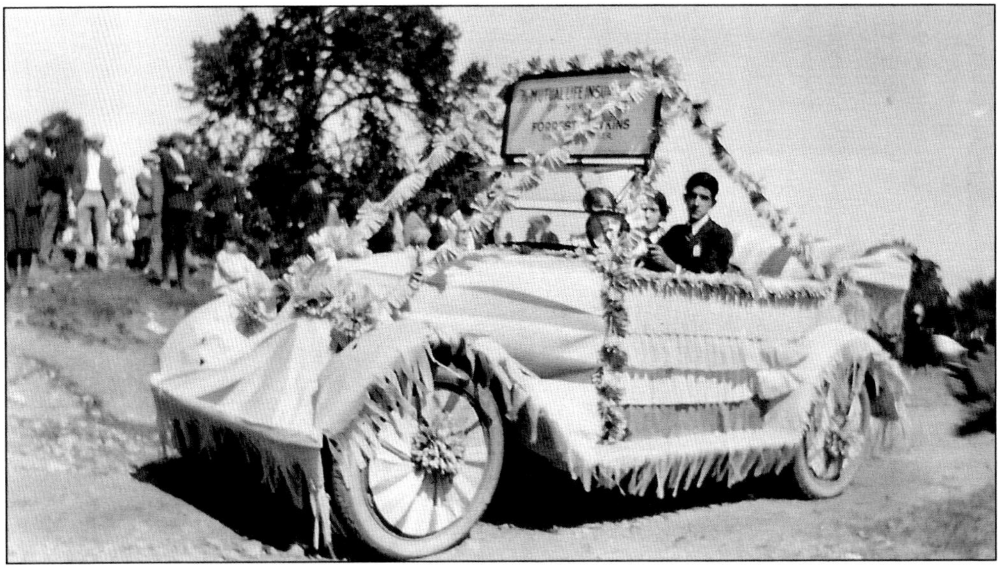

Forrest Hawkins is driving one of the floats in the 1929 Hoover Day parade, part of the celebration welcoming President Hoover, who was building his fishing camp on the Rapidan River near Big Meadows. The festival was held south of the town of Madison at the fairgrounds on the Clore farm, now owned by the county, and named Hoover Ridge. Newspapers reported that 10,000 people turned out for Hoover Day. (Katherine Clore Craft.)

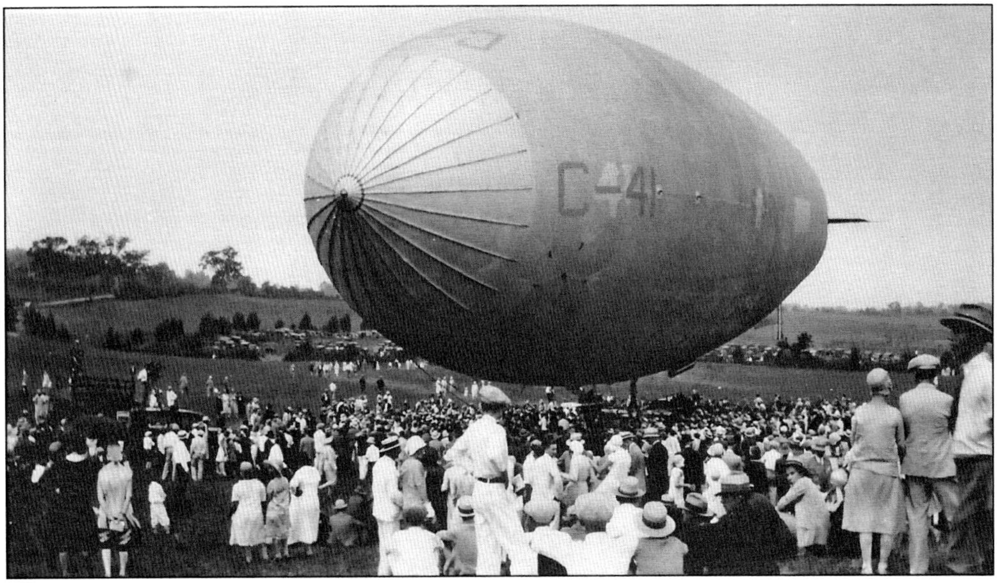

On Hoover Day in 1929, thousands of people swarmed around the U.S. Army blimp as it landed at the fairgrounds, bringing Virginia governor Harry F. Byrd to Madison County. He was then taken by car to Rapidan Camp to pick up the president and first lady and bring them back over miles of bumpy dirt roads to the celebration. (Katherine Clore Craft.)

When Herbert Hoover became president, he looked for a place not too far from the White House where he could relax and fish. A spot was chosen in the mountains of Madison County at the headwaters of the Rapidan River. Madison, being very proud that Hoover had chosen this area, held a huge celebration in 1929 to welcome him and his wife, Lou. In this photograph, President Hoover is speaking to the thousands of people gathered for the occasion. (Madison County Historical Society.)

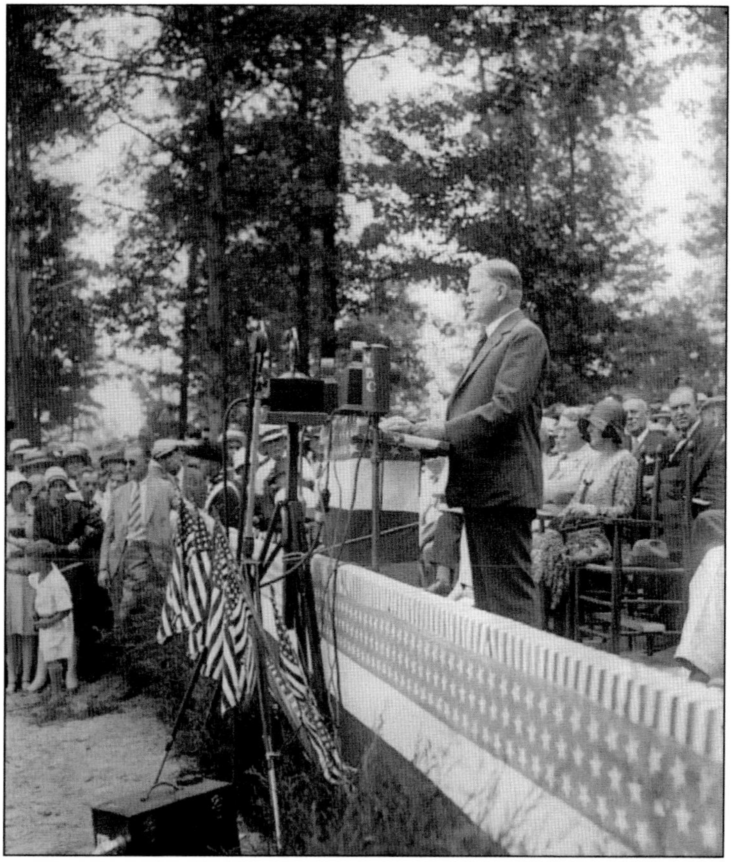

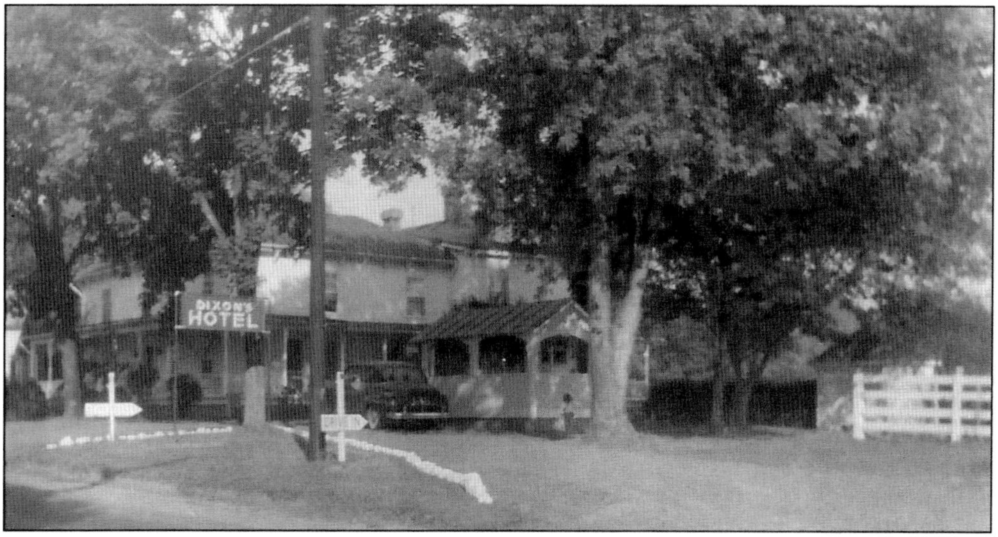

The Dixon Hotel was owned and operated by Randolph and Ervel Dixon in the town of Brightwood in the mid 1950s. The hotel provided rooms and meals to travelers along Route 29 before the bypass took traffic around the town. Prior to the construction of the bypass, Brightwood had a general store, Eddie Smith's jewelry shop, a building and supply store, and a doctor's office in addition to the hotel. Today only the general store is still in operation. (Patti Lillard.)

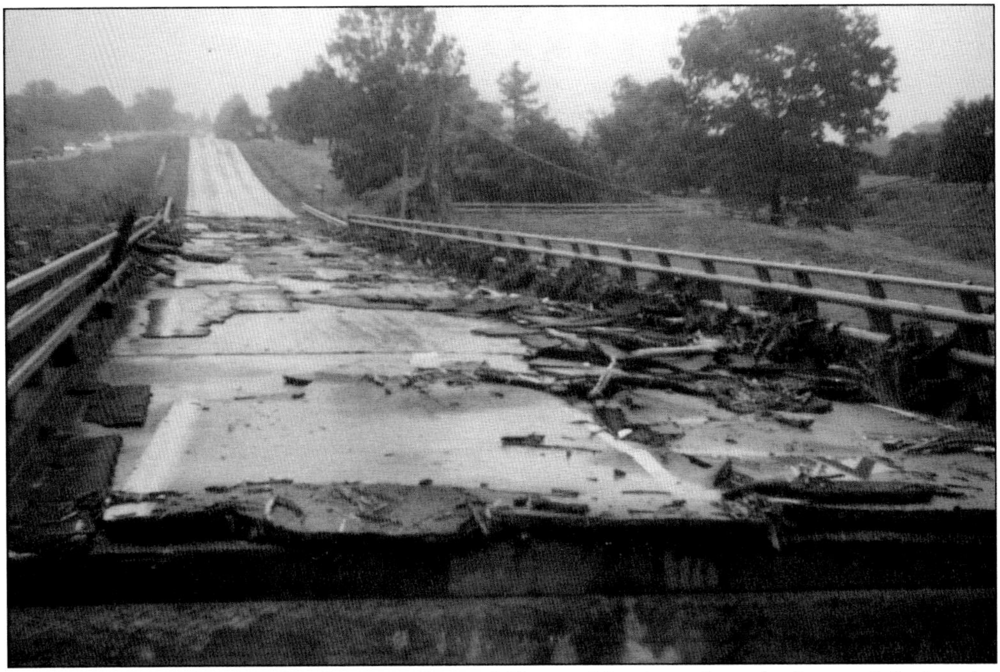

This bridge over the Rapidan River on Route 230 near Hood was heavily damaged during the flood of 1995. A storm stalled over the mountains and dumped as much as 30 inches of rain on Madison County, causing enormous damage to homes, roads, and bridges. Farmland was devastated, crops lost, and many farm animals drowned. (Elmer Miller Jr.)

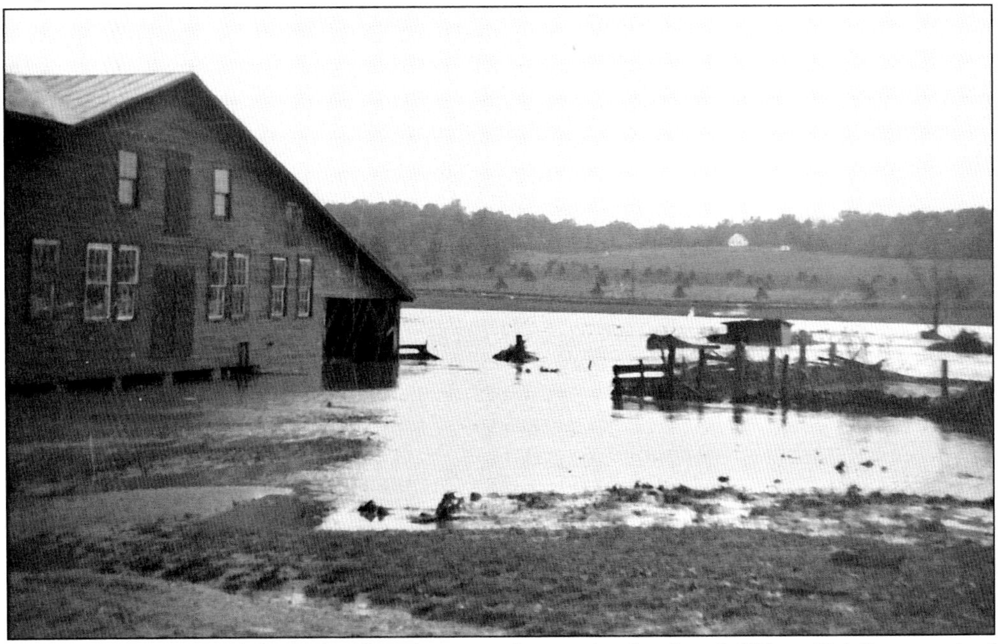

The 1942 flood affected the E. A. Clore furniture factory that lies beside White Oak Run north of the town of Madison and at the southern entrance to the Hebron Valley. Madison's community has pulled together and weathered several floods during the 20th century, including the "2,500 year" flood of 1995, only to be followed by another substantial flood in 1996. (Jim and Margie Lamar.)

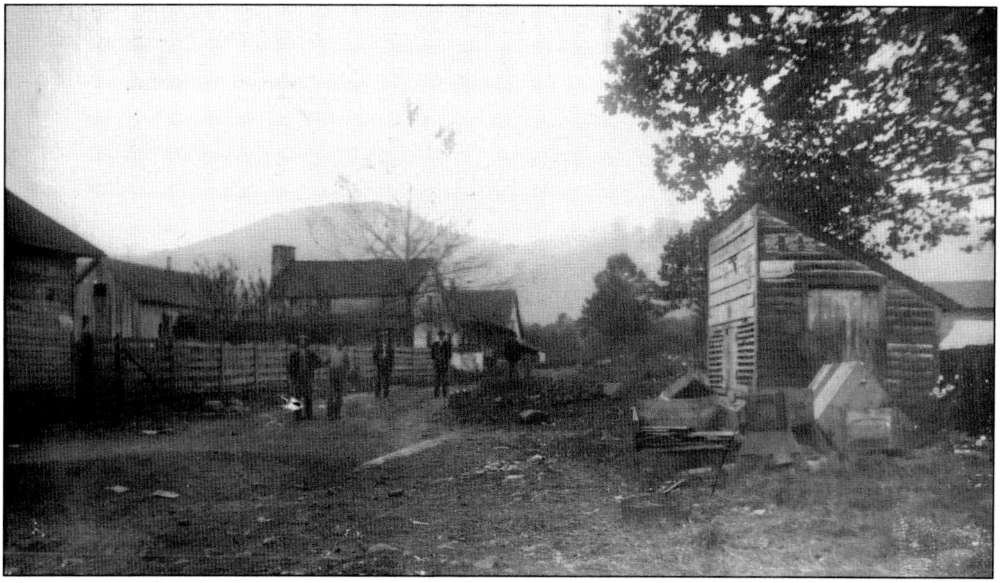

Nethers is a village in the northern part of the county on the Hughes River. It most likely got its name from William C. Nethers, who ran the mill there. Most communities had a mill to grind corn for meal, wheat for flour, and feed for livestock. The reason there were so many mills was because people could not haul their grain long distances for this service. (Dewey Lillard.)

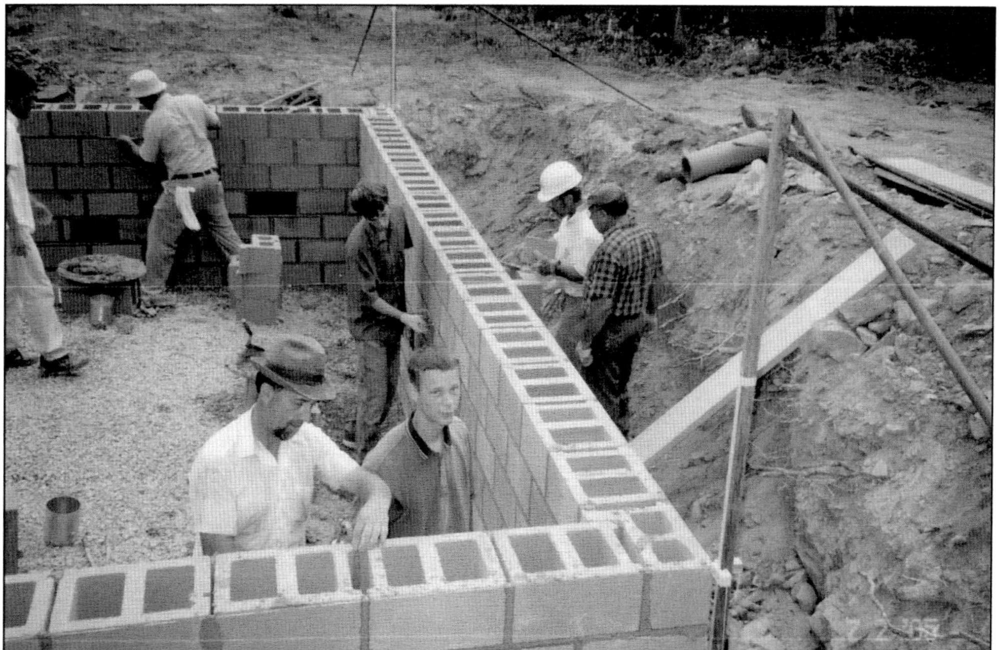

These Mennonites are finishing a basement for one of the Habitat for Humanity houses in Madison County. Habitat started building homes in Madison in 1995. These men work together well and finish basements quickly. They sometimes have young men working with them to learn the trade. The perspective owners also put in many hours on their own home and other homes. (Elmer Miller Jr.)

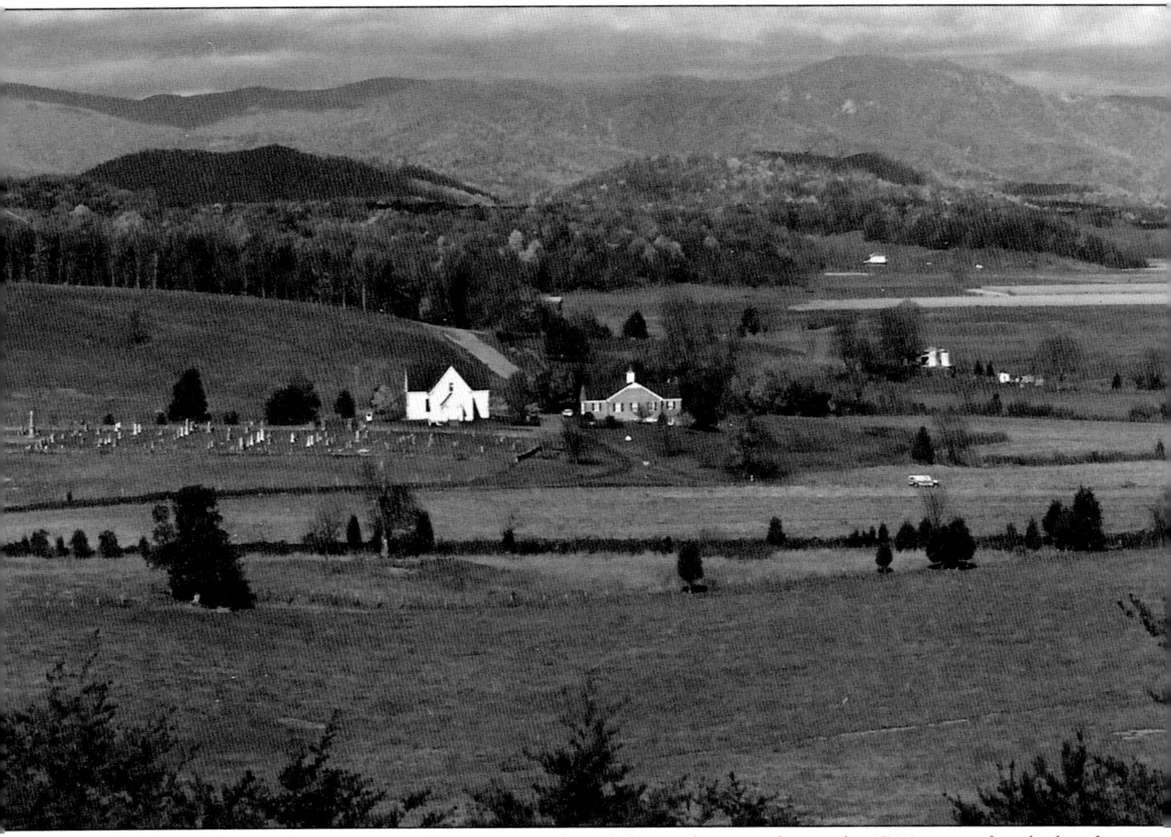

Madison County's Hebron Valley, occupied and farmed since the early 1700s, is a fertile land with streams and rivers meandering through it. It was settled by German Lutherans seeking their own land after working out their indenture to Gov. Alexander Spotswood in Germanna. The surnames of many of those original settlers are familiar names today. Hebron Lutheran Church is seen here at the southern edge of the valley. (Martha Cornwell.)

Three

Business and Enterprise

Early residents of the Madison area wanted land to live on and to farm. Businesses were opened to serve their needs. Mills were built to grind the corn and wheat that farmers raised. Sawmills cut wood for buildings. In the early 1800s, there was a hemp mill in Criglersville to make rope.

Individuals provided services. Blacksmiths made and repaired tools, harnesses, and wagon wheels. Tanneries provided leather. Stores opened to sell goods farmers could not raise or make, although store-bought goods were expensive and homemade was the rule.

Taverns and "ordinaries" served tired, hungry, and thirsty travelers. The James Tavern at James City (now Leon), the Washington Tavern (later the Carpenter Tavern and then Eagle House) in Madison, and the Rose Tavern in Wolftown were stagecoach stops. Spirits were at hand. At one time 52 licensed distilleries were operating in Madison County.

Entrepreneurs found they could provide goods and services for which people would pay. In 1830, Moses Clore began making oak chairs with split oak seats. His grandson E. A. Clore carried on the business. President Hoover bought Clore chairs for his Rapidan Camp. Today Clore furniture is well known throughout the country.

The Graves family of Syria has offered lodging and meals to travelers and tourists for over 150 years. Originating on the Blue Ridge Turnpike as an "ordinary" where prices were set by court order, it moved in 1857 to Mountain View in the Syria Valley, where it also became a vacation spot for families.

More recent enterprises that originated in Madison County are Madison Wood Preservers, nationally recognized as a supplier of pressure-treated lumber; Plow and Hearth, which started in a barn, expanded to a single local retail store, and ultimately grew to a national mail order business; Yoders Country Store, which draws customers from as far away as Washington, D.C.; Weaver Works, which was one man with an idea and is now a major contractor; and Kite's Country Hams, now shipped throughout the country.

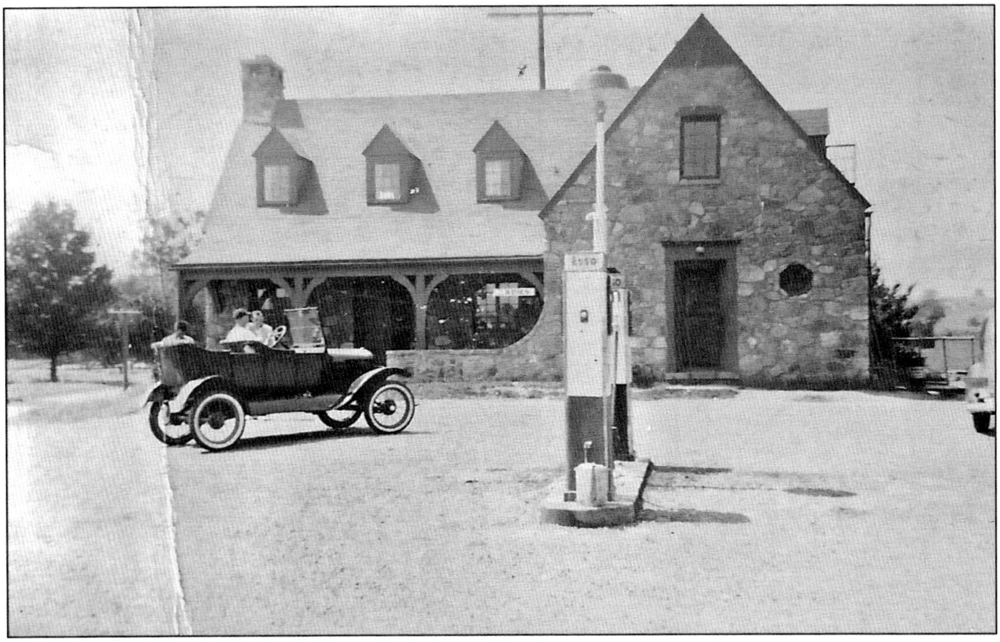

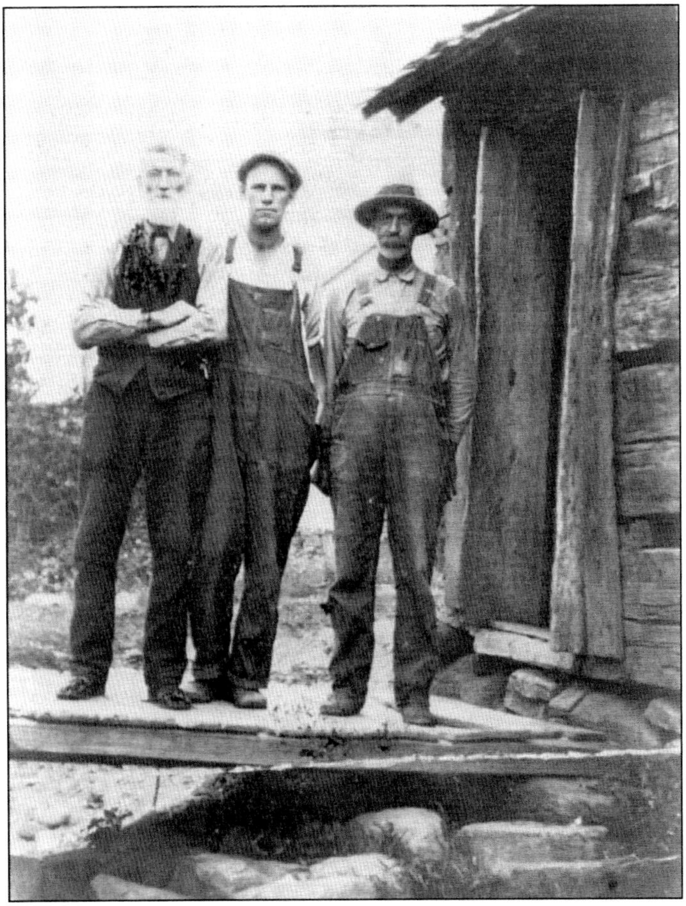

James and Roy Strickler built the old Greystone Inn at Banco in 1935. They ran a store, had gas pumps, and did automobile repair. A post office was located inside the store. Dances were held in what later became the living room and folks came from all over to dance to the jukebox. The store closed in the 1990s. (Robert Finks.)

The Old Rag Post Office, commissioned in 1919, and the store shown here around 1927, served the residents who lived both in and near the mountains around Nethers and Old Rag. The man on the left is the postmaster, William Austin Brown. (Harold Woodward.)

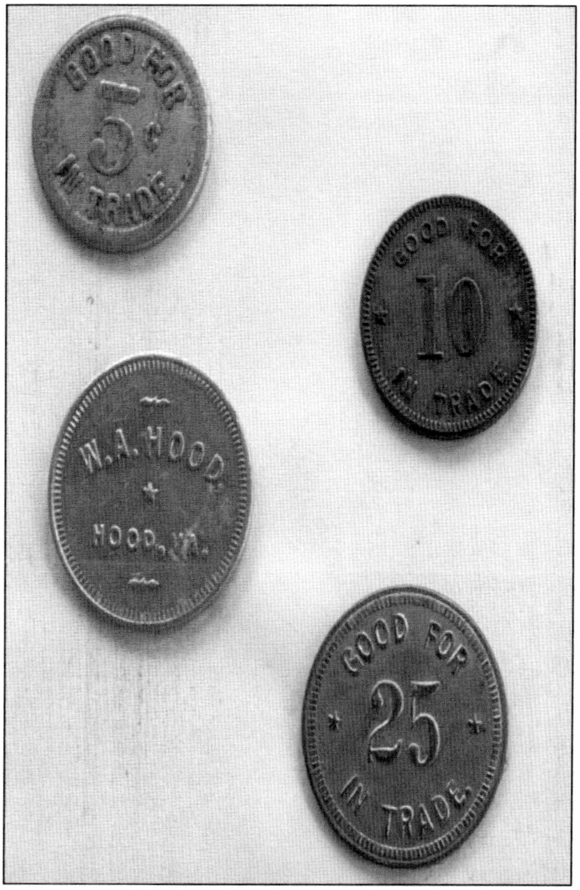

The Hood store and post office was a general full-service store that sold everything from clothes to clothespins, along with food, guitar and banjo strings, and dye. In the picture below, S. Walker Hood and his son W. Alvin Hood look out at the photographer from behind the counter of their well-stocked store. When cash was hard to come by, people dealt in trade or barter. The "store coins" issued by the Hood store could be used to purchase items at another time. The store was a community gathering place. (Right, photo by John Mitchell, below, courtesy of Mary Hood.)

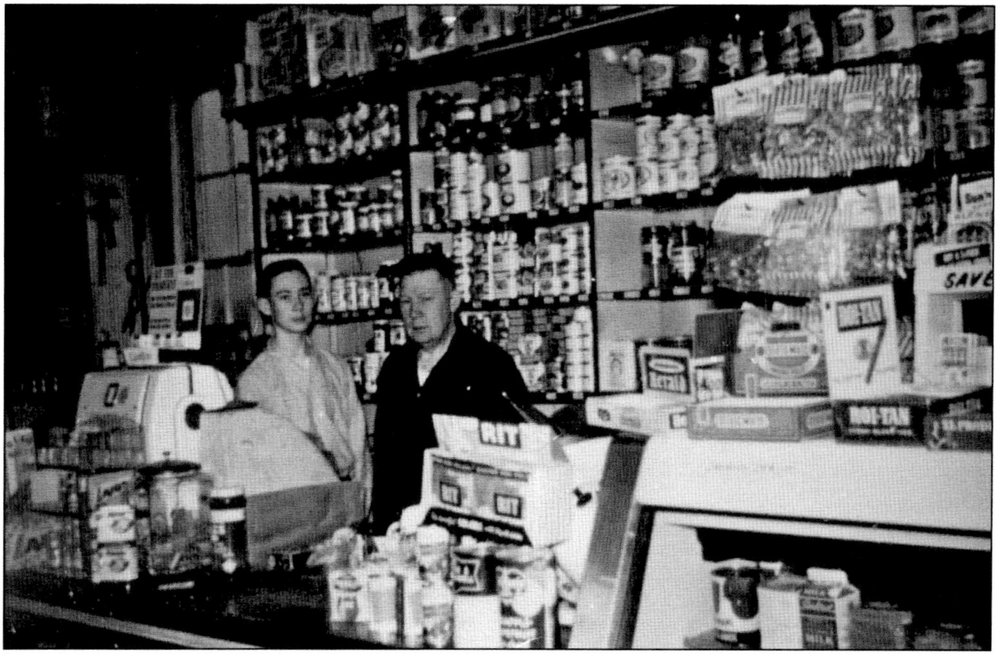

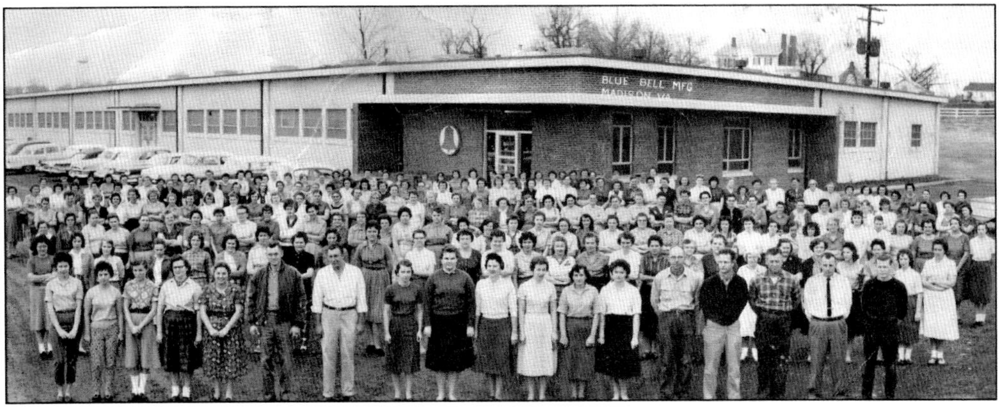

Initially this factory in the town of Madison was called Blue Bell and it made jeans. At one time it was one of Madison County's largest employers. All of its employees gathered for the picture above taken in front of the plant in 1961. The first Blue Bell workshop in the 1950s, with its sewing machine operators turning out jeans, was on the second floor of the Arcade building. In the photograph below, Mary Sacra Yowell is pictured at her sewing machine in the early days. Blue Bell later moved to a larger and more modern building that is now occupied by the MWP Supply Store. Blue Bell's name was changed to Wrangler in the late 20th century and the Madison factory closed its doors in the 1990s. (Both, Charlotte Lohr.)

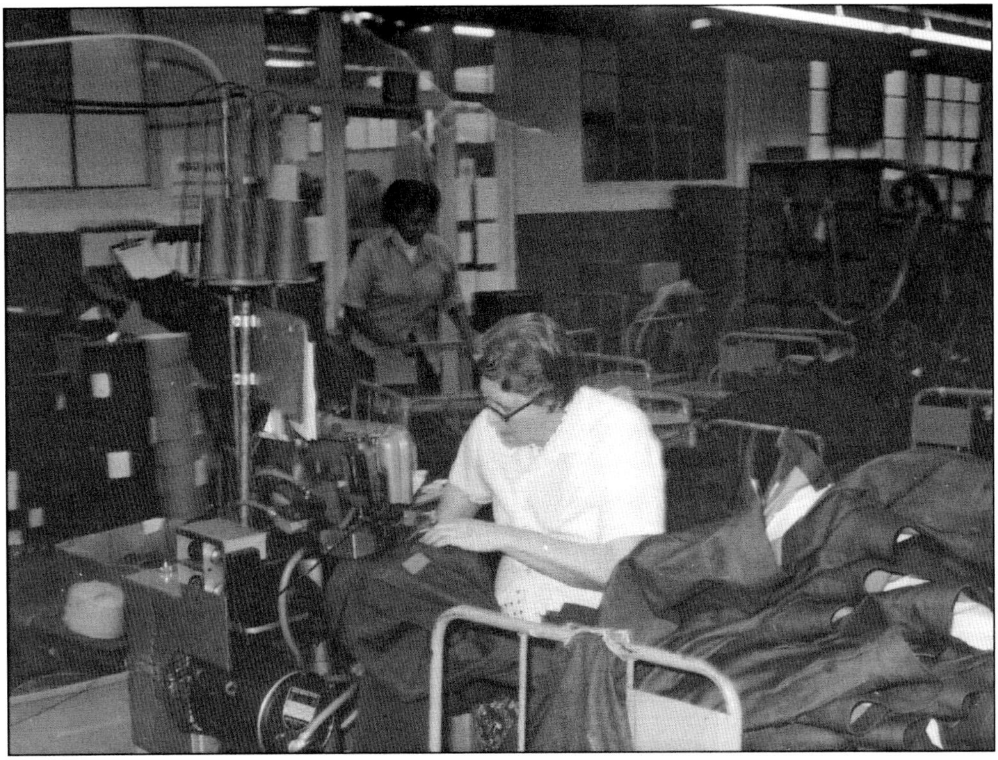

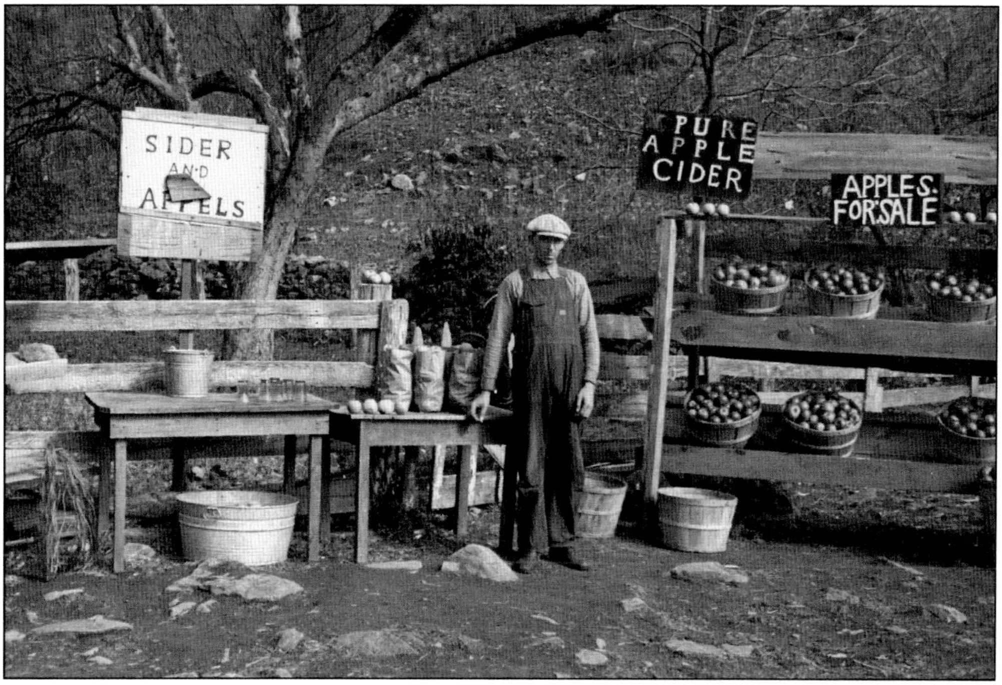

Madison County is known for its fruit products, particularly apples and peaches. Roadside stands like the one above dot the landscape and do a substantial business throughout the late summer and early fall. This vendor is selling both apples and cider from his stand near Nicholson Hollow. The orchard pictured below is at the Coppedge farm at the foot of Utz Mountain. Orchards like this are cultivated throughout the county and much of the crop is taken to larger wholesale dealers. In the 1950s, Madison County was one of the major apple producing counties in the Commonwealth of Virginia. In the last two decades, a number of grape orchards have been added to Madison County's fruit production. (Above, photograph by Arthur Rothstein, courtesy of Madison County Historical Society; below, courtesy of Lillian Mitchell.)

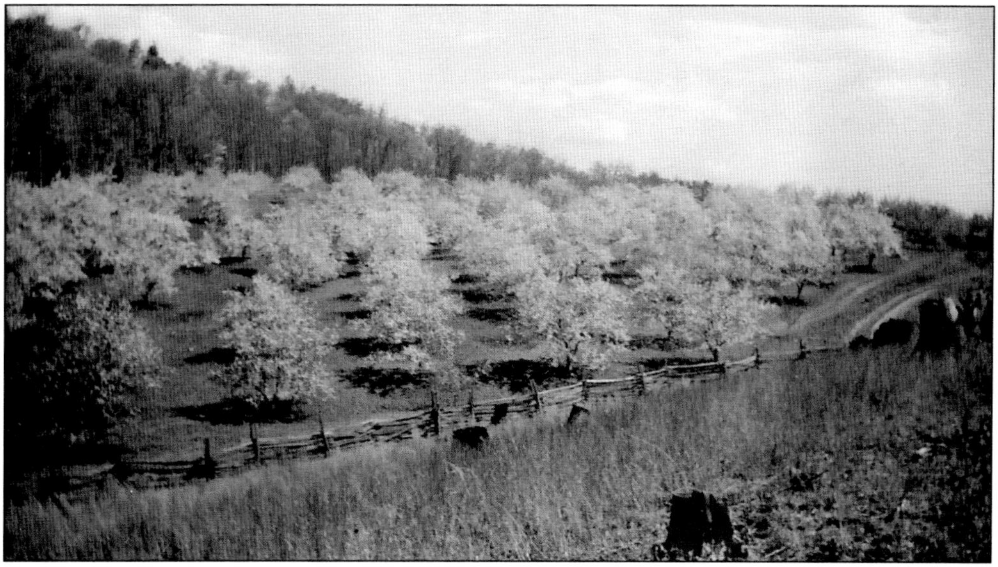

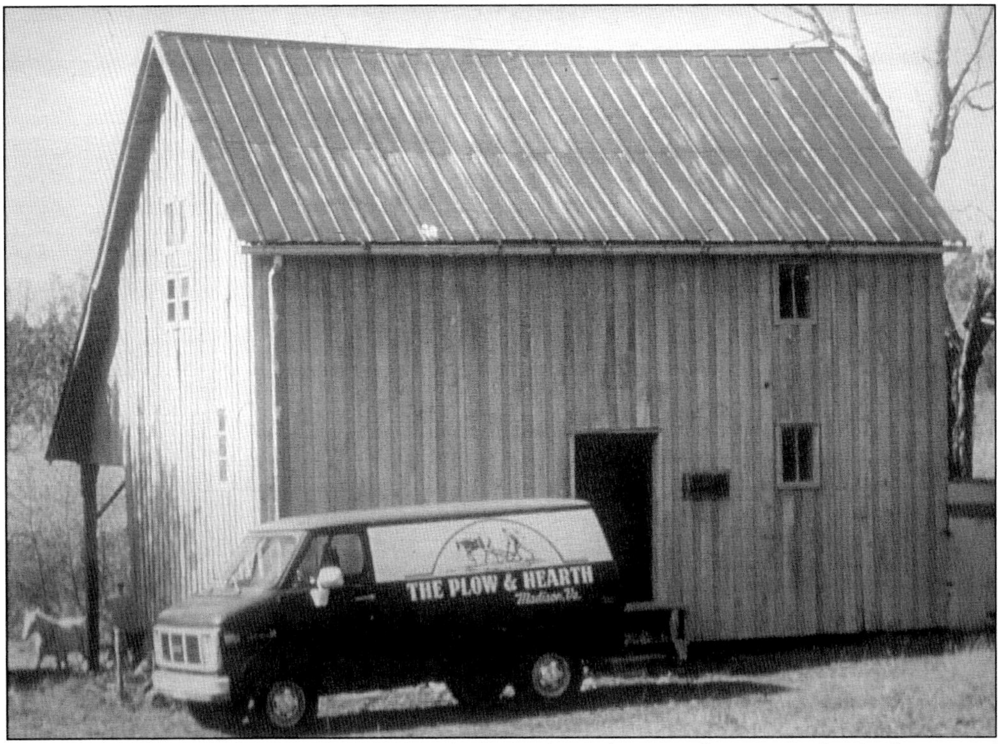

Plow and Hearth, a nationally known catalogue and retail store selling items for the home and garden, got its start in a barn on the property of founders Peter and Peggy Rice near Shelby. Today this giant catalogue company maintains offices and a warehouse on the Wolftown/Hood Road near Madison and employs more than 400 full-time and seasonal workers, making it one of the largest employers in the county. (Nancy H. Knighting.)

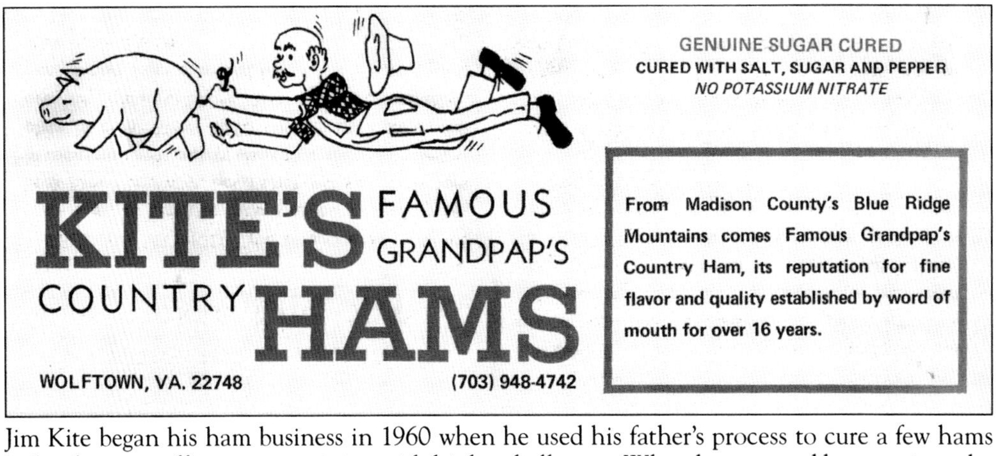

Jim Kite began his ham business in 1960 when he used his father's process to cure a few hams before he went off to spring training with his baseball team. When he returned he went into the business with 400 hams to sell. Fifty years later, in 2010, Kite's Country Hams are sold throughout the country and the company is processing 20,000 a year. (Shirley and Jim Kite.)

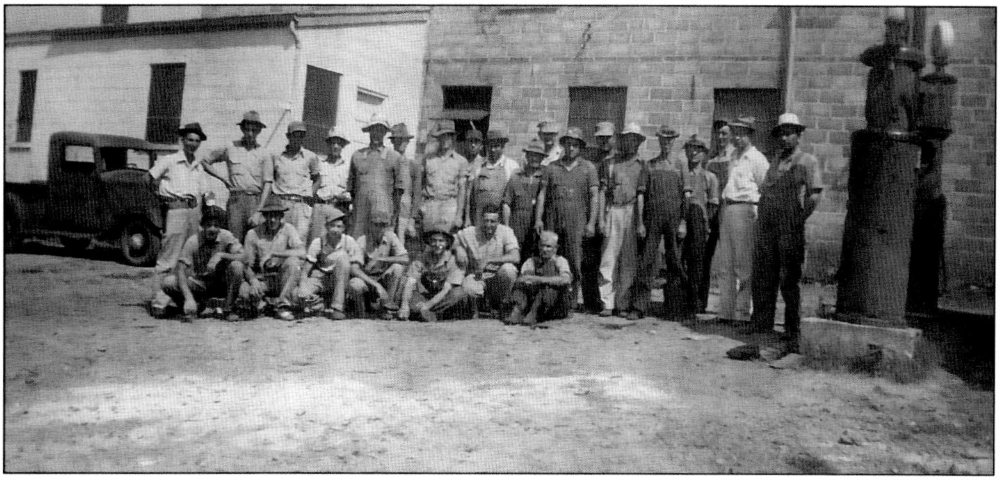

The W. J. Carpenter Company made wooden chicken coops for more than 100 years and went out of business only when metal and plastic coops took over the market. The coops were originally sold to hold chickens, as shown at right, but later people bought them to use for furniture in the home. They made an excellent stand for a heavy television and were always a conversation piece. The 1942 photograph of W. J. Carpenter employees (above) was taken when business was at its height with 40 employees who built about 120,000 coops a year. Lumber for building the coops was stacked over 11 acres. (Above, courtesy of Martha Fishback Breeden; right, courtesy of Thomas Ford.)

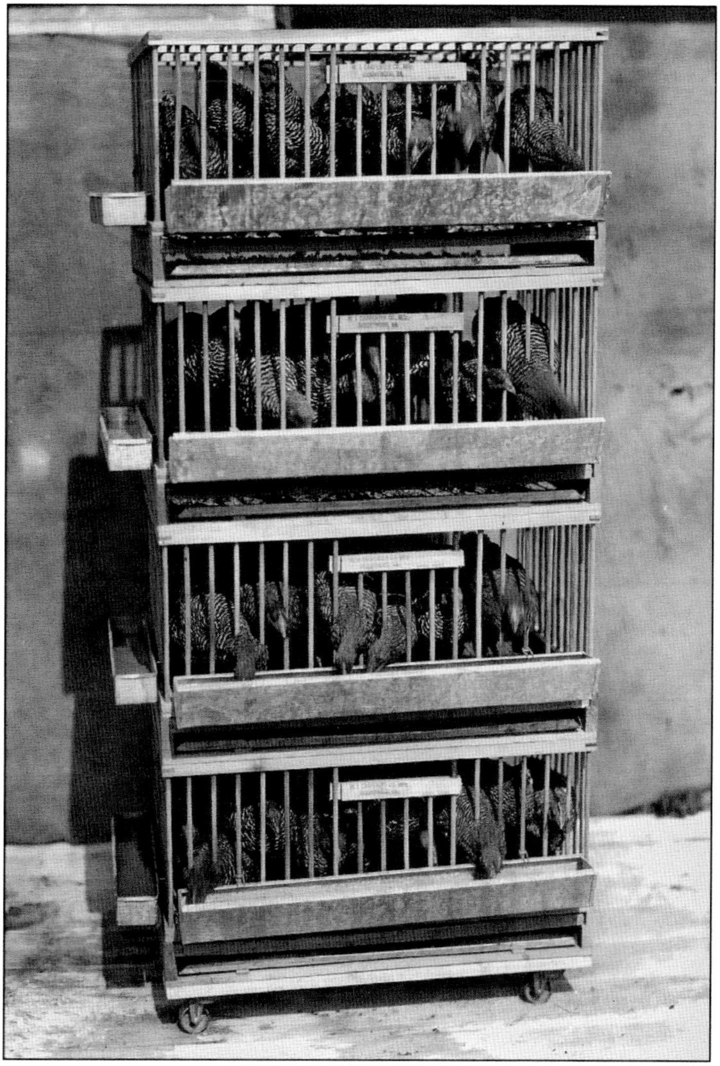

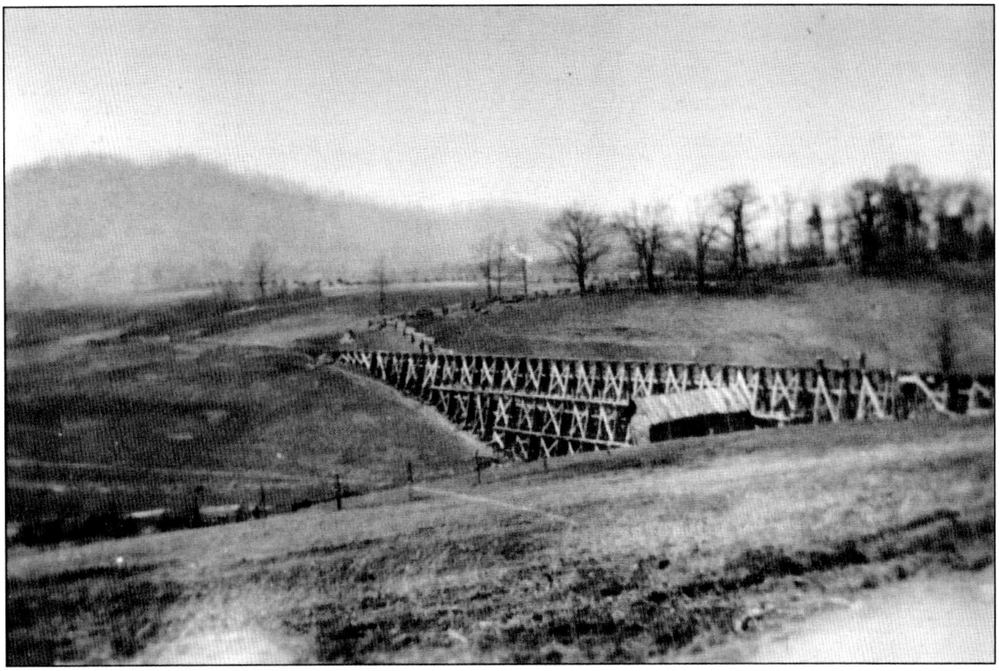

Pictured above is a railroad trestle near Wolftown in the 1920s. The Rapidan Railroad was a narrow gauge railroad constructed in 1920 by the West Virginia Timber Company of Orange. The railroad ran from the town of Orange to Graves Mill in Madison County and hauled lumber from the surrounding mountains back to the sawmill in Orange. Timbering was a major part of Madison County's economy in the 1920s. Gandy dancers like the six men pictured below kept the railroad bed, ties, and rails in working order. Farm products from Madison were also hauled to Orange by rail during the railroad's brief tenure. It closed in 1924 and was dismantled by 1928. (Above, courtesy of Madison County Historical Society; below, courtesy of Nancy H. Knighting.)

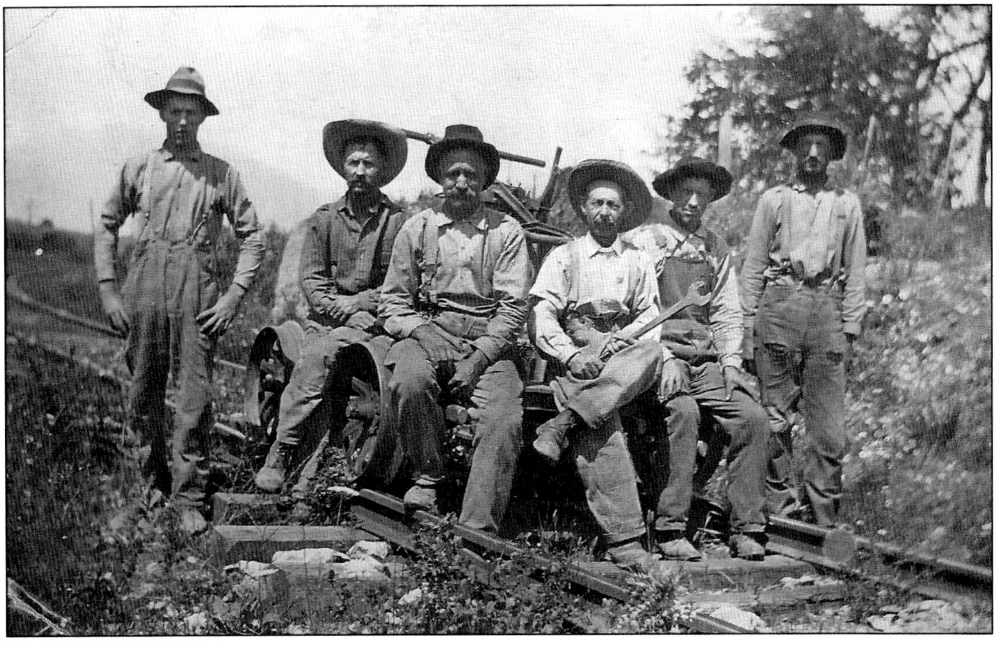

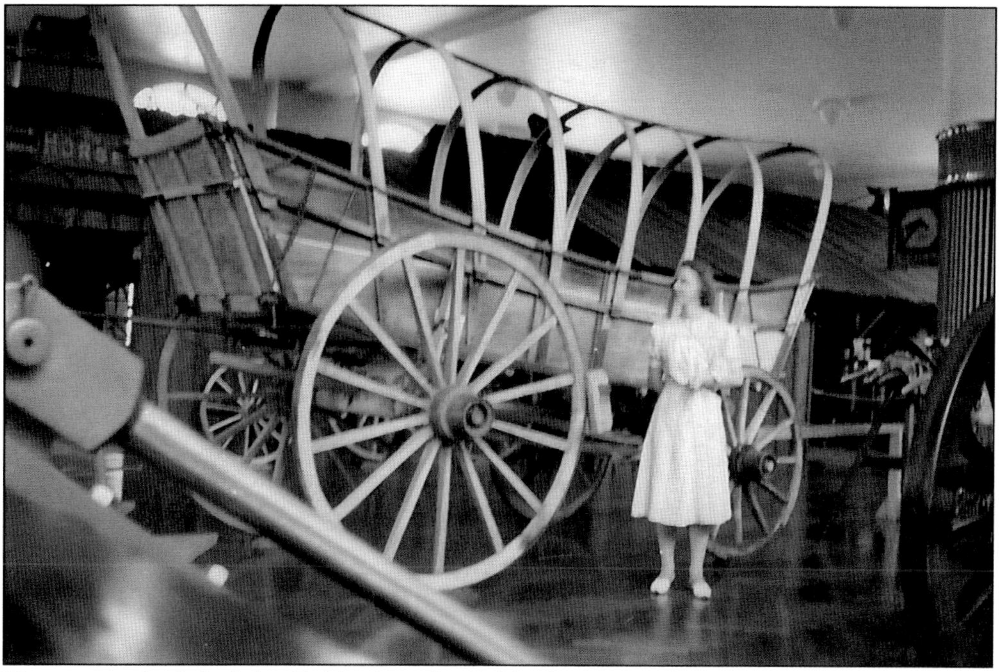

This wagon, built by John Fishback at the Fishback Wagon Shop, stood on his property off Route 29 north of the town of Madison and is now displayed in a San Francisco museum. In the photograph, Dicie Ella Fishback, great-granddaughter of John Fishback, stands by the wagon. John Fishback, born in 1779, is believed to have made many of the covered wagons that traveled west from the Virginia Piedmont. (Martha Fishback Breeden.)

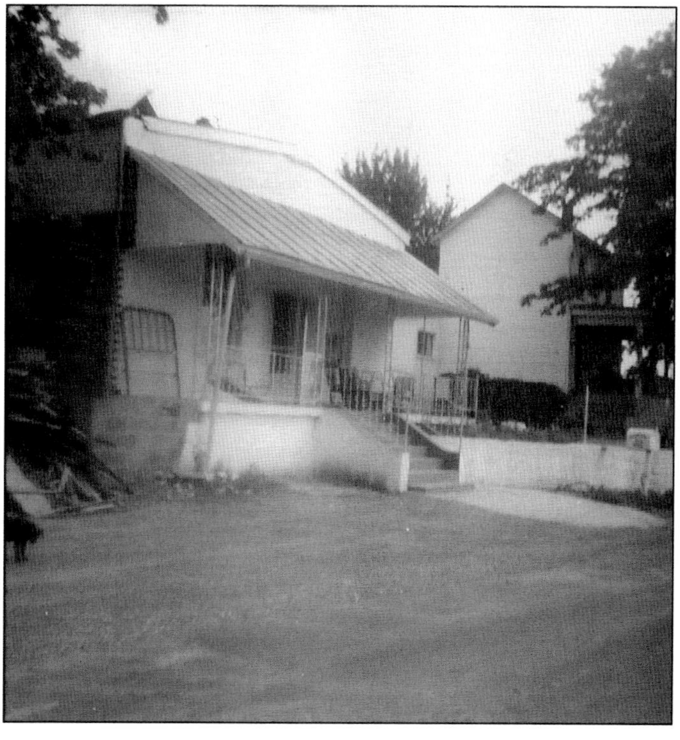

Mountain View Nursing Home had its beginning in this old house and store in 1963 near Elly. It was established by members of the Mennonite community who saw the need for such a facility in Madison County. Nearly 50 years later, after significant renovations and then-new construction, the nursing home is a state-of-the-art facility. There has always been a waiting list for new residents. (Elmina Yoder.)

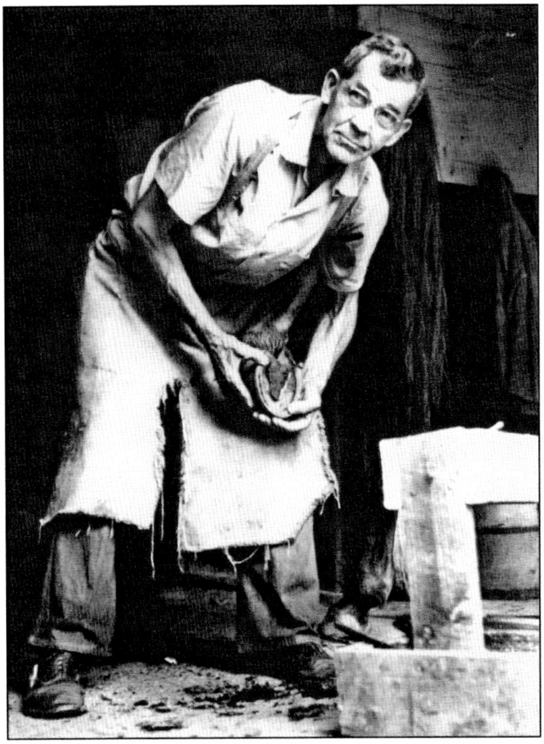

A blacksmithing and wheelwright shop was important to every community. William Arthur Dennis, a farrier and blacksmith, was born at Graves Mill in 1888. In the 1920s he was running his business near Rapidan by the Orange and Culpeper borders. He was said to have been embarrassed about the tear in his apron when he was shown this photograph. (Photograph by Duff Green, courtesy of Kal and Julie Howard.)

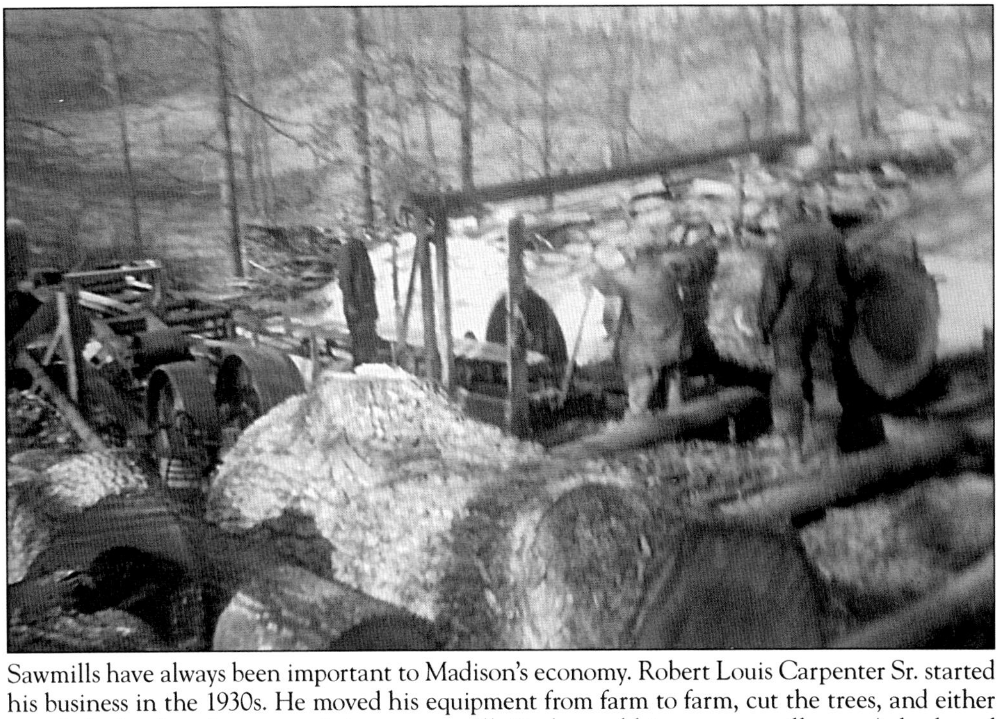

Sawmills have always been important to Madison's economy. Robert Louis Carpenter Sr. started his business in the 1930s. He moved his equipment from farm to farm, cut the trees, and either sawed the lumber there or took it to a sawmill. He located his own sawmill near Achsah and began doing home construction. Now in the third generation, members of the Carpenter family are still engaged in construction today. (Janice P. Carpenter.)

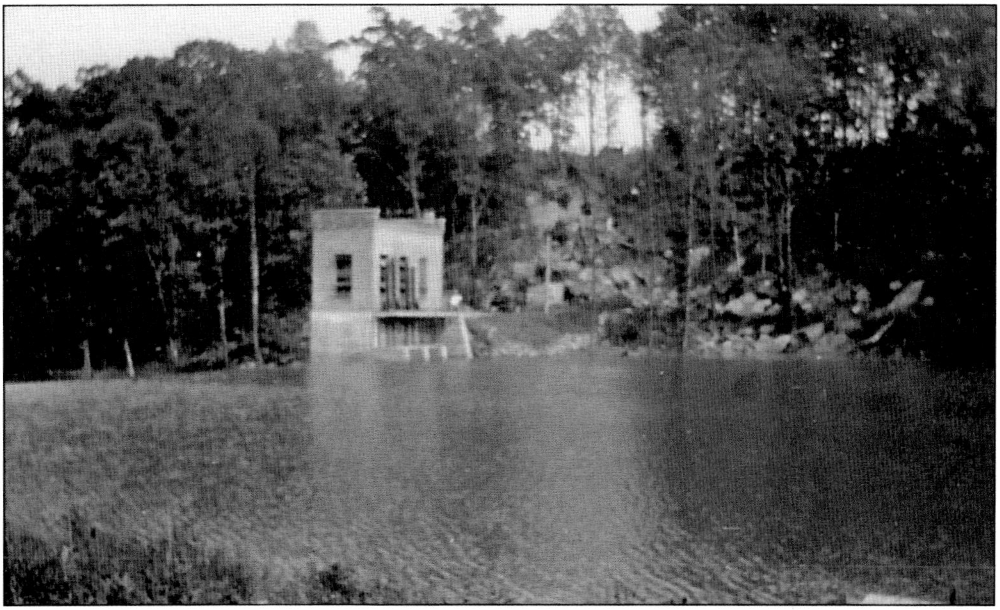

The Madison Power Company was incorporated in 1924 and was the first source for electricity in Madison. A. Hubert Cave organized the power company and built a hydroelectric plant on the Robinson River. The plant served the Brightwood and town of Madison areas. By 1929 the power company could not meet all the demand for electricity and had to purchase additional power from other sources. (Courtesy of Katherine Clore Craft.)

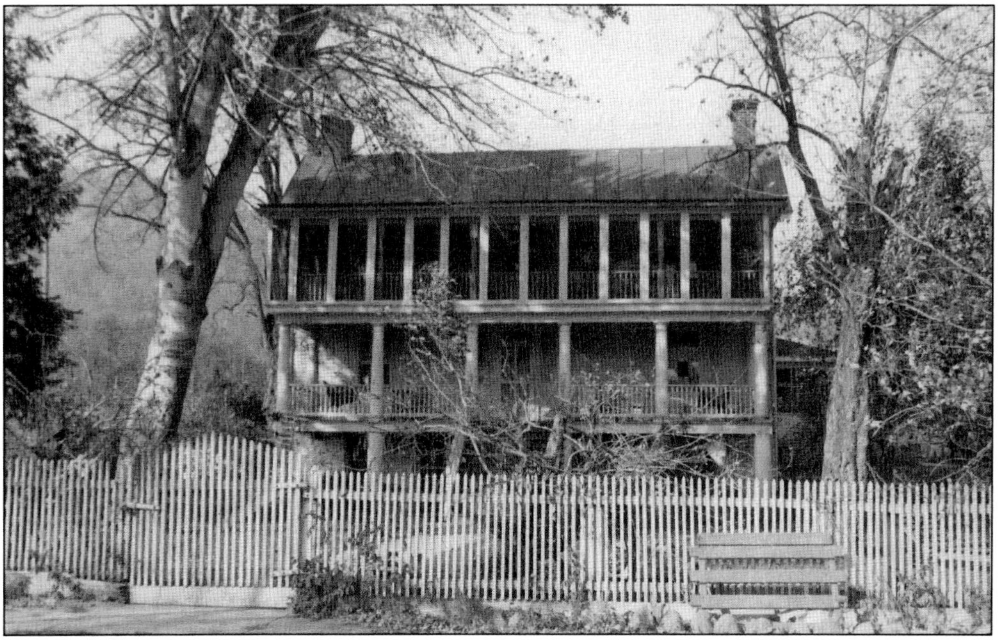

This is a photograph of Mountain View, around 1930, where the Graves family housed and fed guests from 1857 until 1965 when the present lodge was built. In the early 1850s, Paschal Graves opened an ordinary along the Blue Ridge Turnpike in what is now part of Shenandoah National Park. In 1857, the ordinary moved to Mountain View, a rambling three-story farmhouse in the Syria valley. (Courtesy of Rachel and Jimmy Graves.)

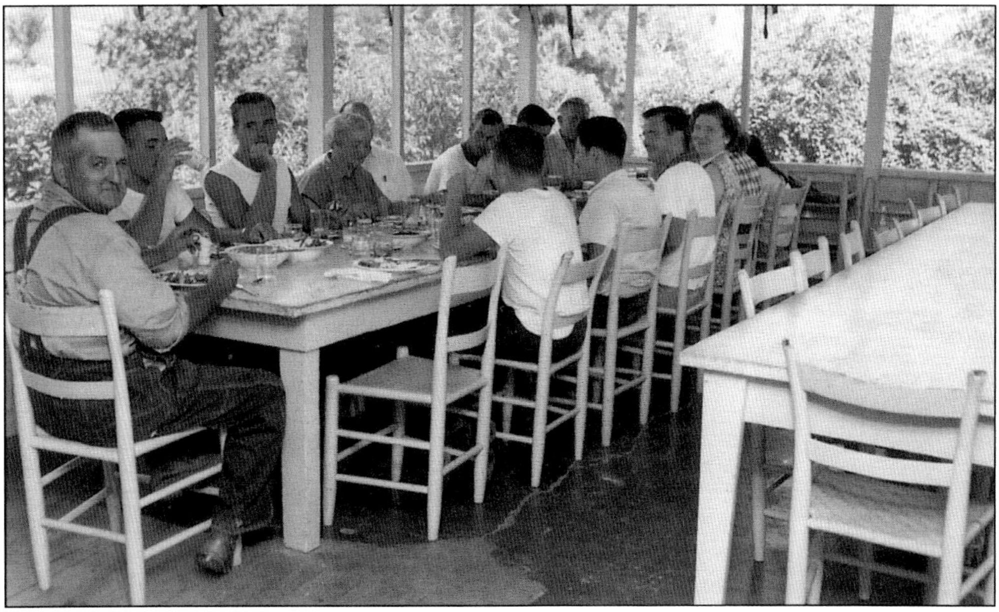

The eating porch at Mountain View, seen above in 1957, was the place where hungry travelers and family members alike had delicious meals. Graves Mountain Lodge opened in 1965. It was built by Rachel and Jimmy Graves to replace the facility at Mountain View, the Graves home that had welcomed guests for many years. The lodge is nestled on a hillside with commanding views of the Blue Ridge Mountains all around. For over 150 years and five generations the Graves family of Syria has offered lodging and meals to travelers and tourists visiting the area. At Graves Mountain Lodge, in addition to lodging and food, guests enjoy hiking, fishing, horseback riding, and swimming. An annual bluegrass festival, a spring fling, a spectacular Fourth of July fireworks display, and an apple harvest festival draw visitors from throughout the area. (Both, Rachel and Jimmy Graves.)

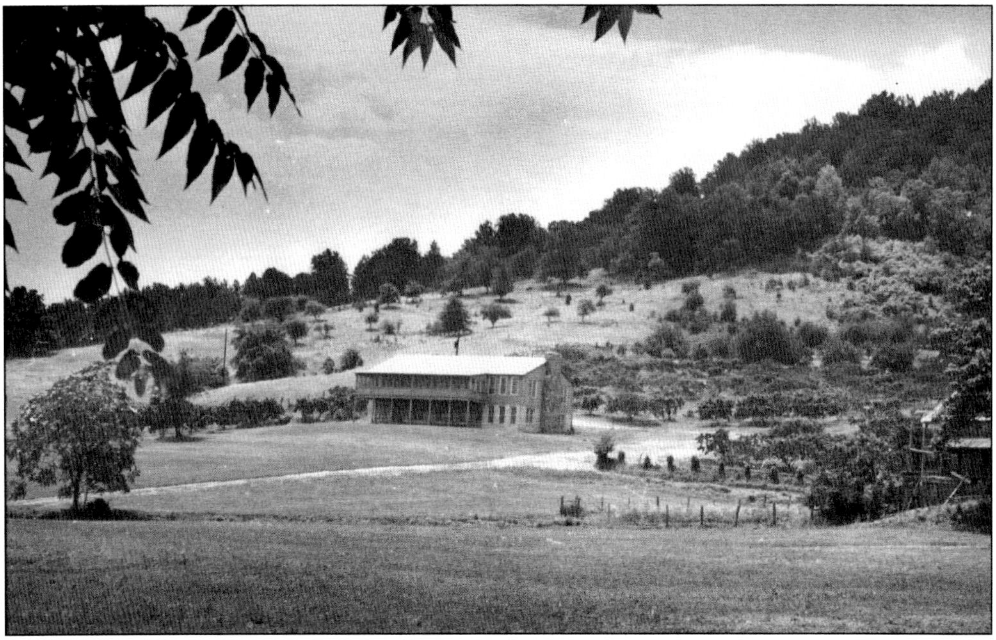

Four

Churches

The church has always been vital to life in Madison County. From the early 1700s, the establishment of churches was a priority. Prior to 1776, Virginia was an English colony. The Anglican Church was the official church of England and of Virginia. All citizens, including dissenters, were required to pay a tax to support it. Encouragement or support of other denominations was unlawful and punishable by imprisonment.

German settlers came to the Hebron Valley from Germanna in 1725. They were Lutherans and established the Hebron Lutheran Church. The first building was a log cabin built in 1727. It was replaced in 1740 by a frame building on the same site, which is still in use. No later than 1748, the church built a community school, which used the German language and may have been the first public school in Virginia. Slaves were bought by the church to work church farmlands, but the church abolished slavery in 1837, three decades before the Emancipation Proclamation.

English Quakers may have established a Meeting House near Criglersville before 1725, as several Quaker families settled there, but this is not confirmed. There is no Society of Friends Meeting in Madison County now. The first Methodist sermon was preached in 1774 at Meander, in the home of Henry Fry. Methodist theology developed within the Anglican Church that may have made dissent easier for the Methodists. Methodist ministers were licensed to perform marriages, but Baptists could not. In spite of legal prohibition, Baptists began preaching in Madison County in 1766. The Rapidan Baptist Church was formed at Wolftown in 1773. Baptist theology spread rapidly through Madison, and there are now many Baptist congregations in the county. The first Episcopal Church in Madison County, Piedmont Episcopal, was built in 1832 in the town of Madison.

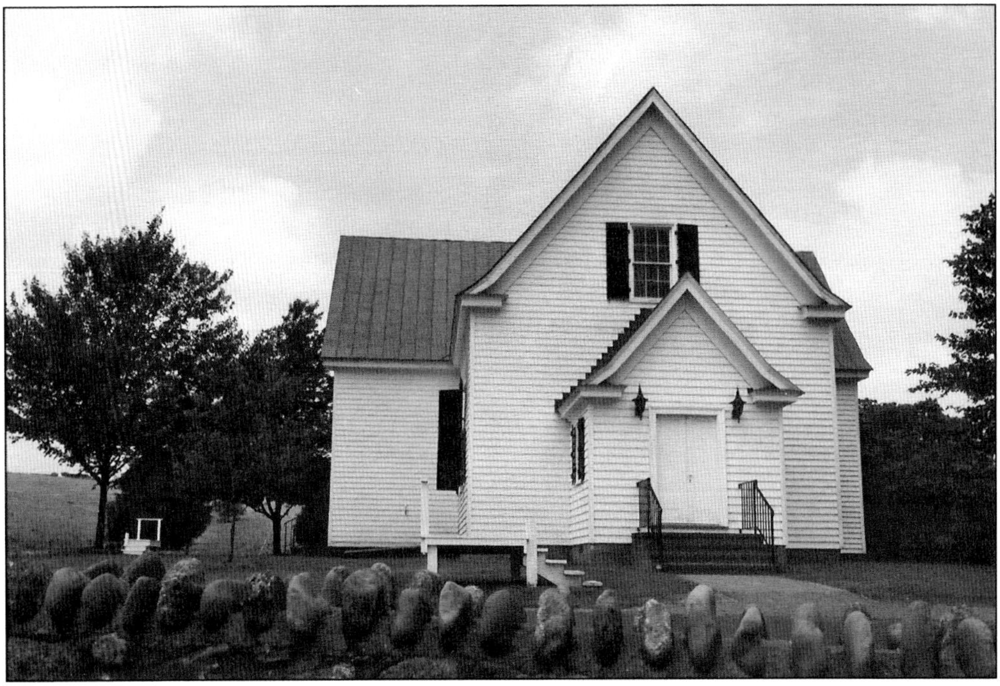

Hebron Lutheran is the oldest Lutheran church in continuous use by Lutherans in the country. It was constructed in 1740 and by 1748 a German school had been built on the property to serve all the local children. The church's 1802 pipe organ is still in use today. (Martha Cornwell.)

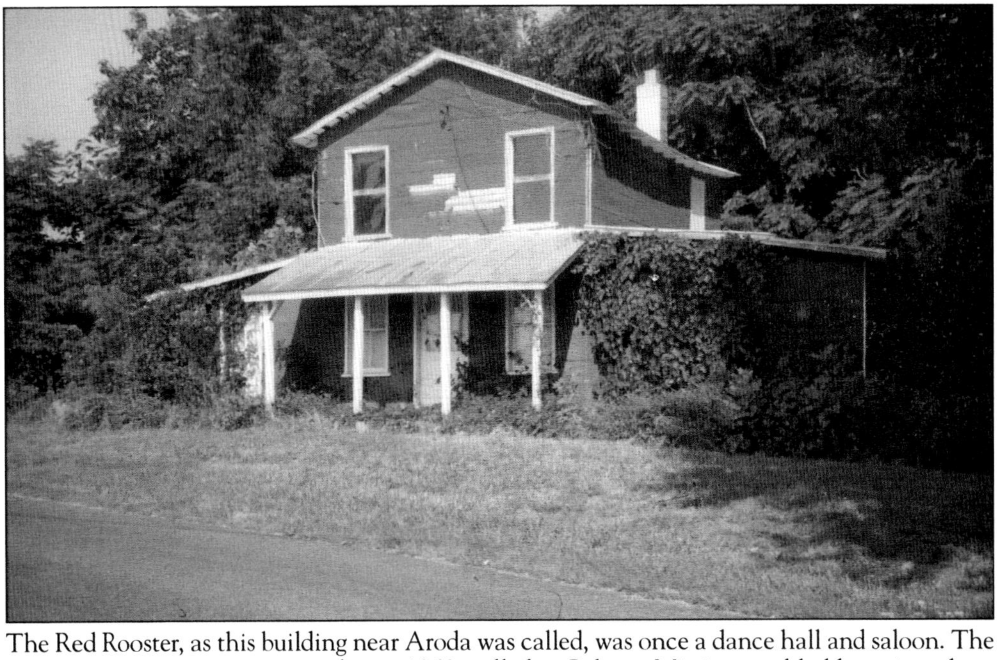

The Red Rooster, as this building near Aroda was called, was once a dance hall and saloon. The Mennonite community acquired it in 1960, called it Calvary Mission, and held services there for African Americans as well as whites during a period when segregation was pervasive. They later consolidated Calvary and their church at Oak Grove and have only one church for worship today. (Elmer Miller Jr.)

Rapidan Baptist Church was organized at Wolftown in 1773 and is the oldest Baptist church in Madison County. Baptists were persecuted before the American Revolution because the Anglican Church was the only officially recognized religion. The congregation, with both white and African American members, opposed slavery and petitioned Virginia's government to abolish it years before the Emancipation Proclamation. (Joyce Jenkins Gentry.)

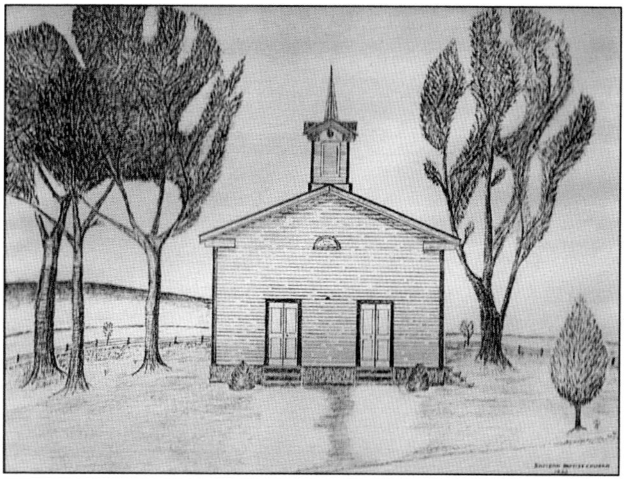

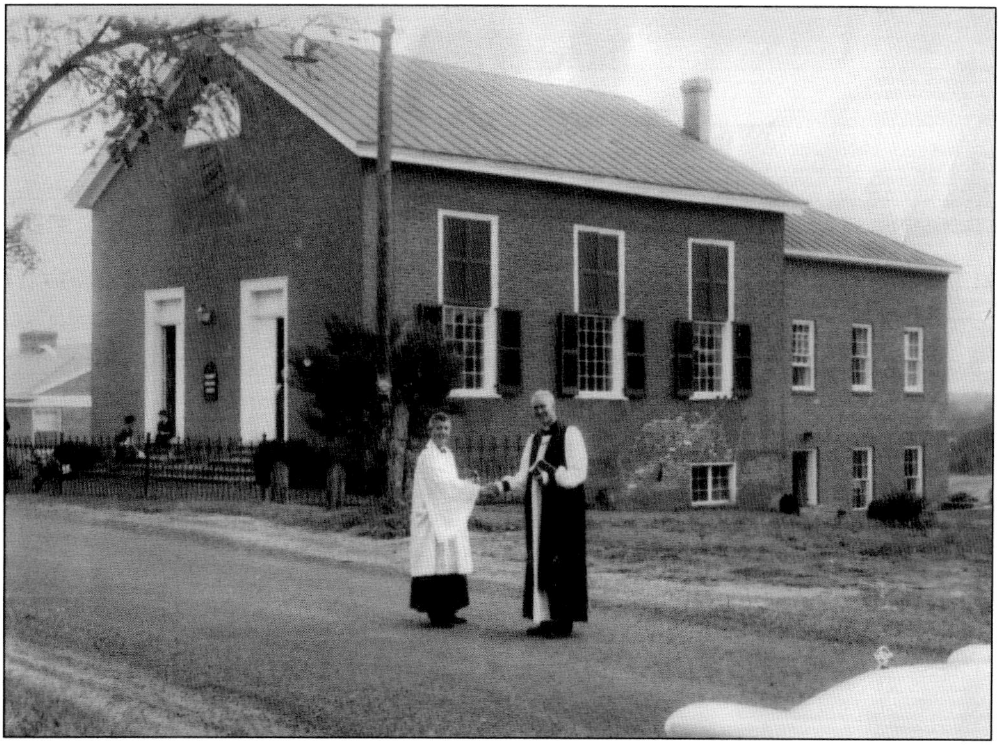

Piedmont Episcopal Church was consecrated in 1834 on land given by Capt. Henry Barnes. It did not have a resident minister until 1895. The church was used as a hospital during the Civil War, with wounded from both sides brought here after the Battle of Cedar Mountain. This photograph shows the Rev. Douglas Pitt (left) and Bishop Robert F. Gibson at the dedication of the parish house addition in 1961. (Rev. Brad Jackson.)

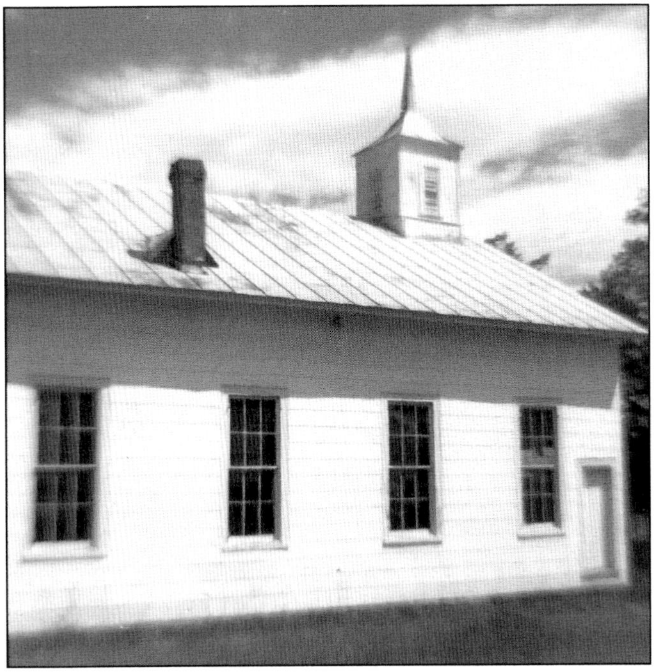

African American members of Beth Car Baptist Church formed Antioch Baptist Church in 1868. Members of Beth Car, both African American and white, built a log building that was replaced by the present church in the late 1870s. The church stands at the corner of Routes 273 and 231 on land acquired from Belfield Cave for $50. It is the oldest predominantly black church in the county. (Lola Poles.)

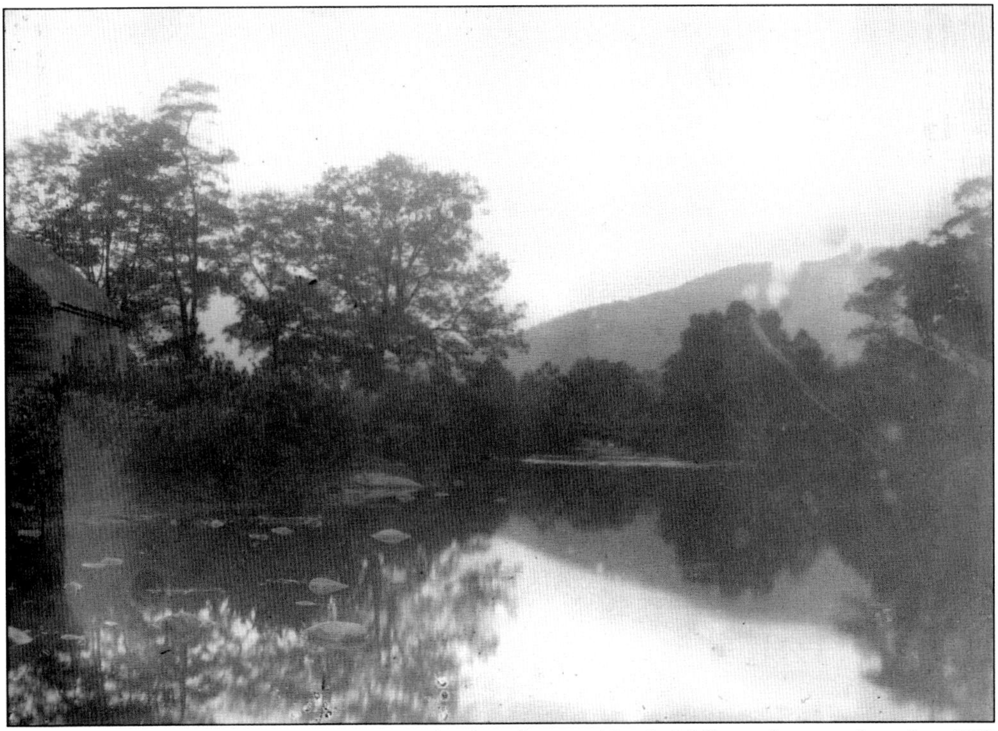

Near Old Rag Mountain and the crossroads of Nethers and Peola Mills residents gathered in 1778 to form a community of worship called the Ragged Mountain Baptist Society. It was one of the first two Baptist congregations in Madison County. This building, on the far left, believed to be the society's house of worship, stood in the early 1900s on the Hughes River and was called the old F. T. Church. (Dewey Lillard.)

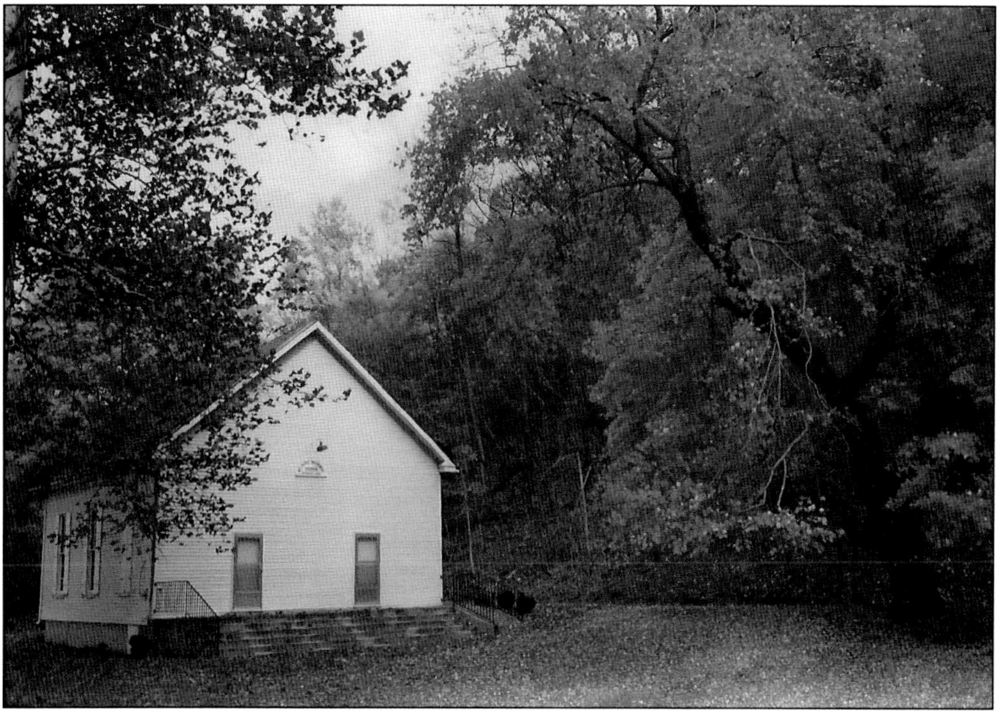

The picturesque Mt. Olivet Methodist Church stands along the Robinson River near Syria. It was established in 1848. A story is told that during the early 20th century, floodwaters carried it off its foundation, depositing it several hundred yards downstream. Local residents used horses and a sled to bring it back and reposition it on its foundation. (Martha Cornwell.)

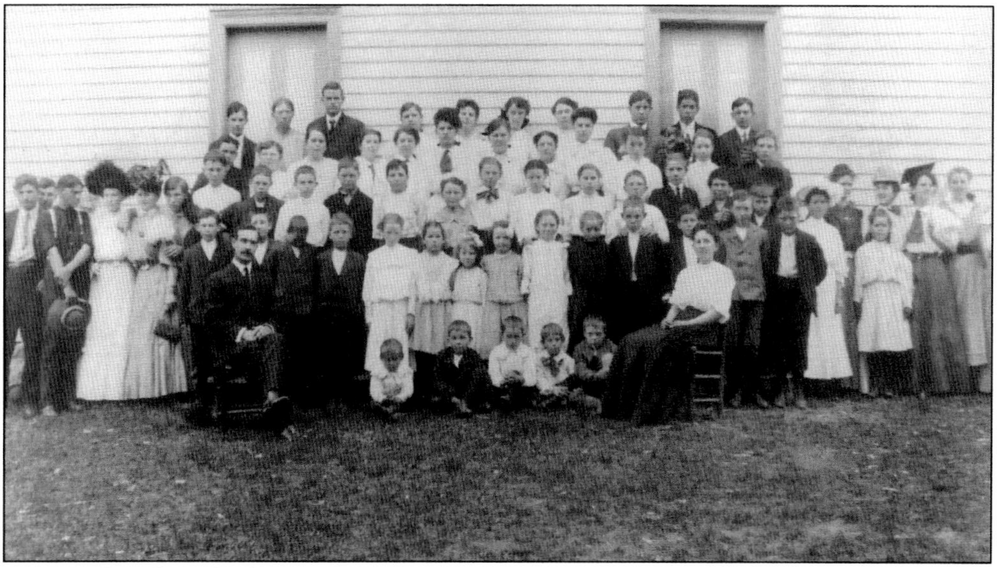

Graves Chapel was built in 1885 as a Baptist meetinghouse. Two doors at the front provided separate entrances for men and women. After the establishment of the Shenandoah National Park, the attendance dropped off and it closed in 1969. Ten years later, services began again and continue on a limited basis today. The chapel is used and cared for by the Graves Mill community and the Piedmont Episcopal Church. (Doug Graves.)

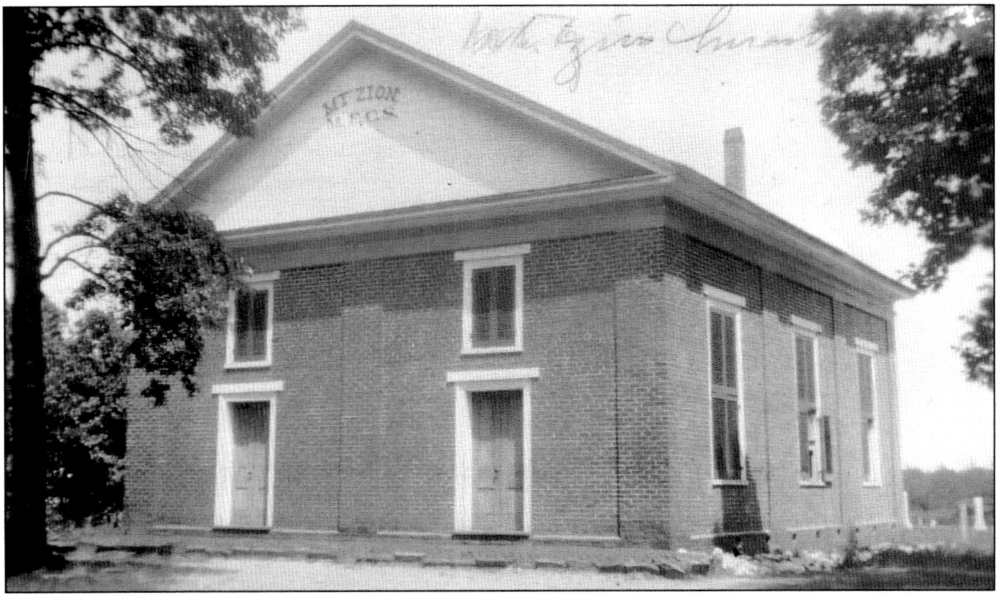

Mt. Zion Methodist Church in Oak Park is one of the oldest Methodist churches in the county. Reverend Isham Tatum is believed to have been serving Methodists in the area as early as 1785. In reviewing marriage records of both Madison and Culpeper Counties, it appears that he performed the marriages of many of the known residents of Oak Park at that time. The current building was dedicated in 1858. (Ruth and Randall Lillard.)

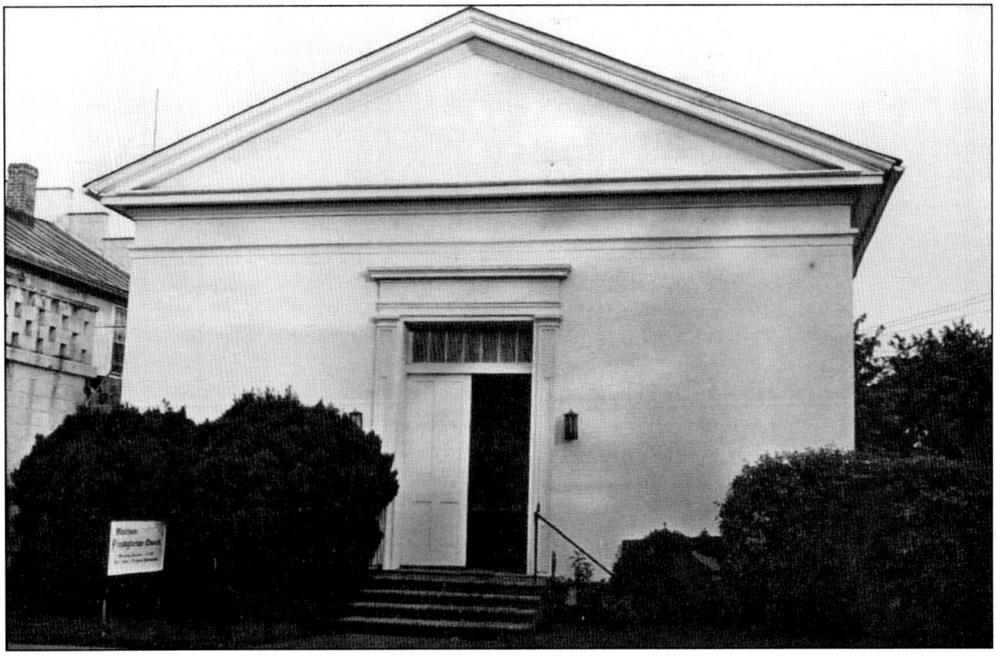

Presbyterians organized in Madison in 1850. The first church was completed in 1852 on a lot on Main Street donated by Angus R. and Jane Eliza Blakey. They eventually outgrew this building and constructed a new church just outside of town in 1984. The Main Street building, pictured here around 1950, is still in use as a business known as That Little Quilt Shop. (John Storey.)

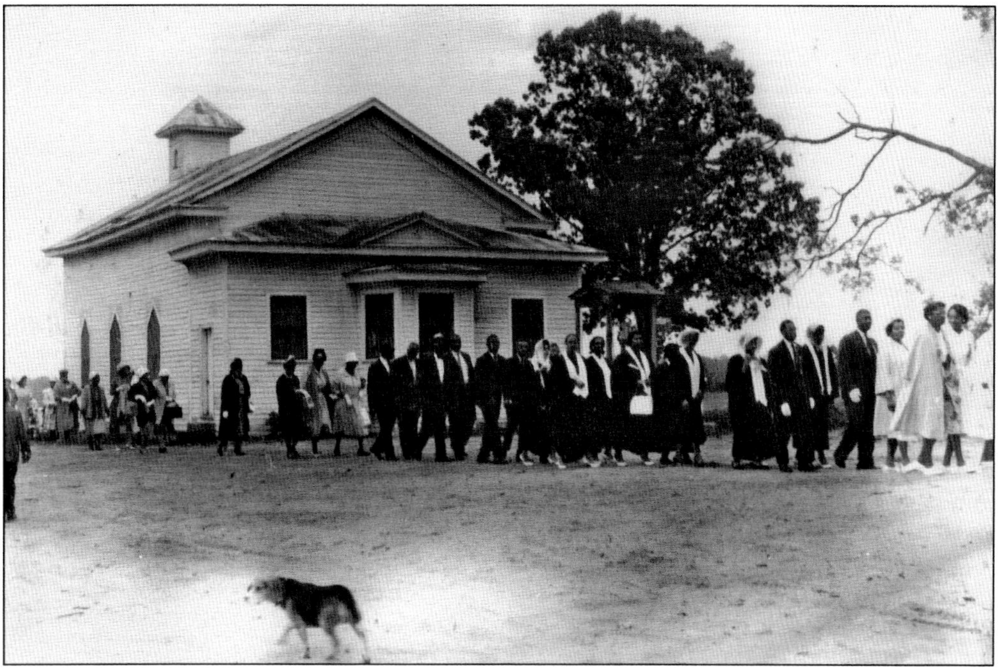

Members of Locust Grove Baptist Church near Radiant leave their old sanctuary in 1963 to march to the newly built church on the grounds. African American members of Good Hope Baptist Church who sought to have their own place to worship after the Civil War formed Locust Grove around 1871. The church was built with the aid and support of the white members of Good Hope. In the lower photograph, church members are entering their beautiful new building on June 3, 1963. (Both, Janice P. Carpenter.)

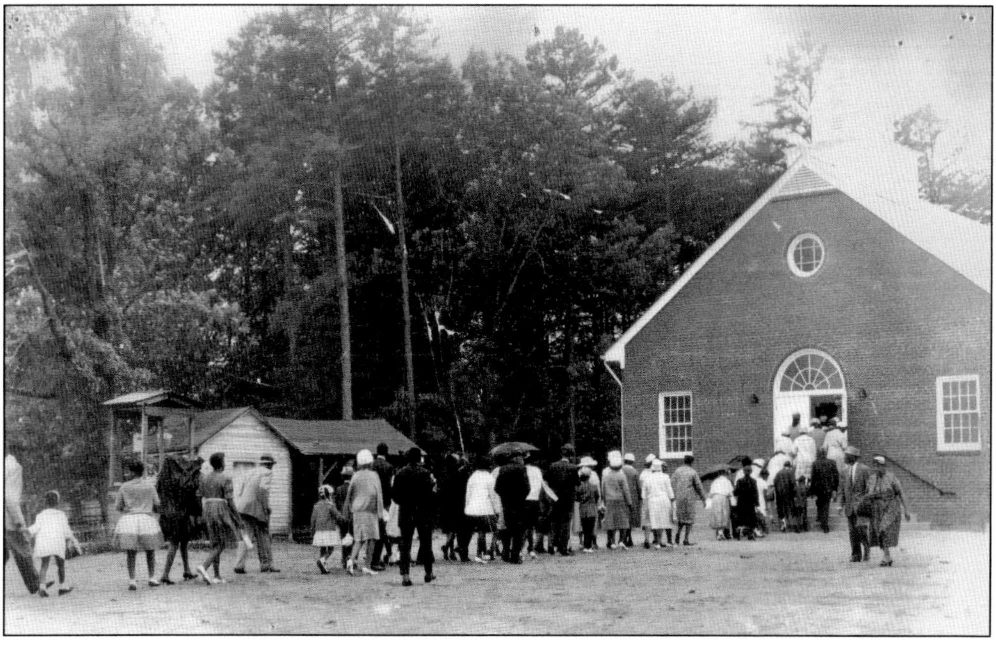

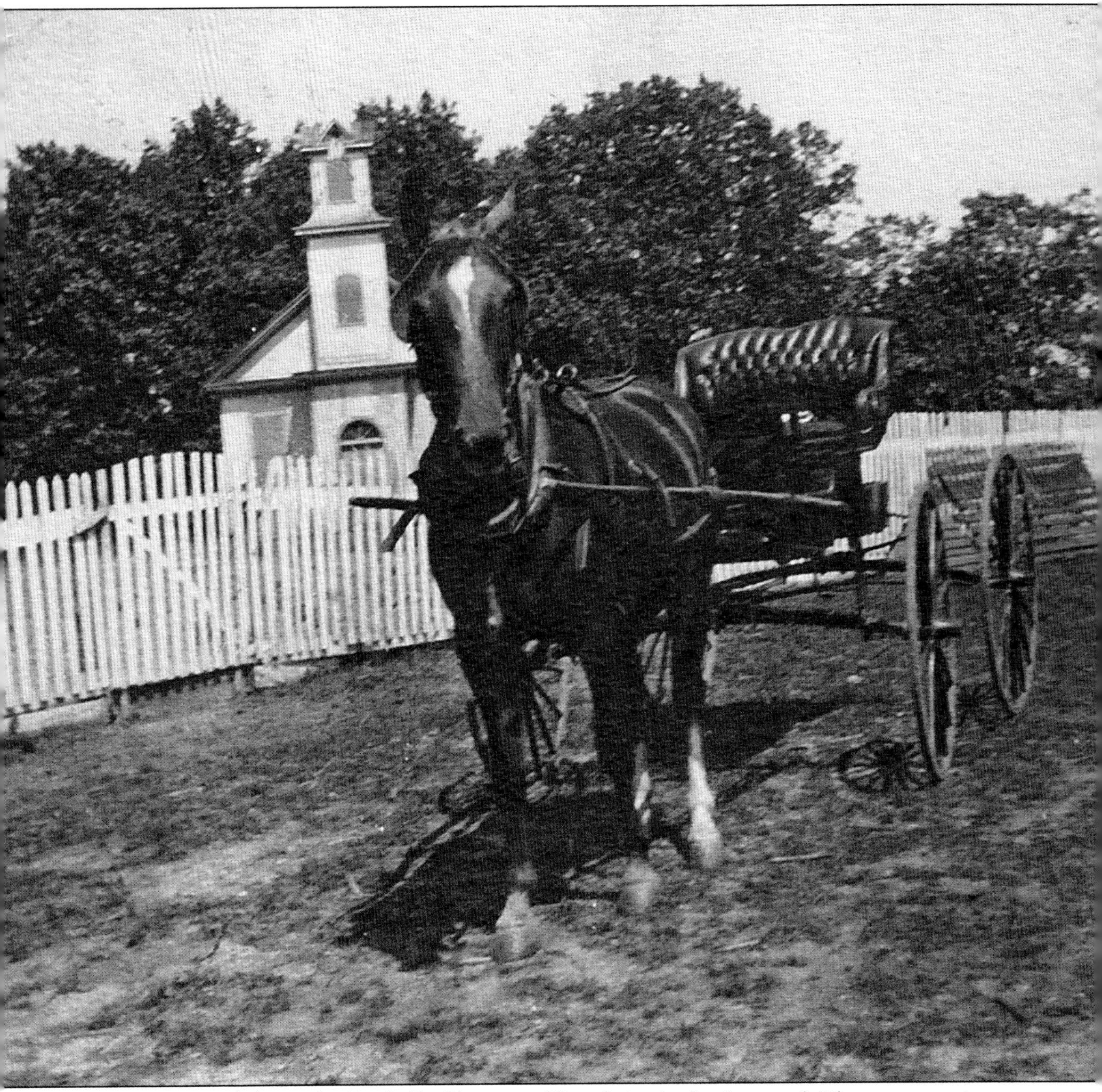

This postcard shows the Rochelle Christian Church in the background. The congregation was organized in 1859 with 23 charter members. A contract for a building was let in January 1860 and the first service was held in the new building on October 27, 1860. Travel was still by horse when this photograph was taken in 1913. (Steve Hoffman.)

Five

Schools

Throughout the years, schools have been an important factor in the life of Madison County. Whether public, private, or parochial, small or large, they have greatly influenced the lives and futures of children. A child's education in the 18th century was heavily dependent on its family. Often a mother or other close female relative would be a child's first teacher. If the family had the means, a clergyman might be paid to teach, either in the home or the parsonage. In 1818, a law required counties to pay teachers for the education of poor children.

Early schools were in homes or frequently in a parsonage. Churches supported some schools. Hebron Lutheran, although its language was exclusively German, was the first public school in the county, as it offered classes to all of the surrounding community. In 1959, the Oak Grove Mennonite congregation opened the Madison Christian Day School in the basement of their church.

The 19th century saw substantial improvement. In 1870, the state assumed responsibility for the establishment of a public school system. Public schools began to be built in 1871 but were poorly funded. Private schools continued to respond to the need, and there were a number of them in Madison County. Locust Dale Academy opened in 1858 and Woodberry Forest School had its first classes in 1889. Both were intended to prepare students for college.

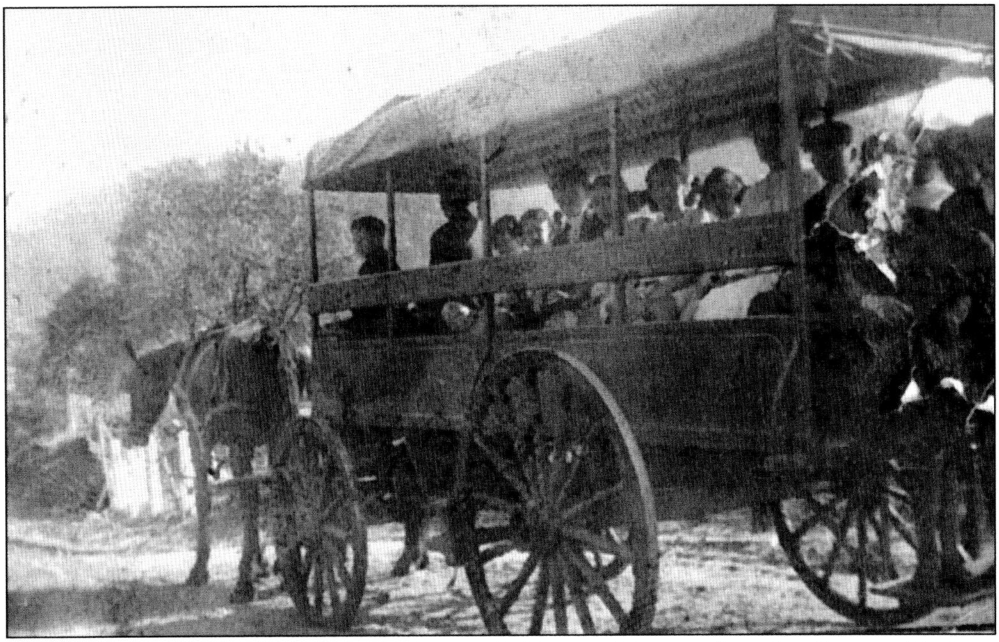

This horse-drawn, specially outfitted wagon is probably one of the very first schoolbuses in Madison County. It took two horses to pull this load. The seats appear to be placed down the middle of the wagon with the children facing outward. School buses were privately owned in the early days. (Betty Lynn Yowell and Barbara Yowell.)

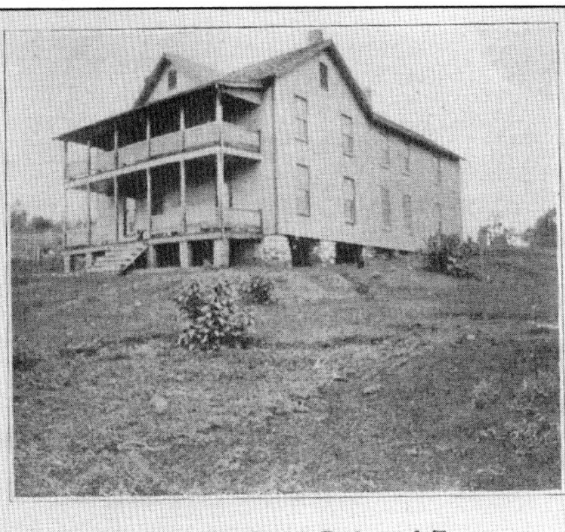

Former Students Referred To

W. J. SMITH, M. D.	SPERRYVILLE, VA.
BURNETT MILLER, LAWYER	CULPEPER, VA.
J. J. MILLER, M. D.	NORFOLK, VA.
Z. L. WEAVER, M. D.	STERLING, VA.
J. C. EASTHAM	CHARLESTON, W. VA.
A. G. FRAY	ADVANCE MILLS, VA.
OTIS MARSHALL	BARBOURSVILLE, VA.
E. N. LILLARD, M. D.	STANARDSVILLE, VA.
W. H. WOOD,	LAUREL MILLS, VA.
F. C. HOOVER	BROADWAY, VA.
HUNTER MILLER, LAWYER	BEDFORD CITY, VA.
L. Y. BOWMAN	NEW MARKET, VA.
ROBT. J. THRIFT, LAWYER	FAYETTEVILLE, W. VA.

.. THE ...

Warwick High School

Location

THE WARWICK HIGH SCHOOL is situated in the county of Madison, Virginia, two and a half miles from the town of Madison, the county seat, at the foot of the Blue Ridge Mountains and immediately in the famous Robinson River valley. The location is distinguished for healthfulness and beauty of scenery. The boys of the school are surrounded by wholesome home influences, which are so largely influential in attaining one of the highest aims of true education—that of character building.

Outdoor exercise is encouraged, tending to healthy physical development, which is almost necessary to real intellectual advancement.

The Fray School, later named Warwick School, was first started on the grounds of Hebron Lutheran Church in 1880. It burned shortly afterward and John D. Fray built a two-room school with 12 dormitory rooms on his property across the Robinson River in 1890. This was a private school for boys that continued functioning until 1916. (John Fray.)

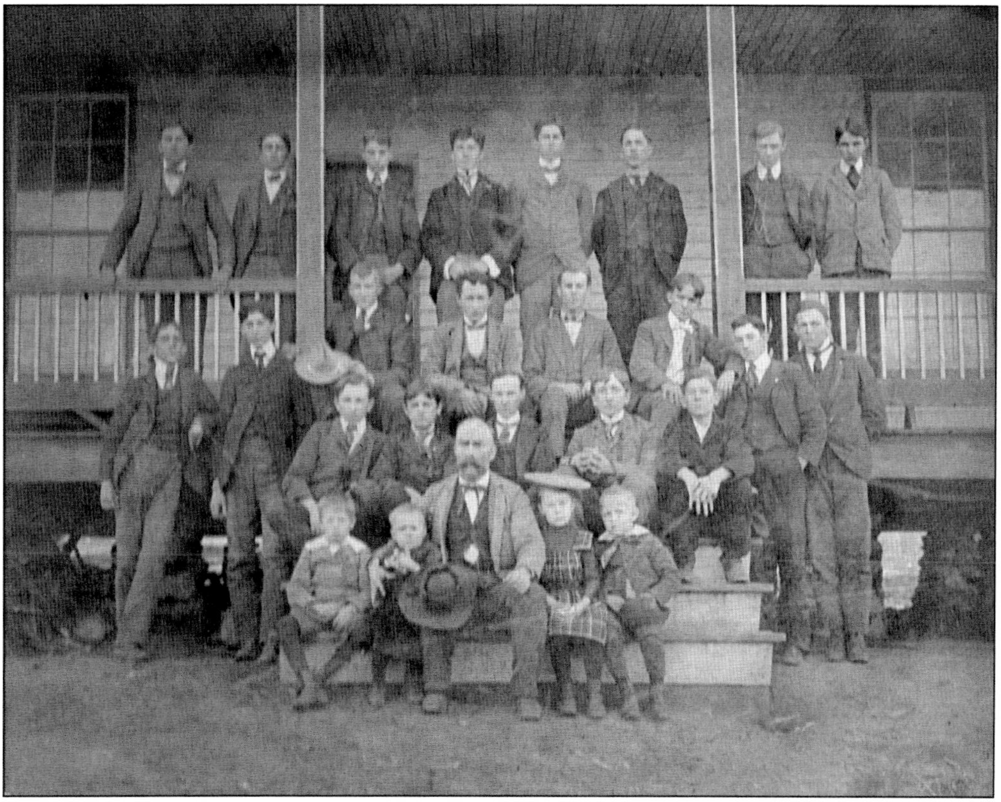

Students of the old Warwick school for boys pose for a picture on the front steps. The school was built by John D. Fray on his property. Pictured in the first row, from left to right, are John W. Taylor, John H. Fray, principal and owner John D. Fray, Hester Fray, and Joe Fray. (Joan Weaver.)

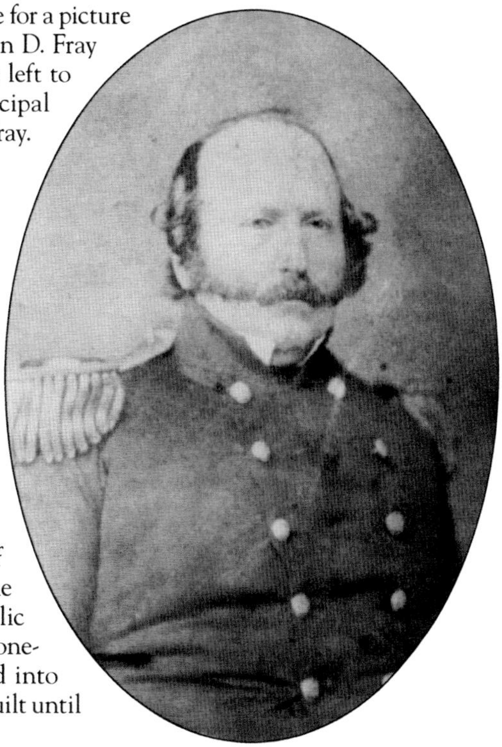

The public school system was established in Madison County in 1871 under the direction of Dr. William A. Hill, pictured here, who was the first superintendent of schools. When the public school system came into effect, most of the old one-room field school buildings were incorporated into the public schools. No two-room schools were built until 1884. (Photograph by John Mitchell.)

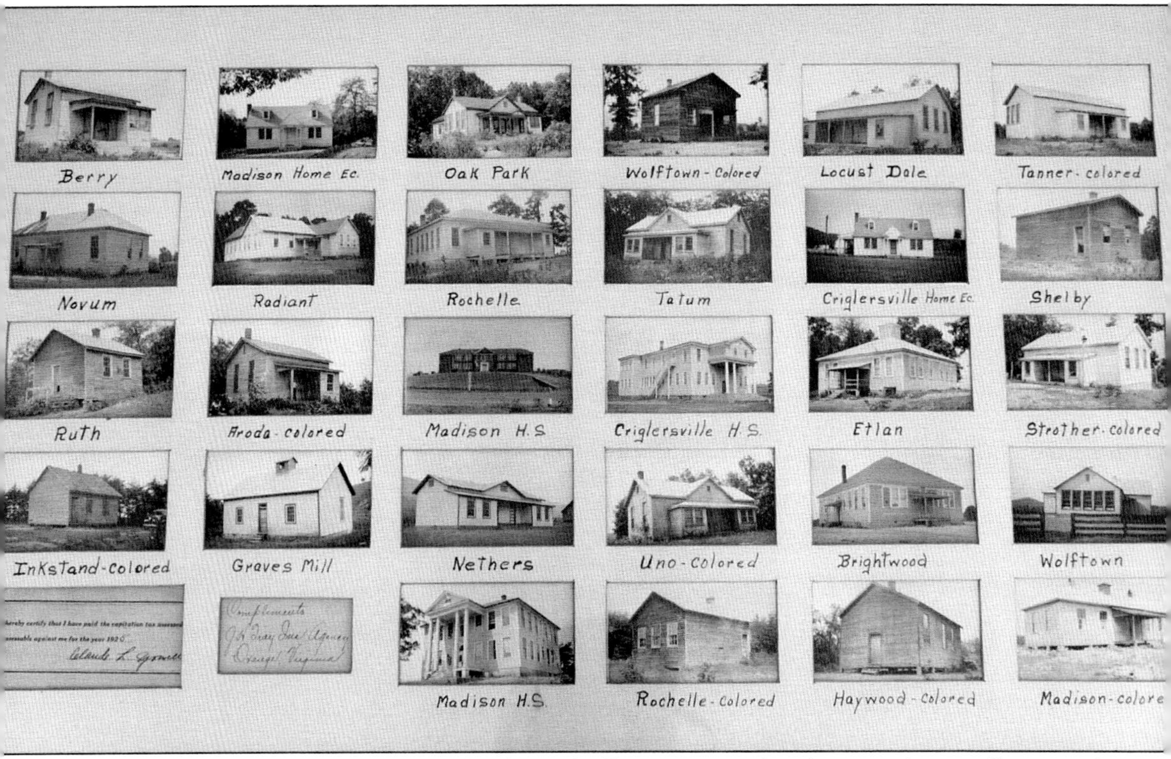

This picture hangs in Madison's School Board office as a reminder of a time when small one- and two-room schoolhouses were common. Between 1915 and 1933, most small schools had sand tables, which had raised edges and were inlaid with tin so the sand could be moistened. The primary grade children illustrated a story they had read by building in sand some aspect of that story, such as a Native American village or a battlefield. In most schools there was an iron wood stove. Once or twice a week the teacher would have the children bring canned vegetables and she would make soup for all of them. Sometimes the water was nearby, but if not, students had to go a long way to get a bucket of water twice a day for drinking. (Photograph by John Mitchell.)

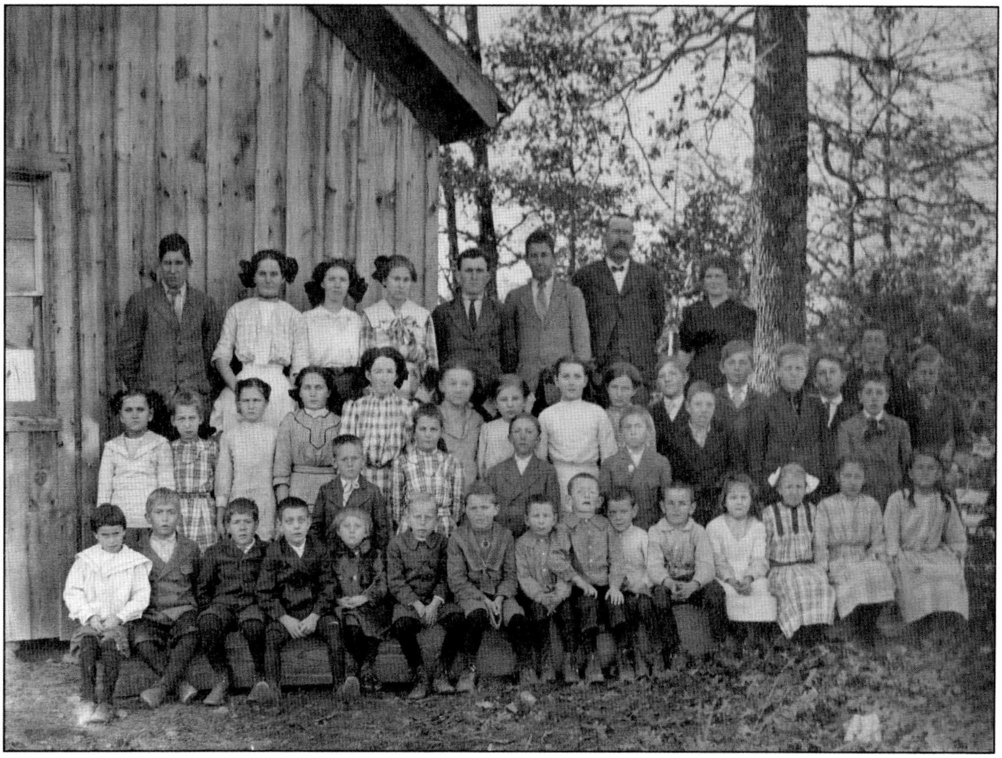

The Brightwood School began in 1913. Soon a third room was added, and by 1929 the Community League requested that the school have five rooms. However, the school board only allowed four rooms and the first two years of high school. Here students pose for their picture outside the school. (John Howard Carpenter.)

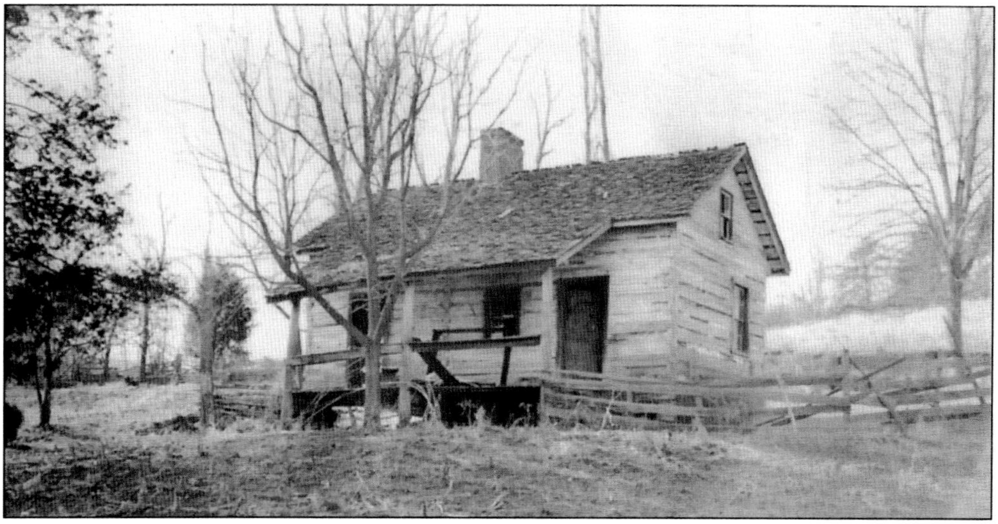

Field schools, the first form of public education, dotted the Madison County landscape from 1800 to 1870. The local community, which also put up the money to pay a teacher, built a field school. These schools were built mostly for convenience because transportation and roads were so poor. This school still stands on the Jim Smith farm off Route 231 just north of the town of Madison. (Dana Smith Faulconer.)

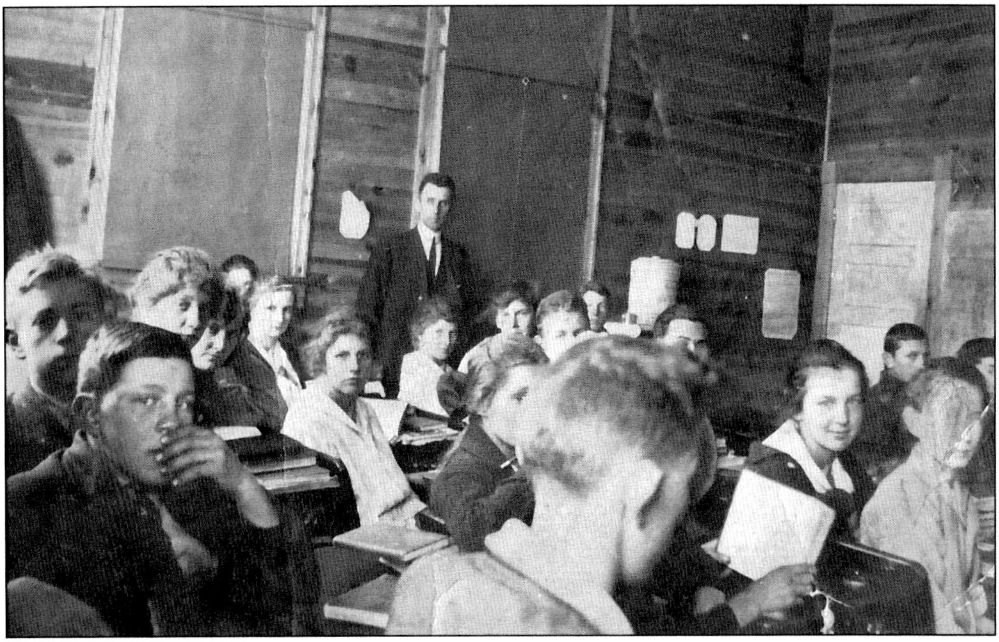

This photograph was taken inside the Etlan High School. Cecil Coppedge is the teacher. The school was enlarged in 1913 to accommodate high school students. A. W. Yowell was the first principal when the school was built in 1911 and kept that job until 1921 when he was appointed superintendent of public schools in Madison. (Lillian Mitchell.)

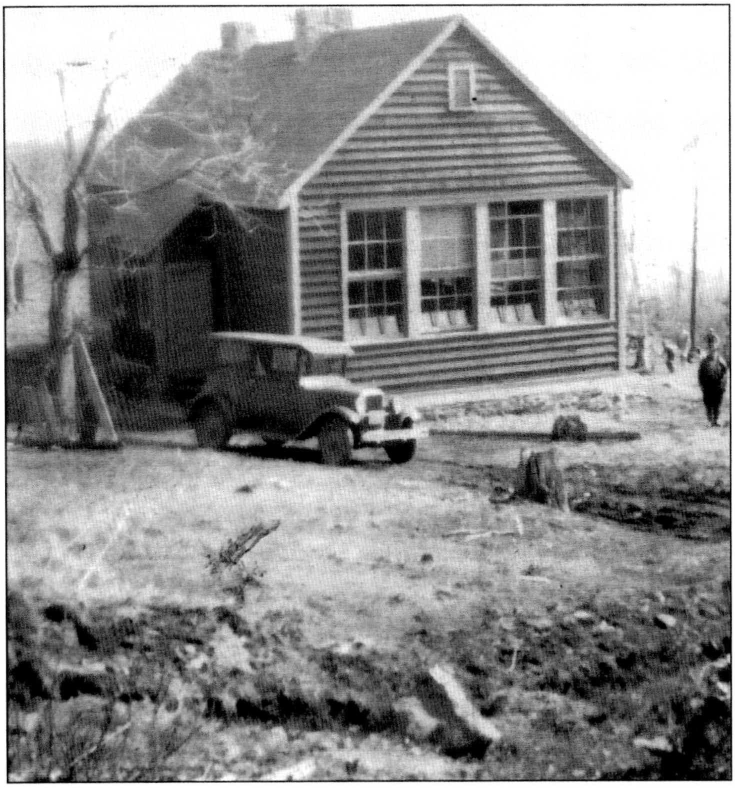

Pres. Herbert Hoover and First Lady Lou Hoover started coming to the mountains of Madison County in the late 1920s. They were good neighbors and took an interest in the education of the mountain children. President Hoover headed the effort to raise funds to build this modern schoolhouse, which had five rooms: a classroom, living room, dining room, kitchen, and bathroom, plus two dormer rooms. Running water was piped from a nearby mountain spring. (Vee Tull.)

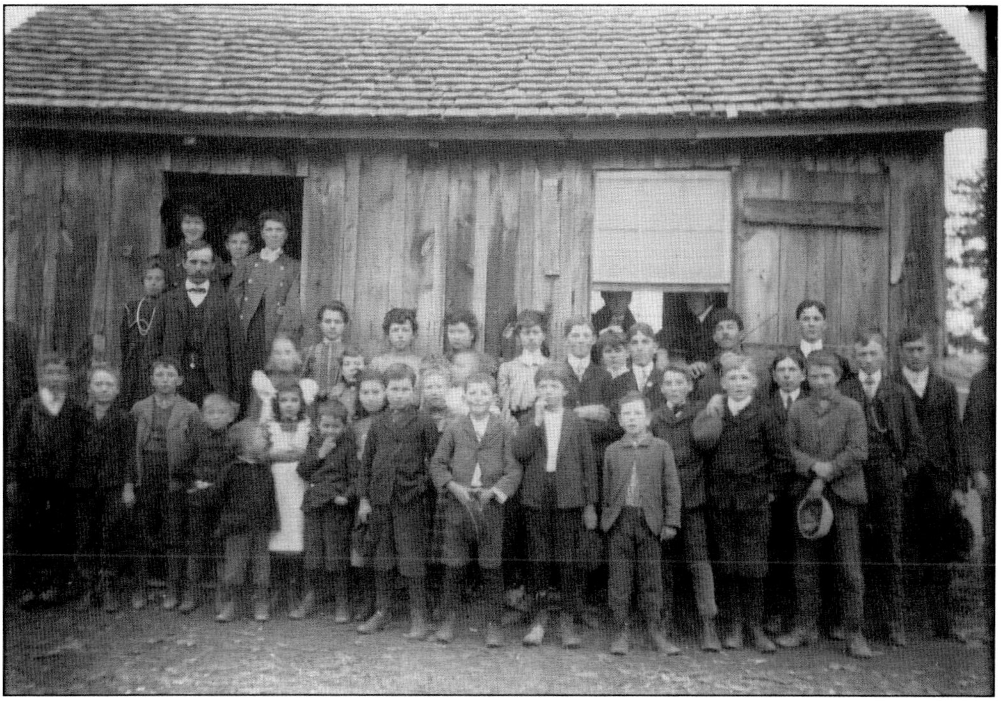

These students pose in front of the Crigler School in 1908. This was a private school on the property of the Crigler family near Brightwood. The school, on Deep Run near Hoffman's Mill, is believed to have opened in the mid-1770s shortly after the first German settlement of the Hebron Valley. (Steve Hoffman.)

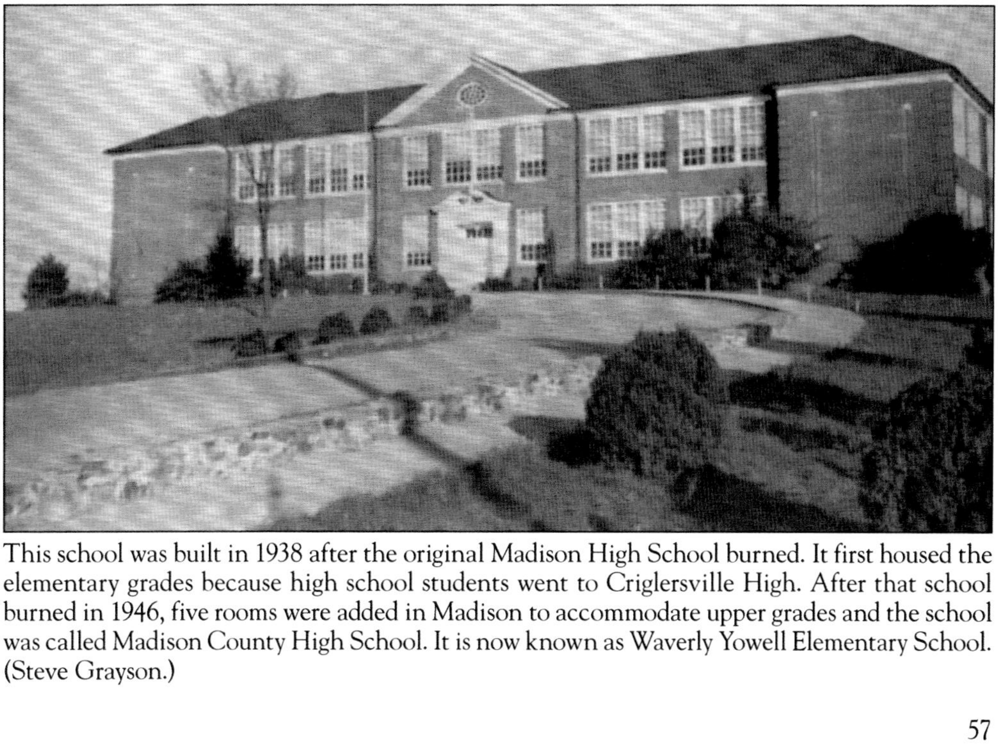

This school was built in 1938 after the original Madison High School burned. It first housed the elementary grades because high school students went to Criglersville High. After that school burned in 1946, five rooms were added in Madison to accommodate upper grades and the school was called Madison County High School. It is now known as Waverly Yowell Elementary School. (Steve Grayson.)

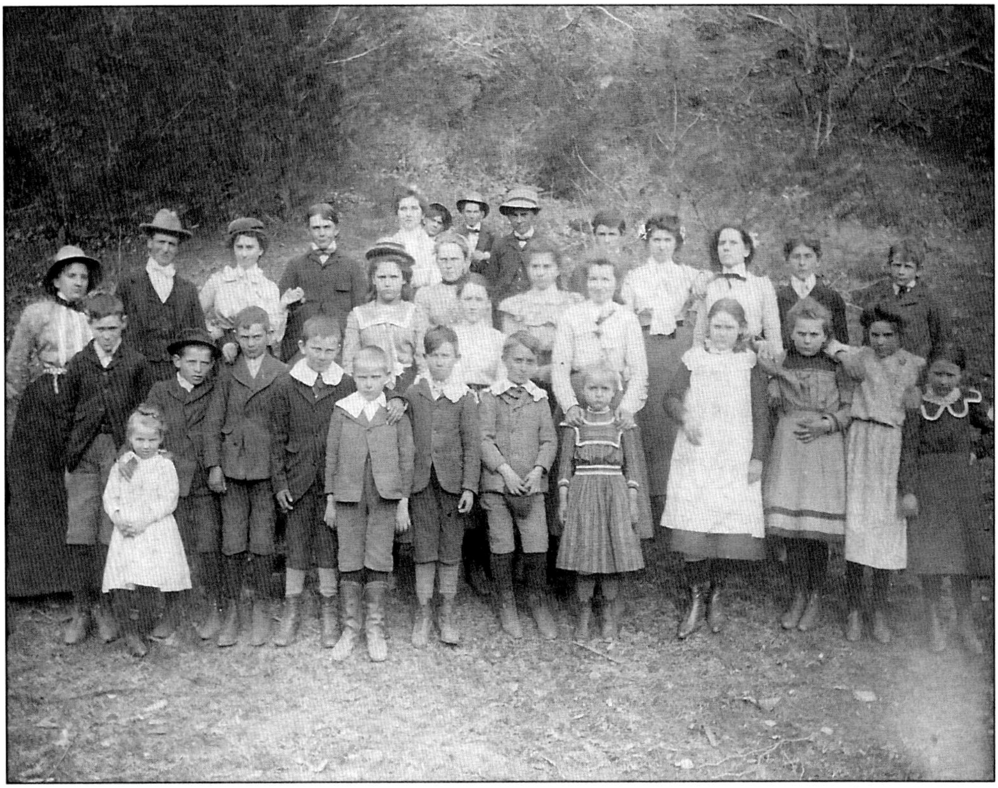

Graves Mill school children pose for their picture in 1902. This earlier school is believed to have been located up the Rapidan River from Graves Mill in a curve of the river near the Goodall place (Rapidan Ranch). It was a one-room building and burned after it was struck by lightning. (Ruth and Randall Lillard.)

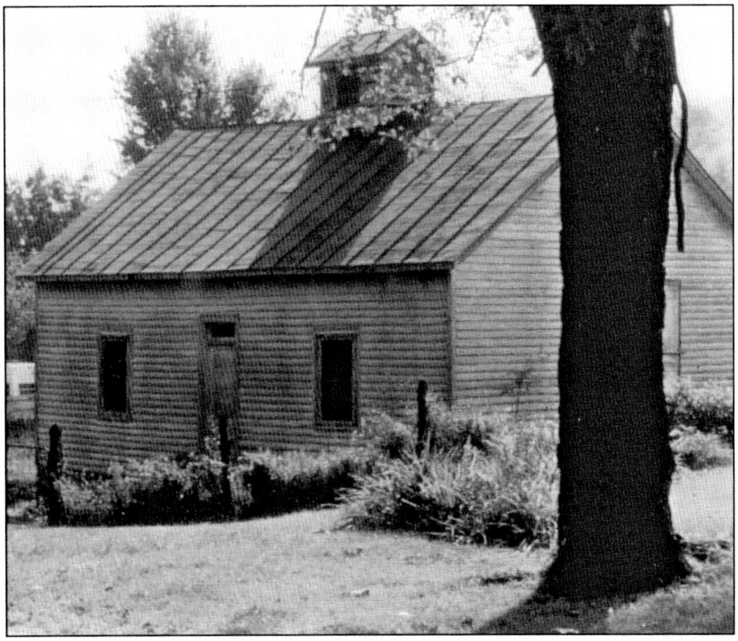

This schoolhouse, pictured around 1929, still stands in the village of Graves Mill as a remembrance of the past. It was built in 1906 on land purchased from James W. Estes and was referred to as the "Estes school" in the early days. The school had one large room, which could be divided into two rooms with a partition. It housed grades first through seventh. (Courtesy of Doug Graves.)

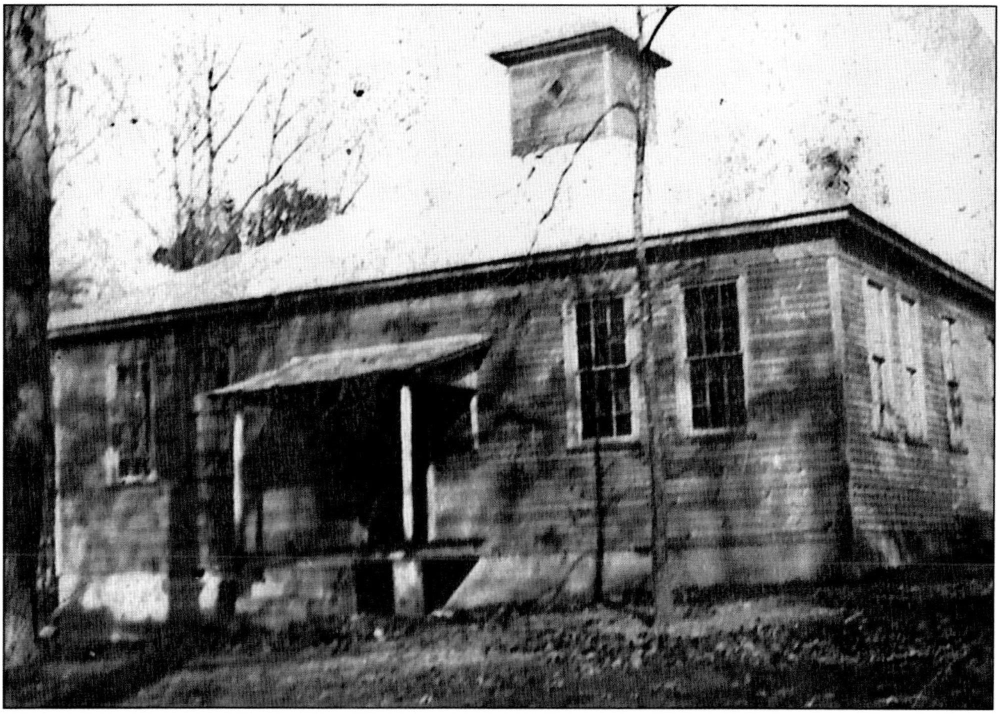

The first two rooms of the Etlan School were finished in 1911. Two more rooms were built and high school classes were added for the 1913–1914 session, making it the first high school in Madison. A. Waverly Yowell was principal at Etlan until he was appointed superintendent of schools in 1921. Claude Lindsey Yowell, Madison County historian, graduated from Etlan High School and went on to the University of Virginia, where he received a master's degree. (Betty Lynn Yowell.)

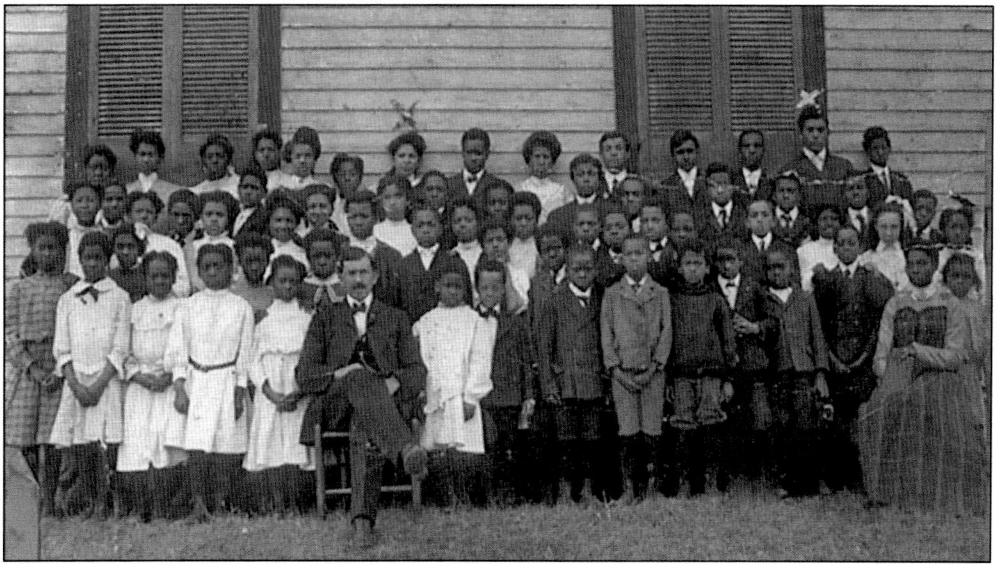

These children attended the African American school in Madison sometime around 1935. They are standing in front of Antioch Church, where for several years classes were held on the second floor of the church building. Later the school was moved to a new building on Fairgrounds Road. Currently this old school serves as the county school board offices. (Eunice Frye.)

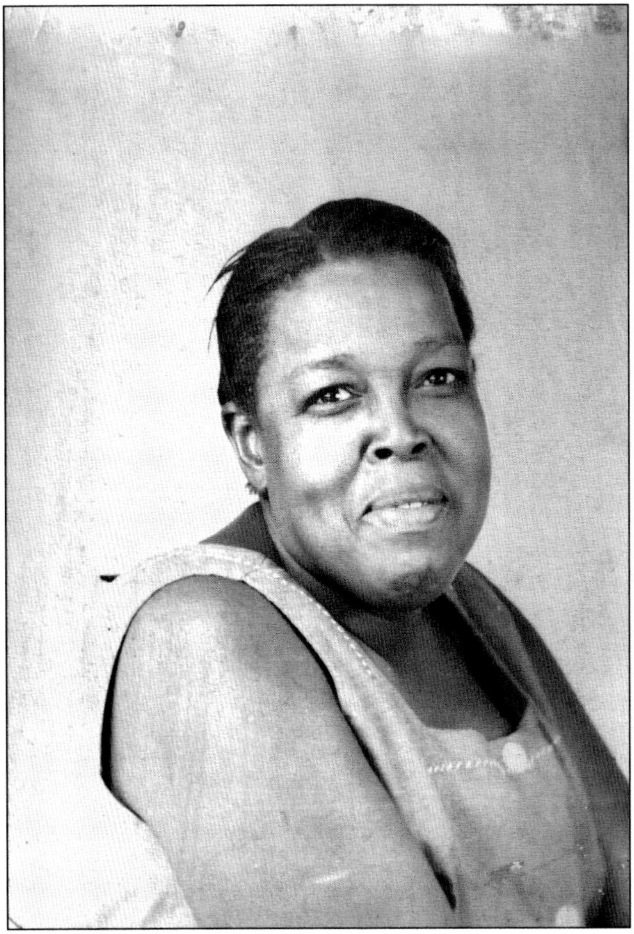

Emma Lee Acty Davis taught at the African American school at Radiant in the 1930s. She was known for being a strict disciplinarian and for her rigorous teaching of penmanship, grammar, math, and geography. Funding of public schools was greatly affected from 1929 to 1933 by the Depression. The length of the school year was reduced and some parents paid part of the teachers' salaries. (Janice P. Carpenter.)

The Madison High School on Schoolhouse Road was built in 1916 and served Madison's young people until it burned in 1937. A brick school was built on north Main Street in 1938, which housed all grades for many years. It is now called Waverly Yowell Elementary School and serves the third, fourth, and fifth grades. It has been remodeled to be a state-of-the-art facility. (Steve Hoffman.)

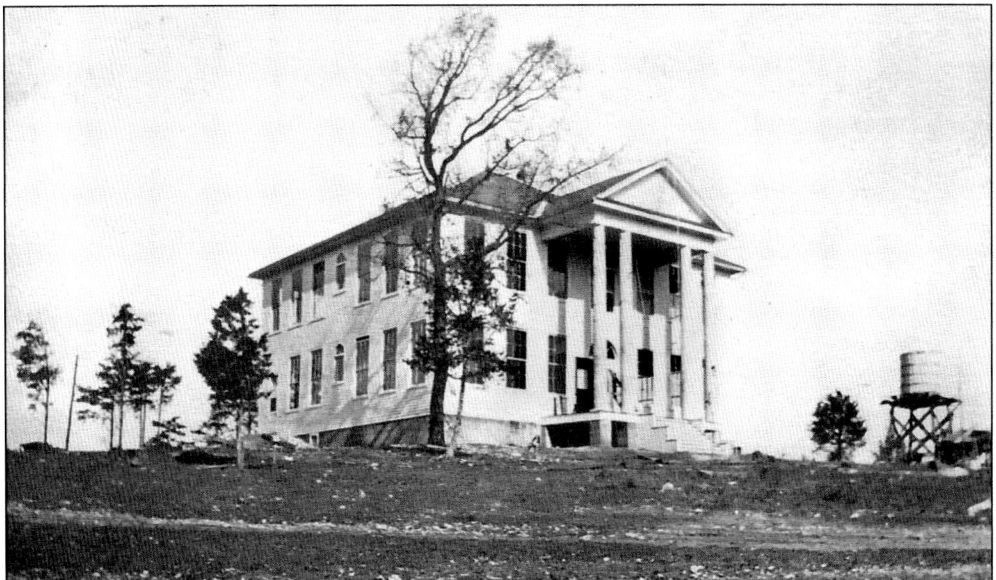

Mary Elizabeth Hale, standing here in front of the Etlan High School, was a revered teacher at this school. She married fellow teacher and principal A. Waverly Yowell on December 26, 1914. Yowell became superintendent of schools in 1921 and served Madison and Greene schools from 1921 until 1949. (Betty Lynn Yowell.)

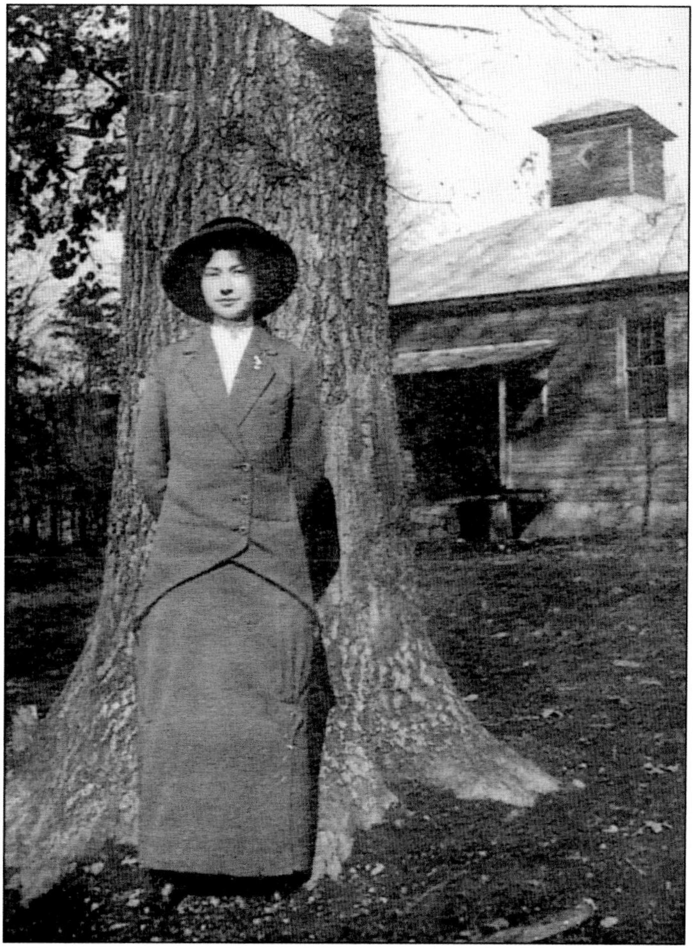

This is the Nethers school house, pictured around 1910. It stood in the shadow of Old Rag Mountain and served the surrounding community. (Madison County Historical Society.)

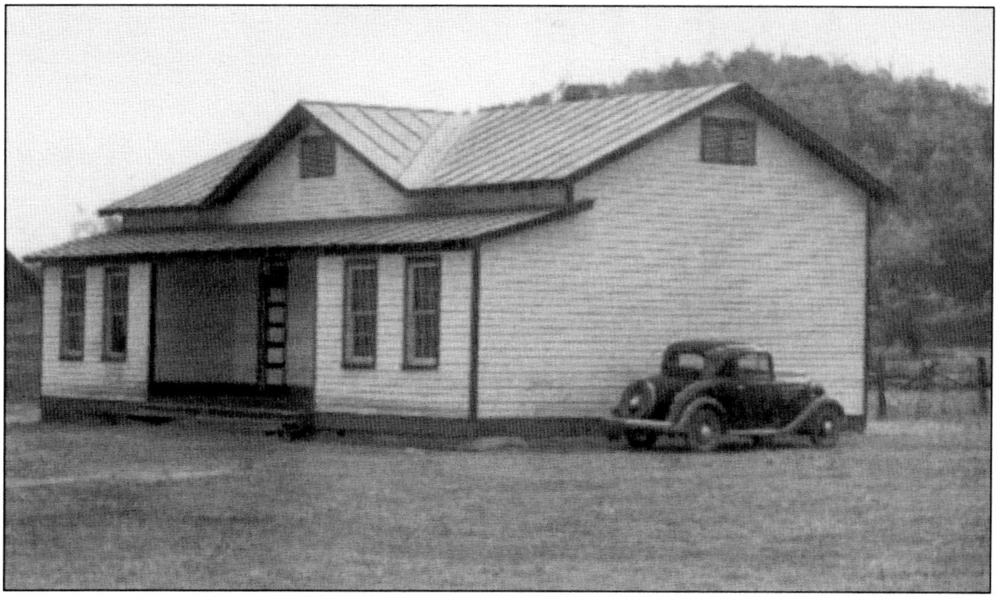

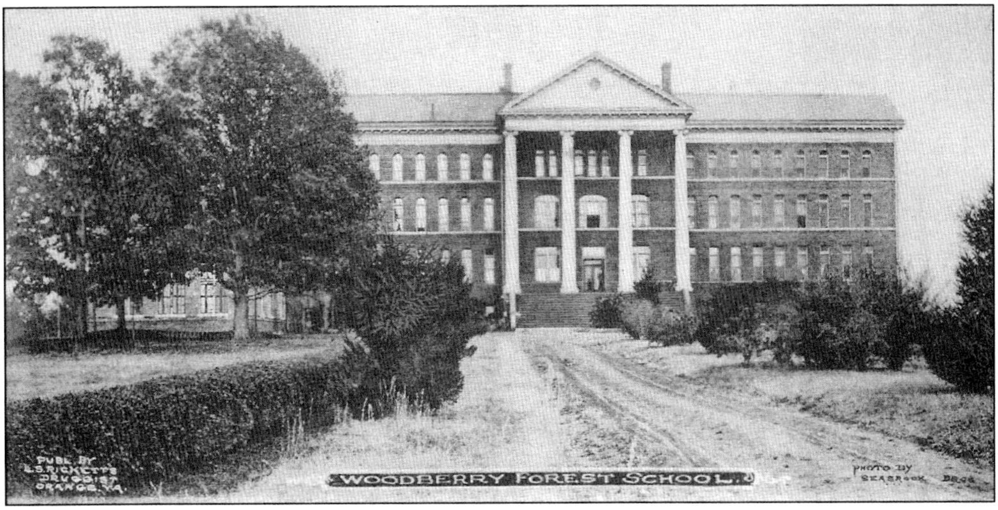

Here is a postcard of Woodberry Forest School. It stands in the southeastern part of Madison County and is a nationally known private college-preparatory school for young men. It was established in 1889 when a tutor, Thompson Brown, was hired to teach the six Robert S. Walker children in their home, which is now called "The Residence" at the school. (Steve Grayson.)

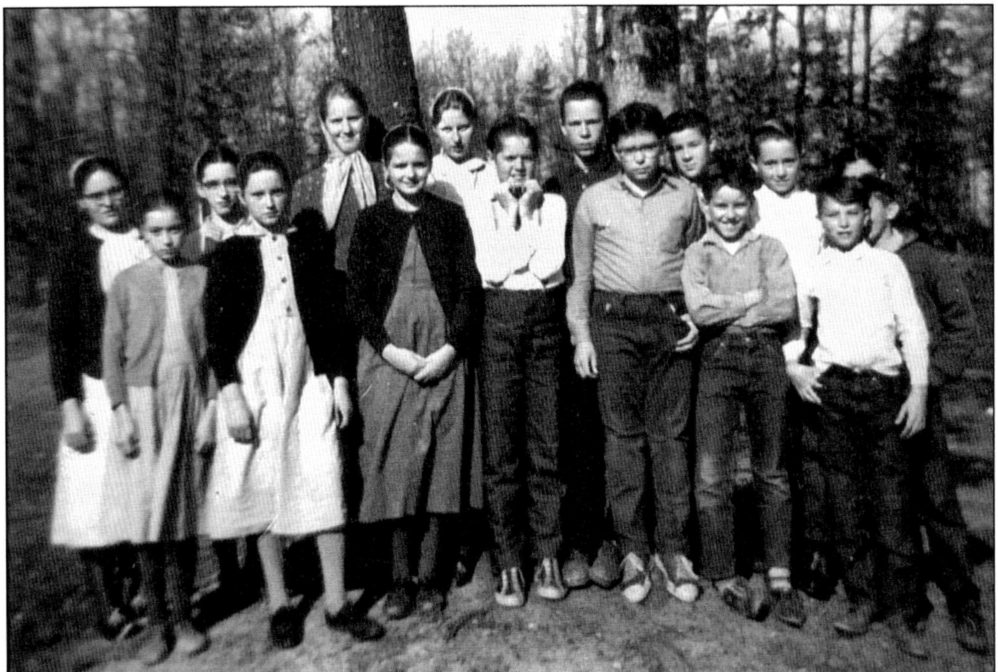

Shortly after the first Mennonite families arrived in Madison County in the 1950s, they started a school near Oak Grove Mennonite Church in Aroda. The school still functions today and teaches students from kindergarten through high school. (Elmer Miller Jr.)

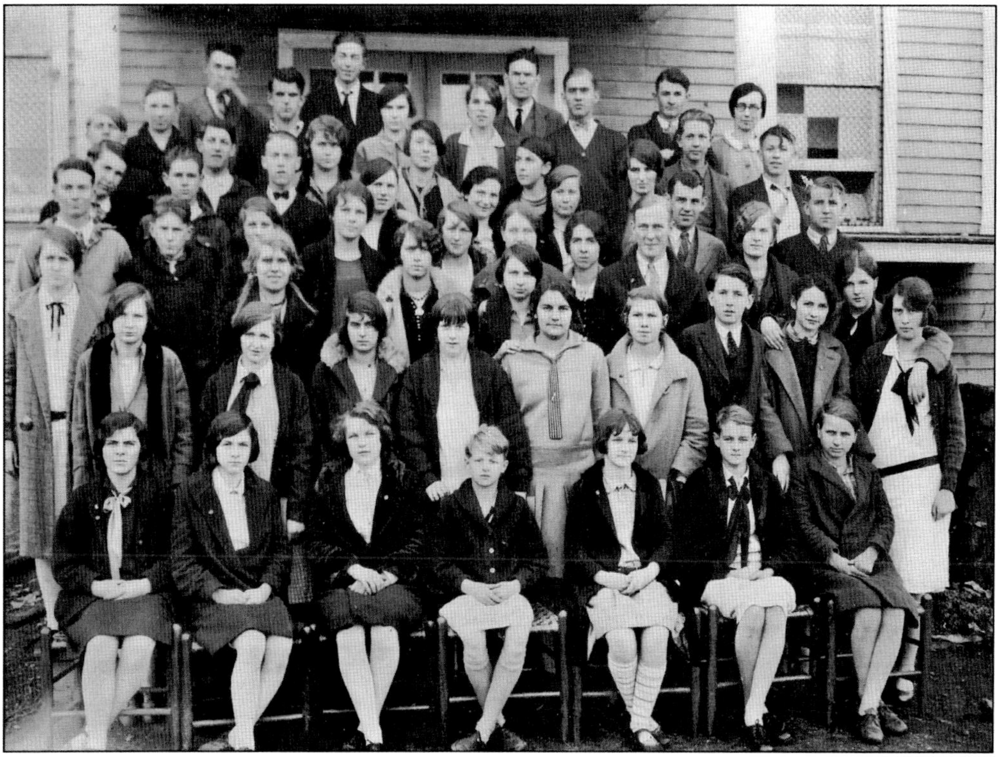

Many Madisonians still remember the old Criglersville High School. It burned at Christmastime in 1946. Students finished the year at a Civilian Conservation Corps camp near Criglersville or were bused to the town of Madison. The students in this photograph represent the class of 1929. (Lillian Mitchell.)

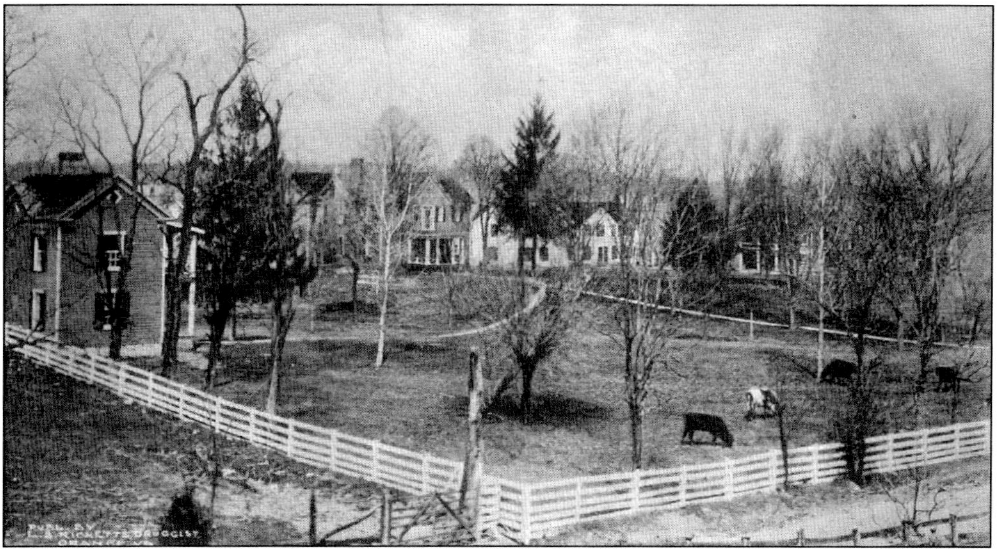

Locust Dale Academy, established in 1858, was a private boys preparatory school. It is believed that two men later to become Confederate generals during the Civil War attended Locust Dale. They were Gen. A. P. Hill and Gen. James Lawson Kemper. Kemper later became governor of Virginia. Locust Dale burned in 1911. (Steve Hoffman.)

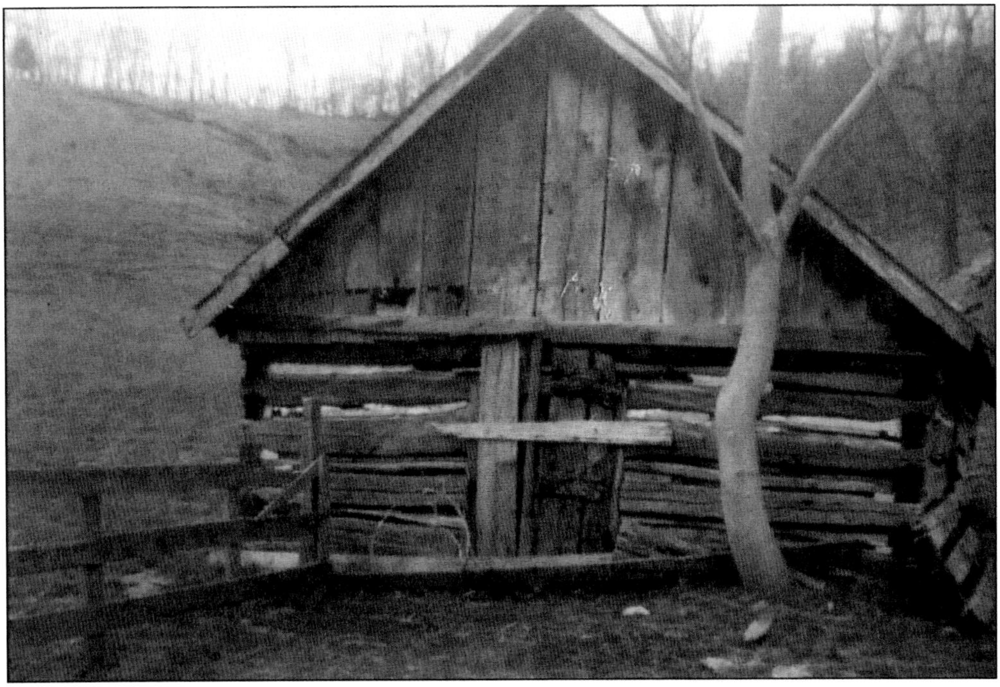

The Old Shotwell Hollow School near Syria, shown here in the early 1900s, is an example of the local community school house. What few books there were in the schools were usually hand-made, which meant that the course of study had to be prepared and presented by the teacher. Most of the work in these schools was memorization and recitation. (Nancy H. Knighting.)

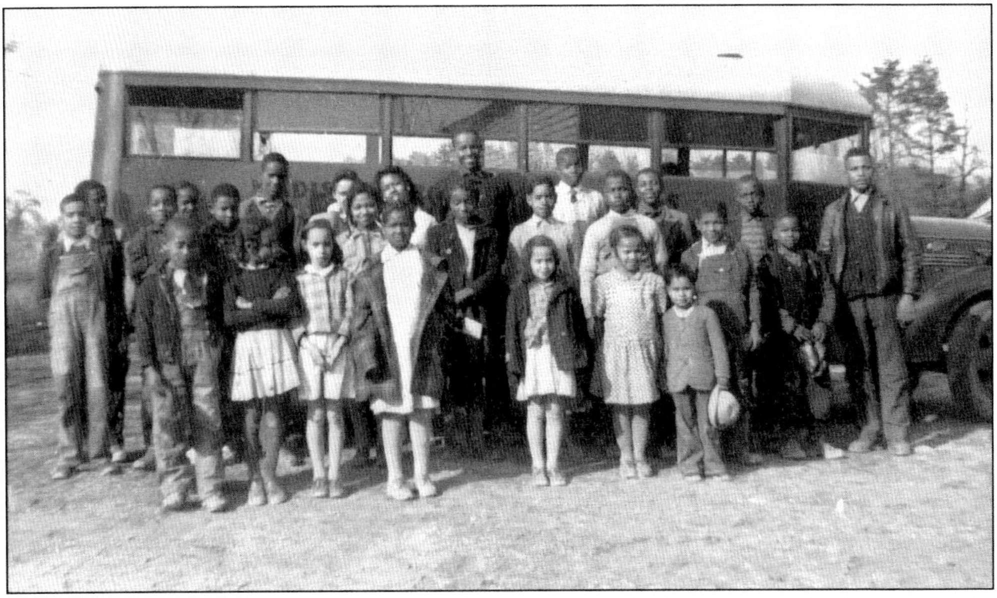

After roads were improved, buses were used to transport children to school. There was only one bus in 1921 but by 1929 there were 13 school buses in the county. This bus was owned and operated by Dan Washington around 1940. It served the African American children in the Haywood area. (Flora R. Washington.)

Six

Faces of Madison County

The faces of Madison County are diverse, multi-ethnic, and many-hued, and they span more than three centuries. The earliest photographs of Madison County faces are from the mid-1850s when photography was still in its infancy and was a great novelty. Having one's picture taken meant keeping absolutely still during a long camera exposure. The very serious expressions on the faces of some of these men and women sitting for formal portraits show what a trial it must have been.

Madison County faces are of the rich and the poor, mountain people and flat-landers, yeoman farmers and landed gentry, tradesmen and teachers, artisans, lawyers, and doctors. They are of men and women, both old and young. A few of the families in Madison County have some Native American ancestors, but most of their ancestors emigrated from the old world to this new one. Many came voluntarily but others did not. Some Europeans came indentured; almost all Africans came enslaved. In the early 19th century there were more African American people than there were white people in the county. After the Civil War, many black families moved north to find greater economic and social opportunity but others remained and became integrated into the life of the county. Some of their pictures are here.

Today the population of Madison County stands at nearly 14,000 people. What unites the vast majority of them is their love and concern for their families and their appreciation of the sustaining gifts of the land and the mountains.

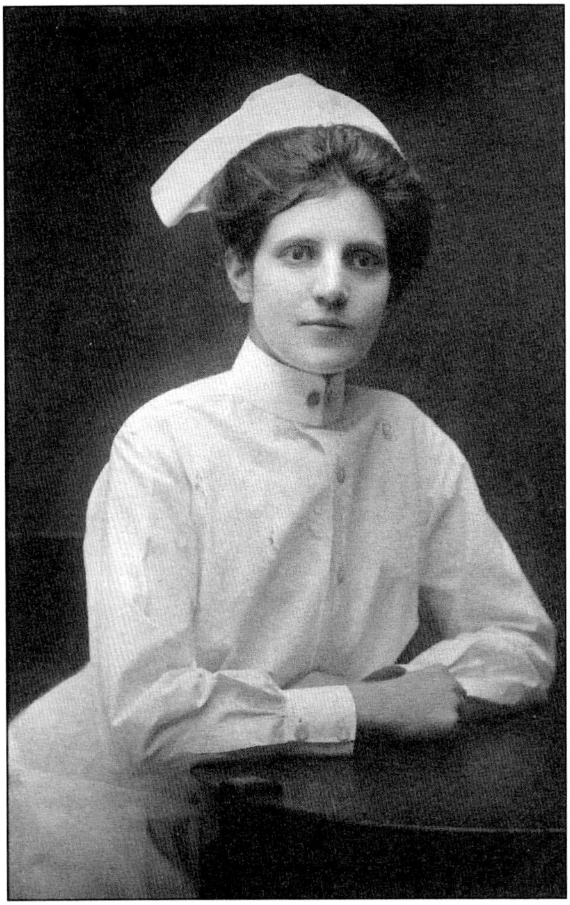

Anna Lewis Hood, nicknamed Sug, was born in 1879 at Hood. When the United States entered World War I in 1917, she volunteered with the Red Cross and was sent to France for the duration of the war. She married Walter Rogers Lamkin in 1925 and, after many travels and adventures, returned to Hood where she died and is buried. (Ruth and Randall Lillard.)

E. A. Clore, founder of E. A. Clore and Sons Furniture Company, sits astride his horse in front of the T. T. Mitchell service station in downtown Madison. In 1921, he built his first factory and made chicken coops, coffins, and chairs. Today furniture made by the E. A. Clore and Sons Furniture Company is known throughout the country. He and his wife, Alma, were the parents of 12 children. (Katherine Clore Craft.)

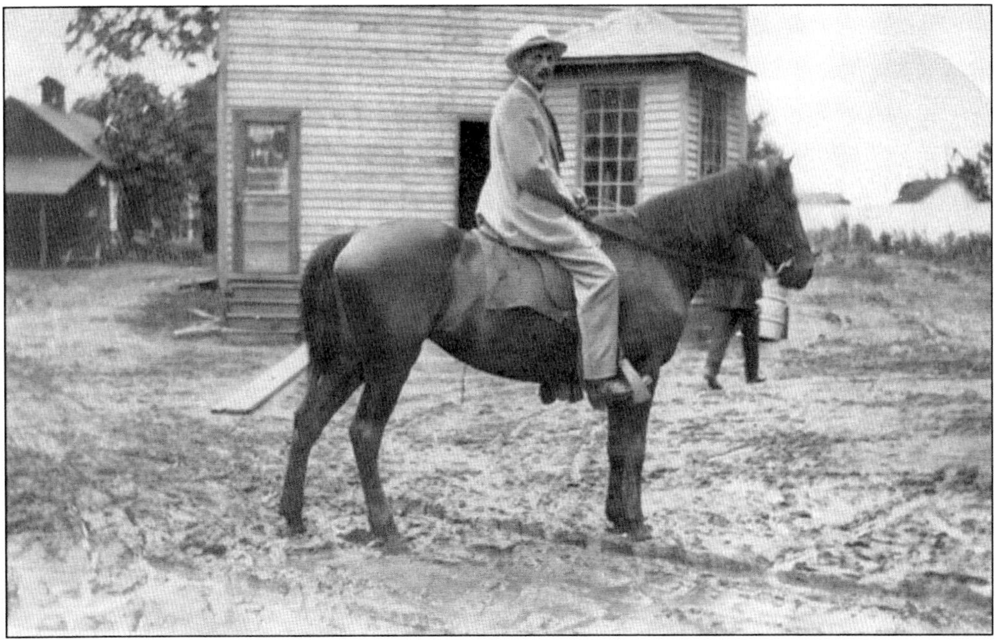

Alvin Schrock and his wife, Maggie, were among the first Mennonite families to come to Madison County in the 1950s. For some years they farmed near Aroda. Eventually Alvin began working for the state forestry department, a job that he loved. He worked as a forest ranger until his retirement in 1992 from Cumberland State Forest in Cumberland County. (Elmer Miller Jr.)

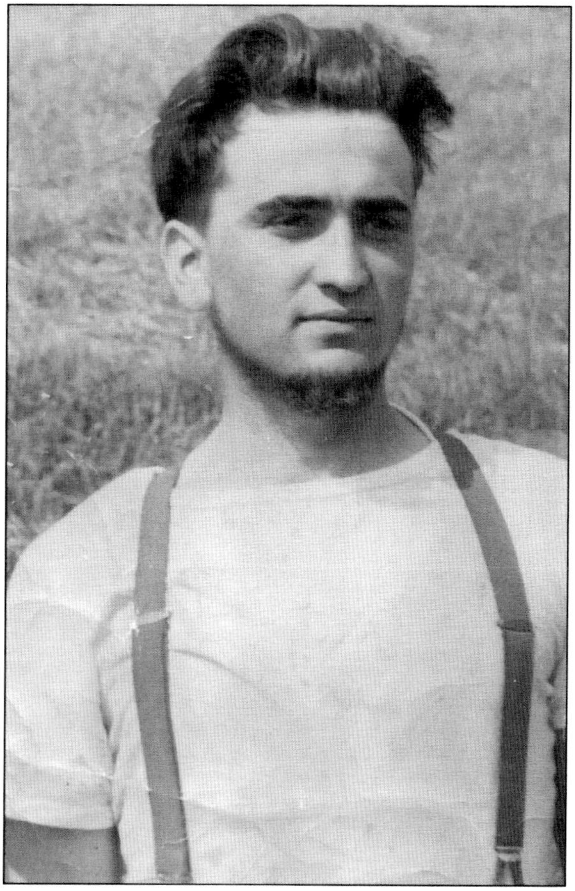

Dr. Robert Lee Taliaferro (1866–1938) of Greenway and his family go for a ride in his 1909 Maxwell, believed to have been one of the first cars in Madison County. The bearded man at left is Taliaferro's father, Civil War veteran Fitzhugh Taliaferro (1828–1923). Robert Taliaferro was married to Virginia Walker (1870–1942) from nearby Edgewood. (Gilbert Queitzsch.)

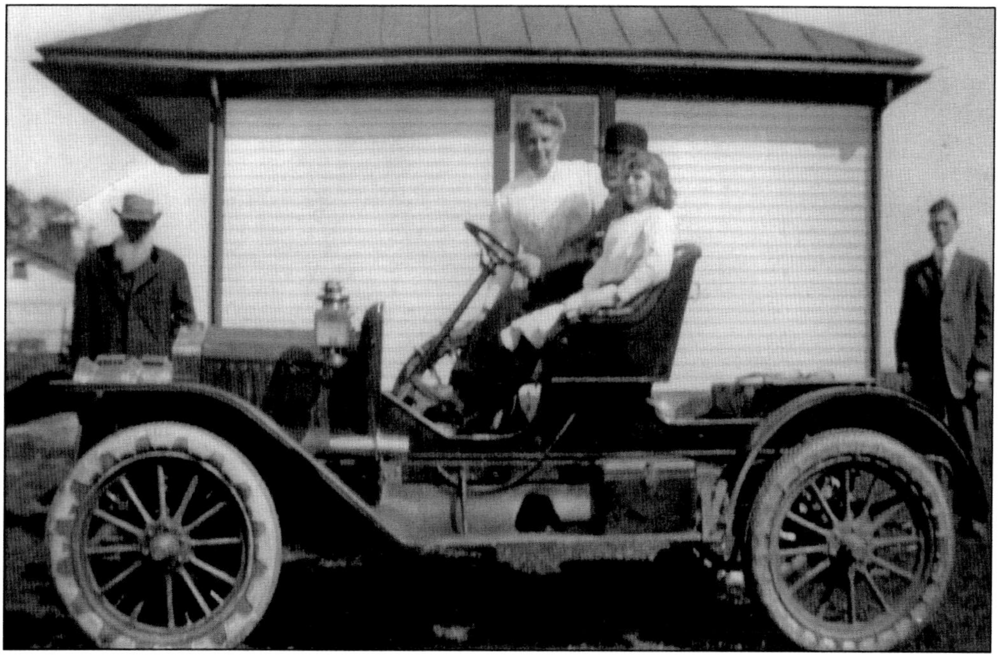

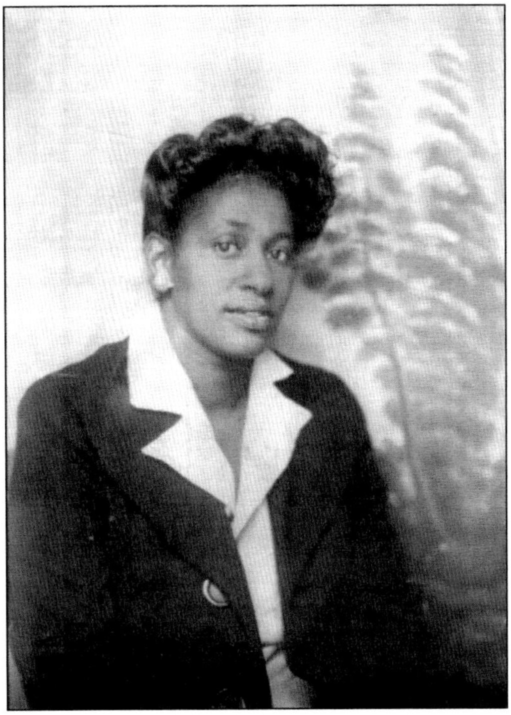

Gertrude Price Turner, born in 1909, was the daughter of Ernest Price and Bessie Jefferson of Madison. She married James Randolph Turner and the couple had 13 children, including two sets of twins. James Turner was the cook at the Hunton Hotel in the 1930s. In the 1940s, after Turner's service in World War II, the couple went to Washington, D.C., to find work. The children stayed with relatives in Madison. (Lillian Turner Holly.)

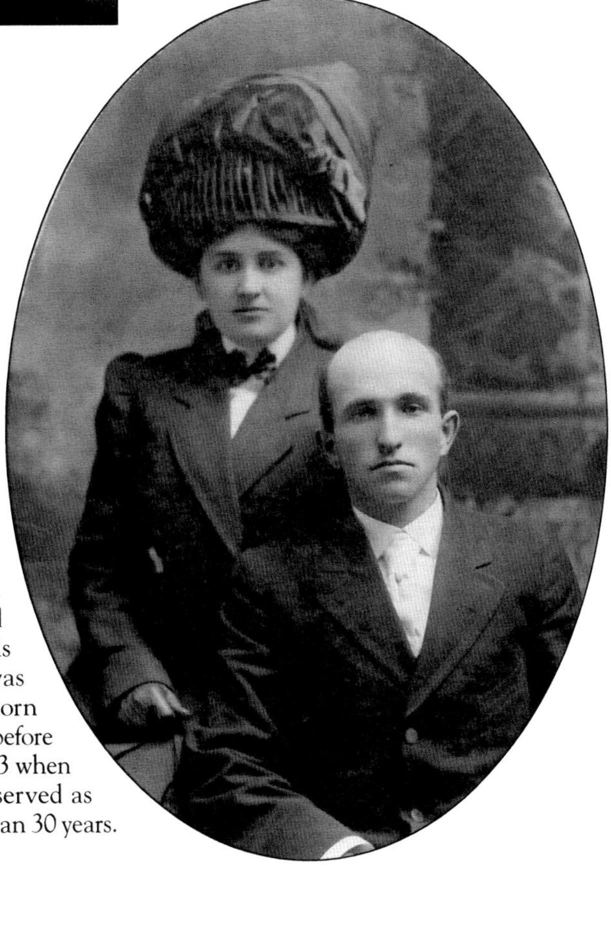

This is the wedding photograph, taken around 1912, of Thomas Hume Lillard (1885–1962) and Carrie "Patsy" Custis Utz Lillard (1884–1969). Thomas was born at Graves Mill and Carrie was born in Rocklin. They lived in Graves Mill before making their home in Madison in 1933 when he was appointed sheriff. Thomas served as sheriff of Madison County for more than 30 years. (Ruth and Randall Lillard.)

Frances Powell Hill was born in 1891. Her father was Roland S. Hill and her mother was Epha Garnett Hill. The family lived at Belle Plaine. After school she went to work in Washington, D.C., at a feed company and then as a realtor. She was very successful and became a real estate broker. She was one of the first women to achieve such a position in the Washington, D.C. area. (Frank Gray.)

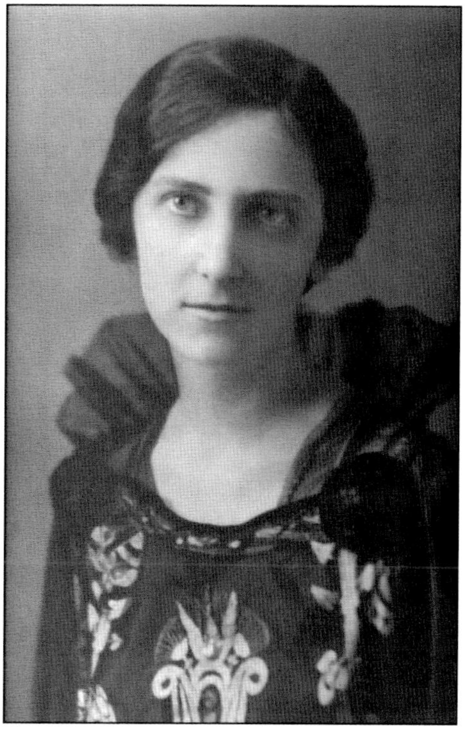

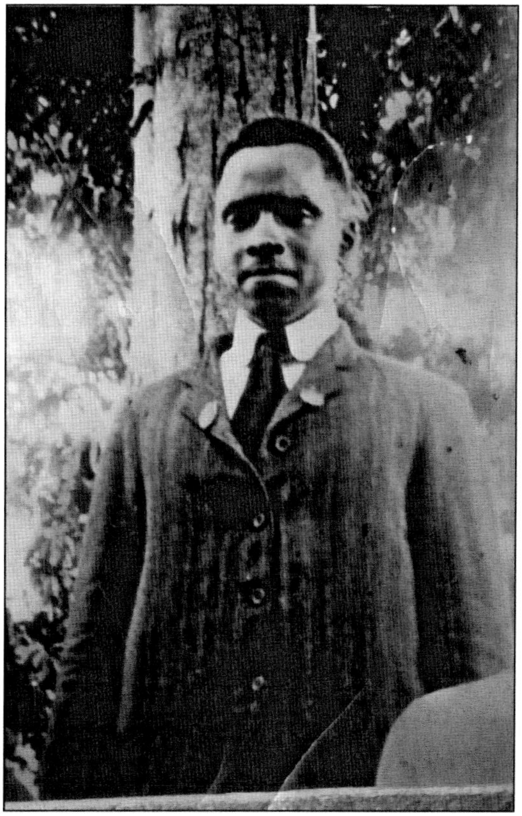

Ashby Clay was born in 1891 near Criglersville, the son of Washington and Amanda Allen Clay. He married Sarah McDaniel of Culpeper in 1917 and moved there. He was a grandson of Henry Clay, a farmer, who was born around 1828 in Madison County. The Clay family has deep roots in the Criglersville area. (Leontyne Clay Peck.)

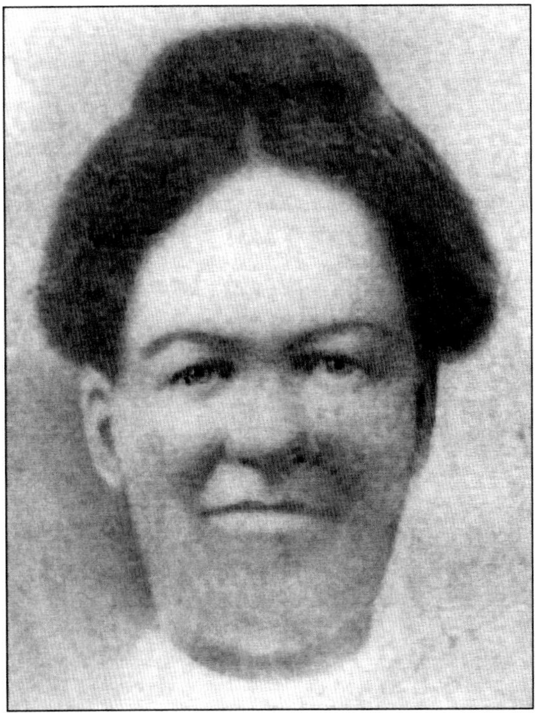

This 1908 photograph is of Leila Price, who was born in 1888 near Criglersville. She was the daughter of Laura Fannie Smith, who was born in 1864. The Criglersville Smith family line goes back to the 1700s when Moses Smith acquired land in the area. Other family names are Clay and Price, all with their roots at Criglersville. (Leontyne Clay Peck.)

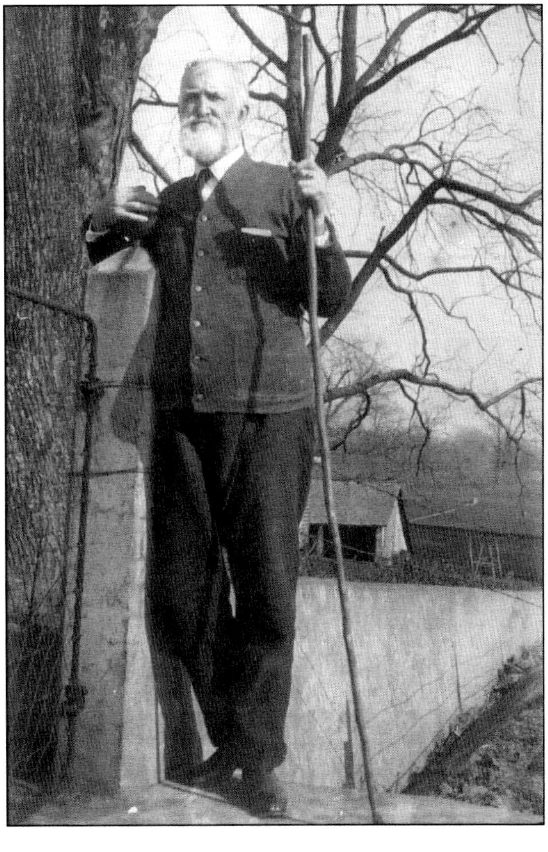

Rowland Flint Hill Sr. stands at his home, Belle Plaine, near Locust Dale, around 1894. Hill was born in 1852, the son of Edwin F. Hill of Indian Trace. He married Etha Garnett, daughter of Jeremiah Cave and Elizabeth Willis Garnett, in 1881. They had 10 children. Hill was commissioner of roads for Madison County in the early 1900s. (Frank Gray.)

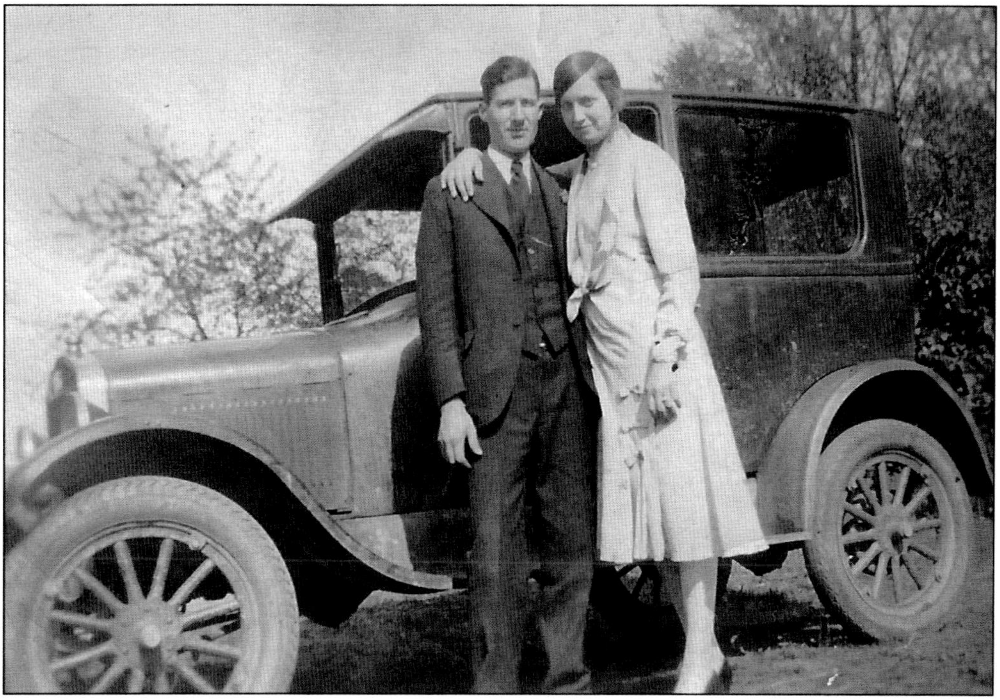

William Howard Carpenter and Lucille D. Hitt, posing with their Model T, were married on April 16, 1930. "Mr. Willie," as he was known, served four terms as a Madison County supervisor, from 1963 until 1979. The couple lived in Brightwood and Carpenter worked for many years as a mechanic with furniture manufacturers. (John Howard Carpenter.)

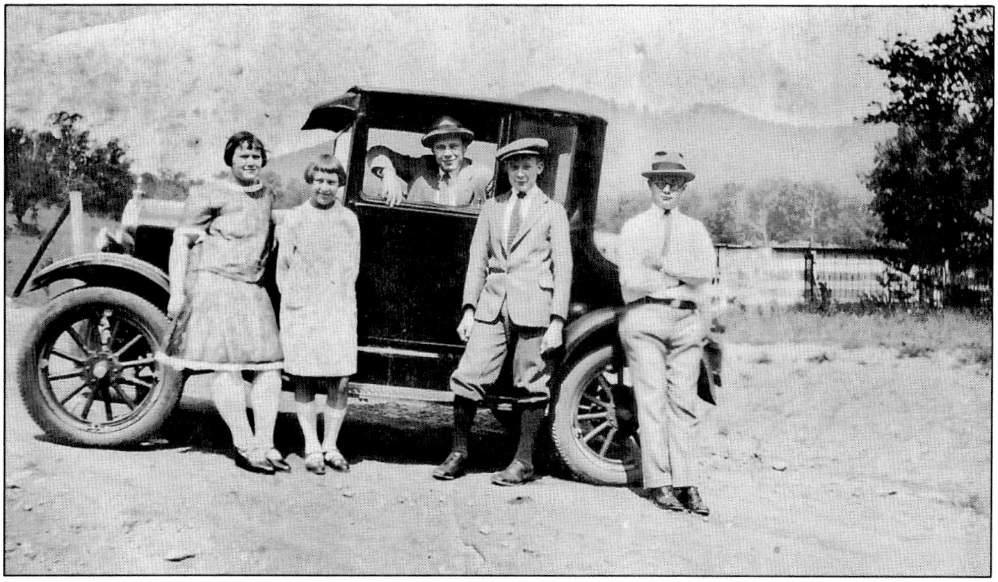

These members of the Hood family are proud of their Ford car, pictured here around 1929. The Hood family ran a store and the post office at Hood for many years. William Addison Hood served as postmaster from 1896 to 1940. The store is closed now but the post office remains and a member of the Hood family is still postmaster today. (Mary Hood.)

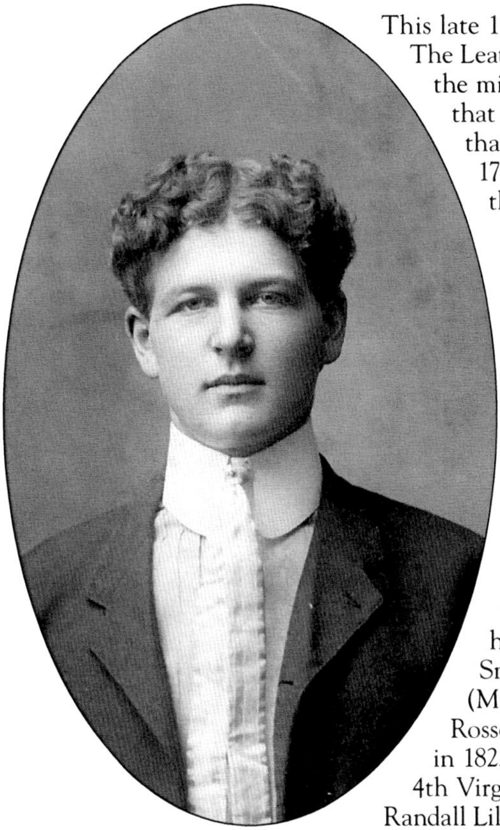

This late 19th century portrait is of Haywood Leathers. The Leathers family has been in Madison County since the mid-1700s and was among the group of Germans that settled in the county at that time. Records show that they acquired property in the Syria area in the 1790s. Members of the Leathers family still live on the property today. (Lillian Mitchell.)

This is the William Nelson Smith family of Criglersville, pictured around 1895. From left to right are mother Mary Elizabeth Berry Smith holding Jesse Fielding Smith, Earle Winifred Smith (Mrs. Robert Mercer Coates), Nina Smith (Mrs. Thomas Aylor), Susie Smith (Mrs. Edward Rosser) and father William. William Smith was born in 1823. He was a farmer and served in Company C, 4th Virginia Cavalry during the Civil War. (Ruth and Randall Lillard.)

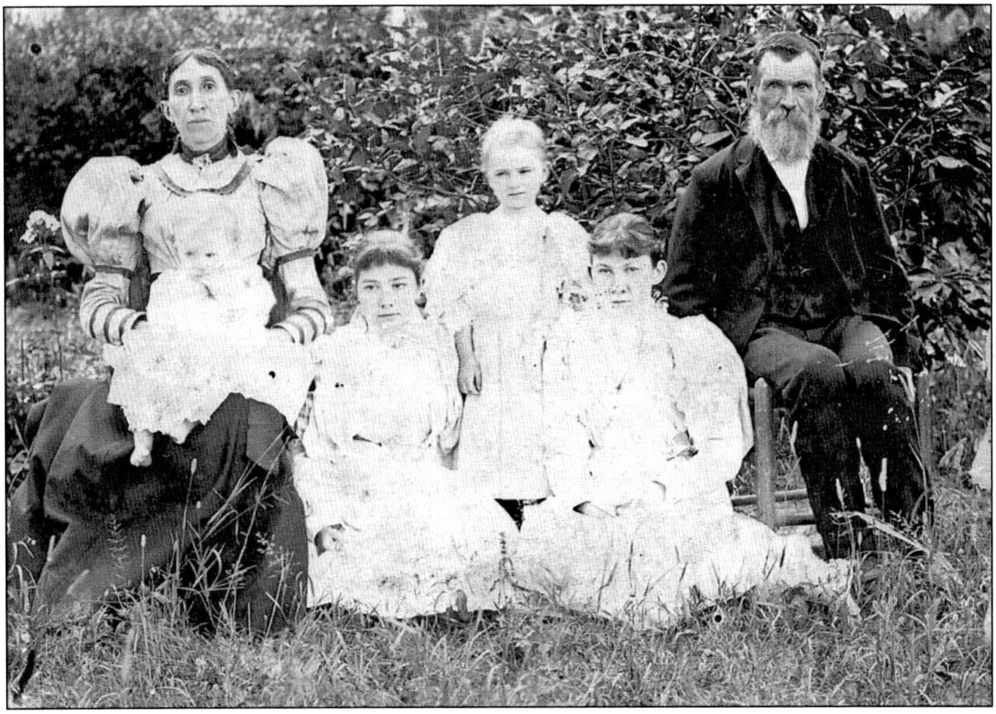

The 1932 wedding of Katherine Earle Gibbs, daughter of Cornelia Estes and Bernard Scott Gibbs of Pratts, and James Osborn Clore, son of Alma Crigler and E. A. Clore of Brightwood, was quite an event. The ceremony took place at the opening of the Madison County Fair and was witnessed by approximately 3,000 people. The bride's dress was a copy of the wedding gown worn by Martha Washington. (Katherine Clore Craft.)

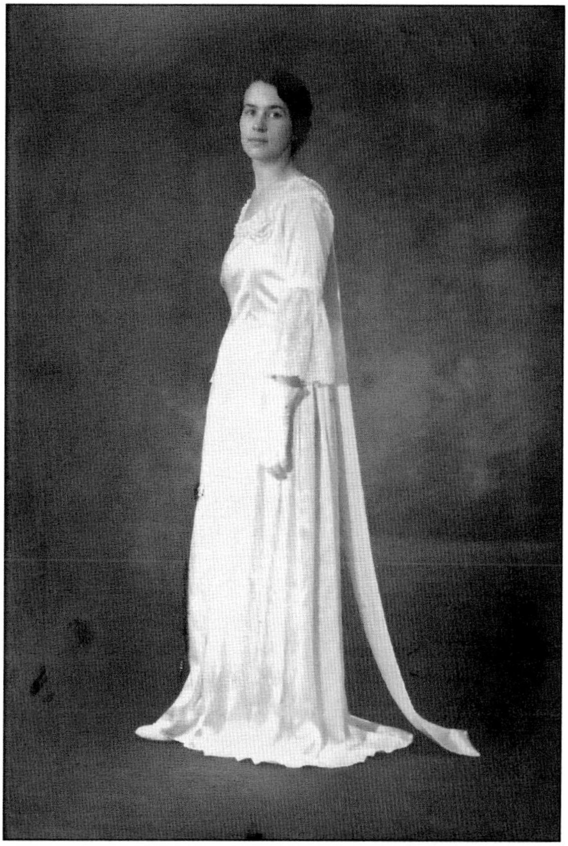

Carroll (left) and Hume Lillard were ages four and six in this picture taken around 1923. Hume and Carroll both became deputies under their father, sheriff Tom Lillard, when they turned 21. Hume served part time and later full time as a deputy for 53 years. Carroll was appointed sheriff in 1953 and served in that capacity for nearly 20 years. (Ruth and Randall Lillard.)

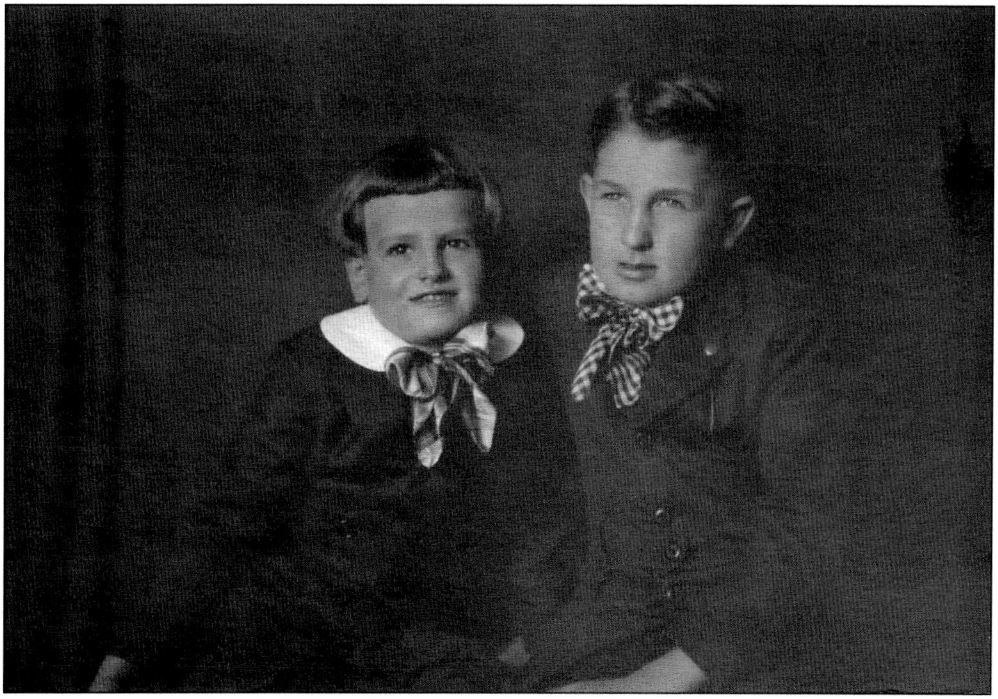

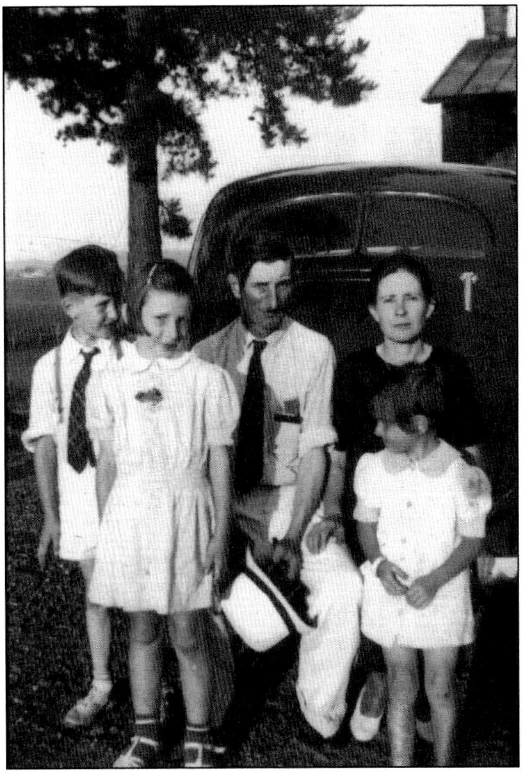

The William Durham family, pictured here around 1937, returned to Madison County when Durham lost his job at an automobile factory in Pennsylvania during the Great Depression. He supported them by working as a tenant farmer on a farm near Locust Dale until the 1950s while his wife, Grace, worked at the silk mill in Orange. The youngest daughter, pictured here at right, and her husband later bought part of the farm. (Jean Busboso.)

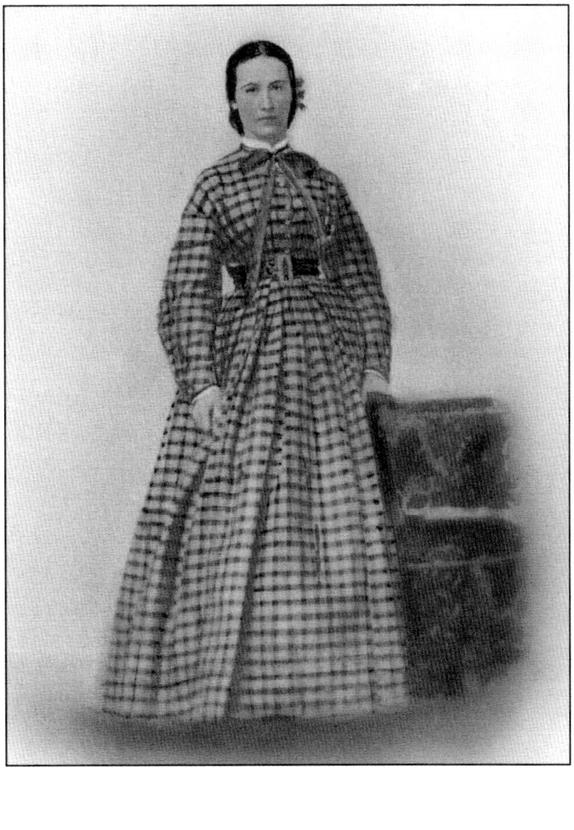

Mary Elizabeth Aylor, pictured here around 1865, was married to Capt. Jason Cornelius Crigler, a veteran of the Civil War. They lived on the old Crigler homestead near Brightwood and raised a large family there. They were members of Hebron Lutheran Church. Her tombstone can be found in the Hebron church cemetery. (Sarah Crigler.)

This photograph of "Mr. Jack" Graves was taken around 1967. He was the father of Jimmy Graves, who, with his wife, Rachel Norman, built the present Graves Mountain Lodge. Mr. Jack was in the third generation of Graves innkeepers, and he was also an avid fisherman. He was famous for his phrase, "Take what you want, but eat what you take." (James and Rachel Graves.)

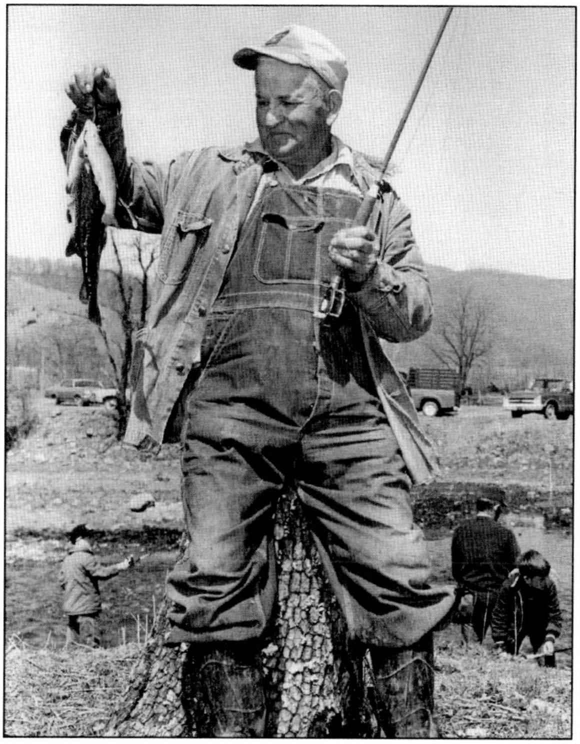

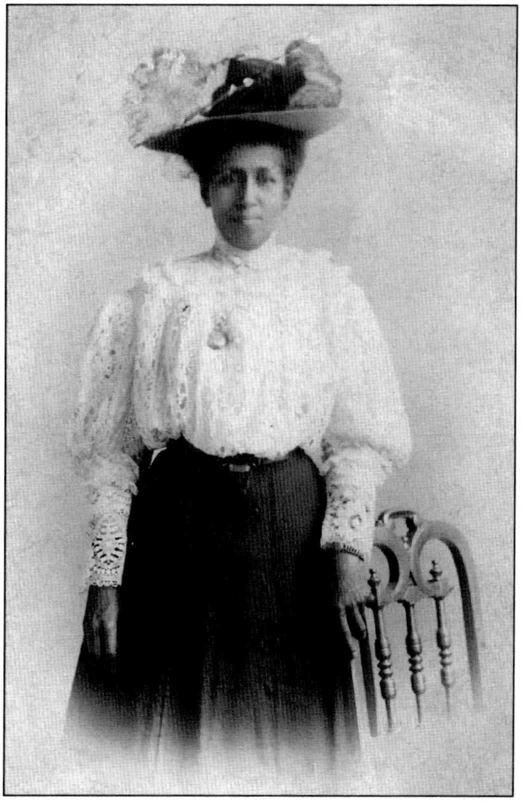

Dolly Ann Gordon was born in the late 19th century. She married George Young and they raised a large family in Madison and provided a tourist home at their house. The kitchen and dining room were separate from the house and in the 1940s, when Dolly Young was in her 80s, a fire broke out in the kitchen. Dolly's body was found there. She died of smoke inhalation. (Martha Turner-Riddick.)

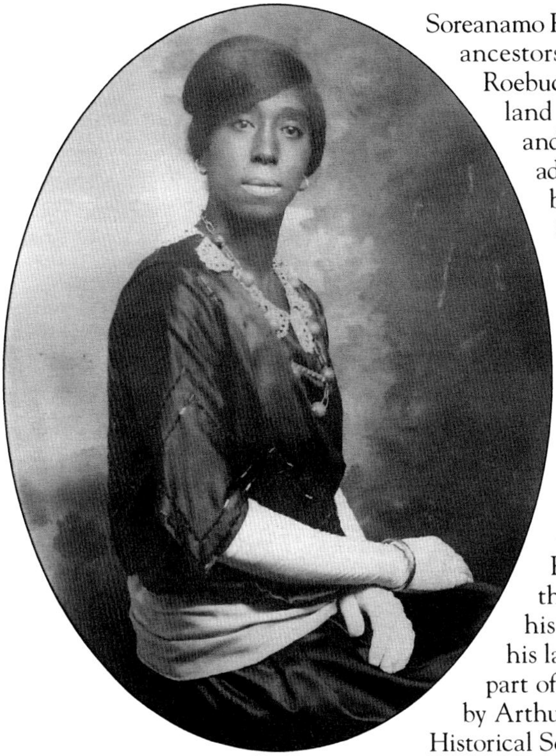

Soreanamo Roebuck Evans, who had Native American ancestors, was born to Wallace and Sally Baker Roebuck near Radiant, where her family owned land dating back to 1877. After her marriage and after living in Pennsylvania much of her adult life, she and her husband, James, moved back to Radiant to care for aging parents. She became well-known in the community for her cooking and sewing skills. (Janice P. Carpenter.)

William Austin Brown was the longtime postmaster and storekeeper in the village of Old Rag that lay on the back side of Old Rag Mountain near Weakley Hollow. In this *c.* 1935 picture, he reads by lamplight at his home. He was a large landowner but all of his land and the remains of the village are now part of Shenandoah National Park. (Photograph by Arthur Rothstein, courtesy of Madison County Historical Society.)

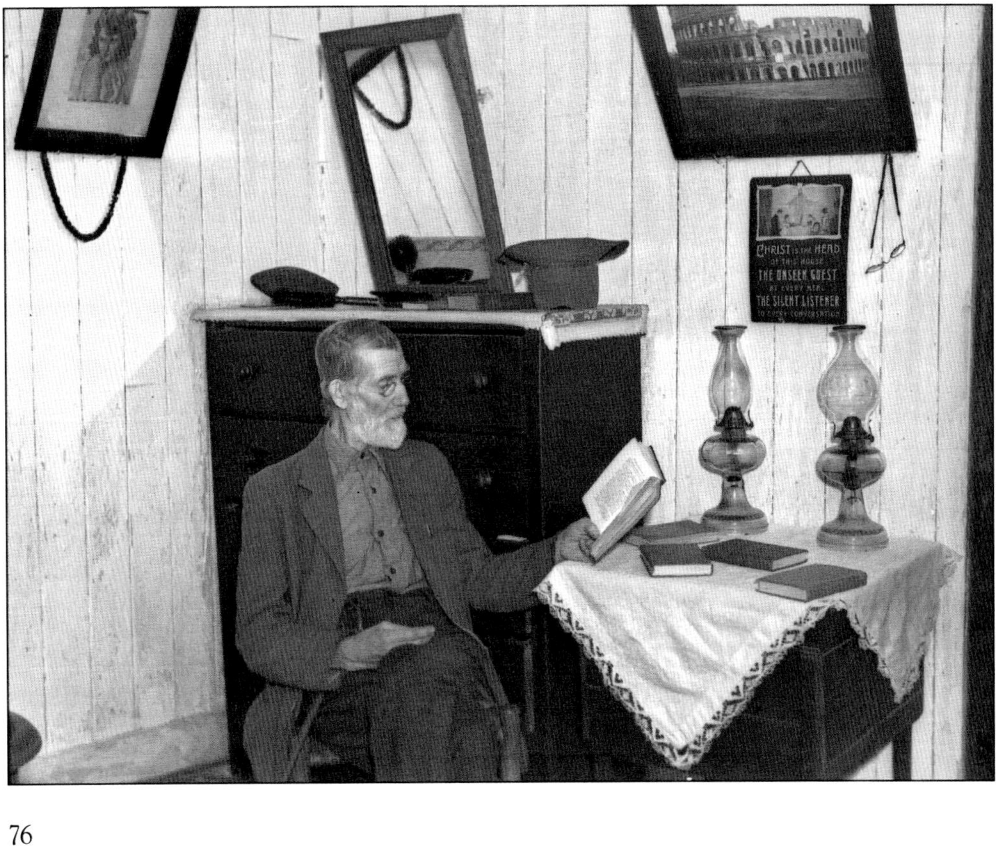

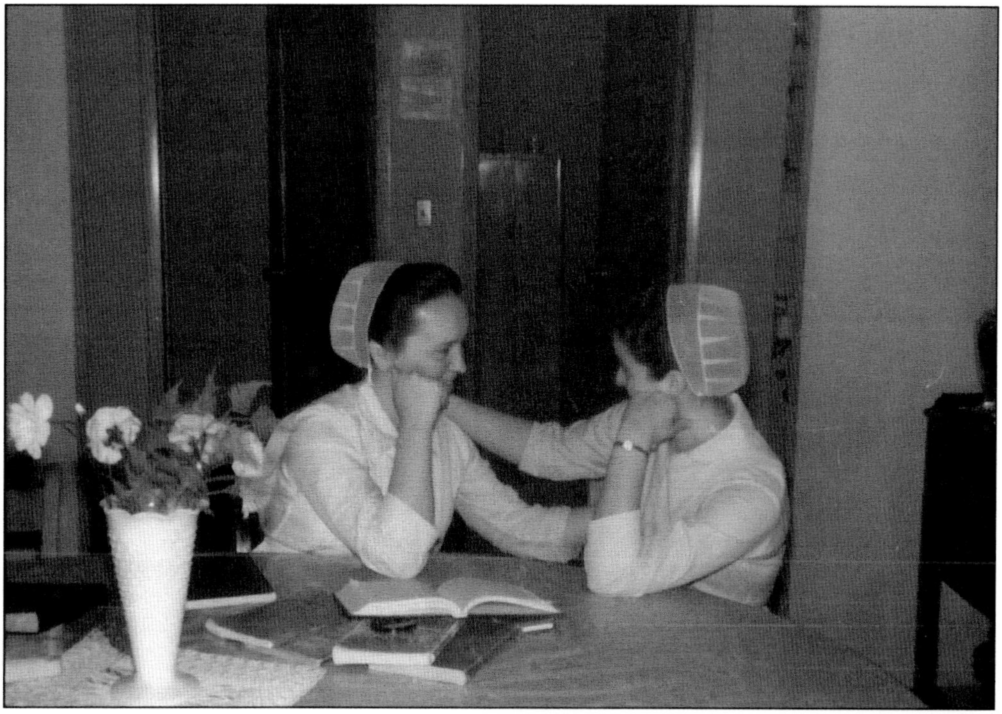

These two Mennonite girls, Elmina Yoder and Alma Yoder, sing and entertain the residents at the first Mennonite nursing home around 1963. Music and singing continue to be an important part of the daily schedule for the residents, an activity that they love and in which all are encouraged to participate. (Elmina Yoder.)

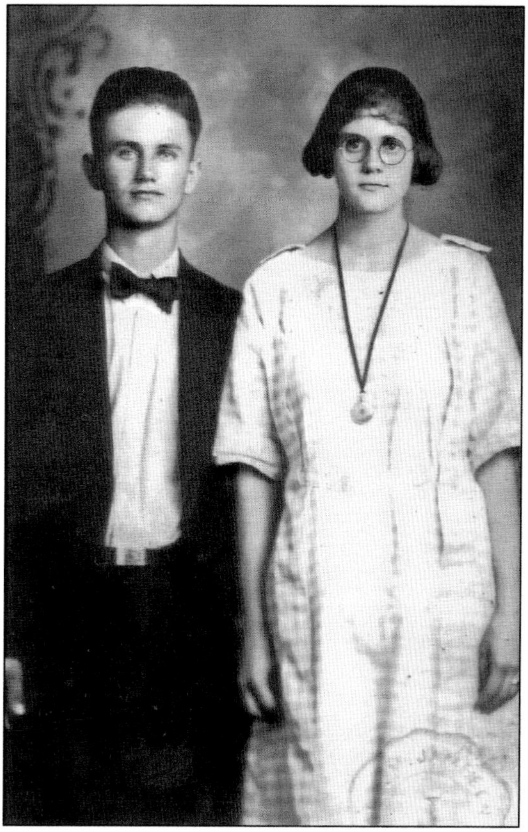

This is the wedding picture of Luther Wilson Knighting (1904–1985) from Syria, and Dollie Ryder (1903–1991) from Locust Dale. They were married in 1922 and lived in the Knighting home place at Shotwell Hollow near Syria where they raised nine children. Luther Wilson Knighting both farmed and worked in Madison for the highway department. (Nancy H. Knighting.)

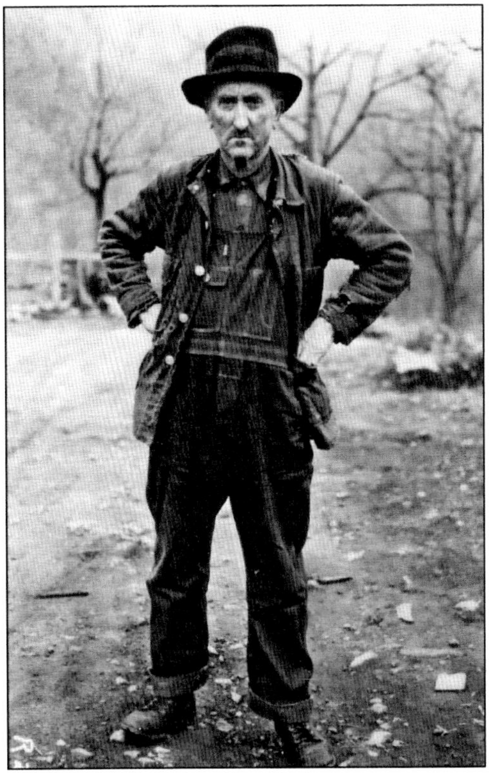

Lester Cave was a notorious moonshiner who lived in the mountains between Richards Hollow and Dark Hollow near Nethers. He was active in the 1930s and was arrested for his moonshining activities many times. Finally he was asked by the authorities to leave the county. He relocated to Baltimore. His father and two of his brothers were Methodist ministers. (Harold Woodward.)

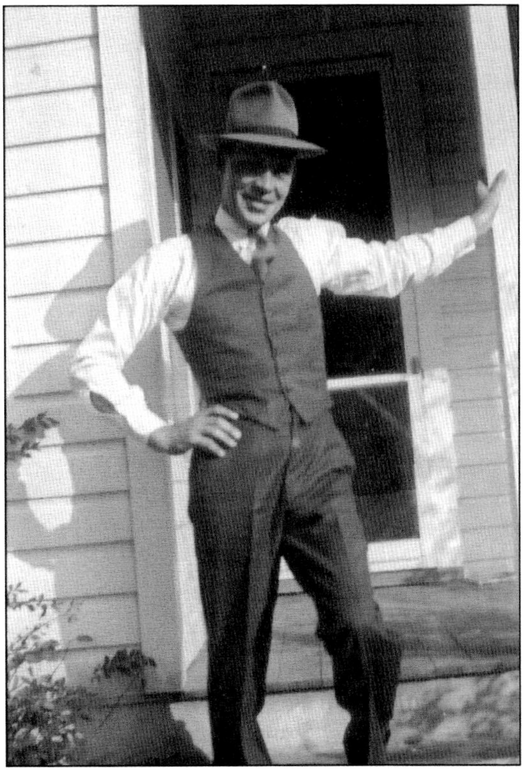

Ralph Clinton Hawkins was born on the Hawkins home place on the Rapidan River in 1917. At the age of 11 his father let him use the family car to drive marines from Hoover Camp to Culpeper for recreation. He married Linda Davis and the couple lived at Rochelle. Both worked at the silk mill in Orange during the 1940s. Later he worked as a bus mechanic for the Madison school system. (Nancy H. Knighting.)

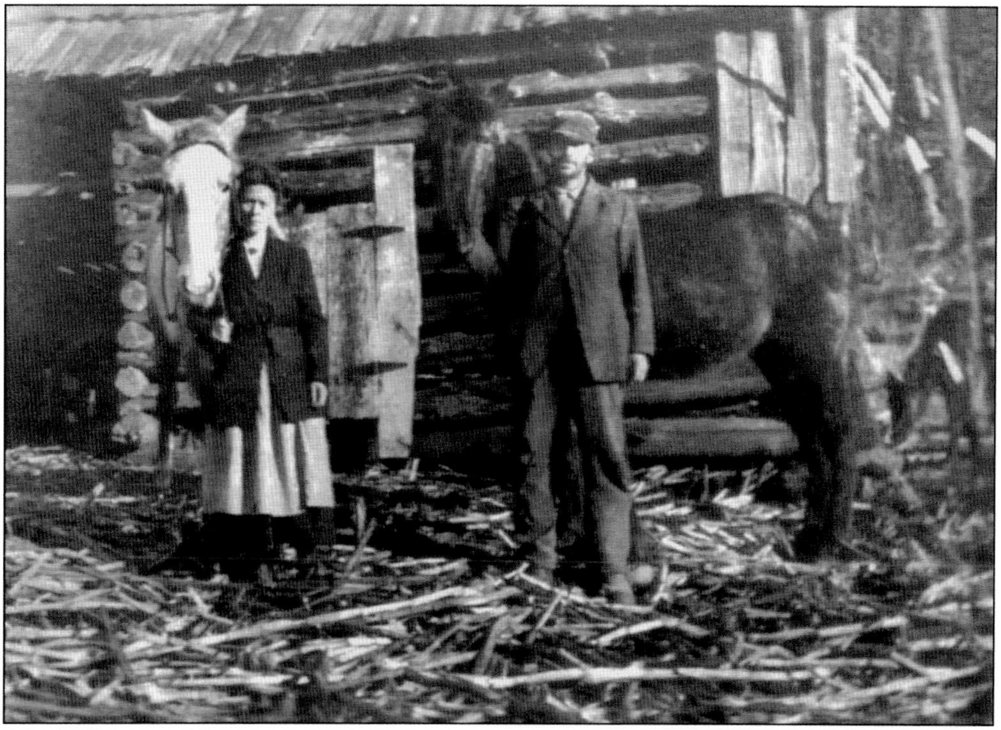

Charles Edgar and Minnie Lee May Hawkins lived on this property along the Rapidan River near Hoover Camp around 1910. They had 172 acres of land on which they raised corn and maintained orchards. They built a six-room log home and raised 13 children. In the 1930s, they had to move when Shenandoah National Park was created; they were compensated $1,419 for their land and improvements. (Nancy H. Knighting.)

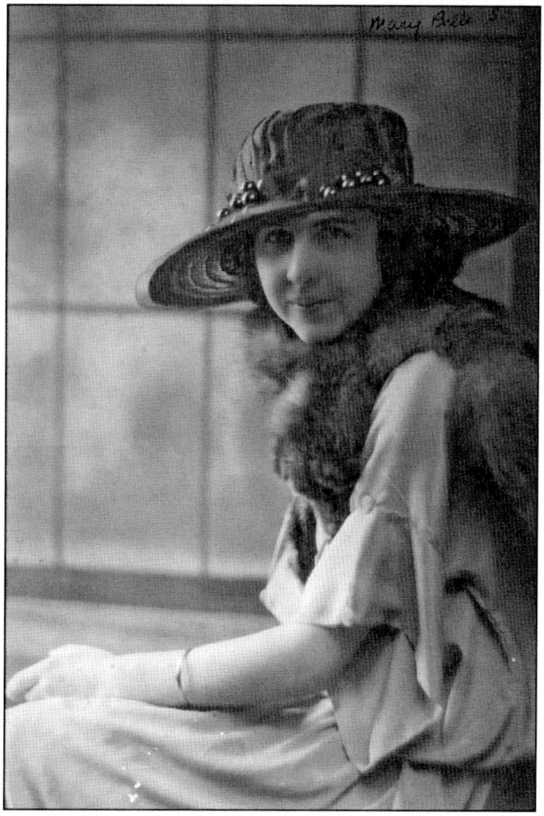

Mary Belle Smith, born in 1901 near Brightwood, was the daughter of Jim and Nellie Crigler Smith. She was a much beloved teacher of English at what is now Waverly Yowell School and taught there for many years. Five of the six children of Jim and Nellie Smith attended college and two were teachers. (Dana Smith Faulconer.)

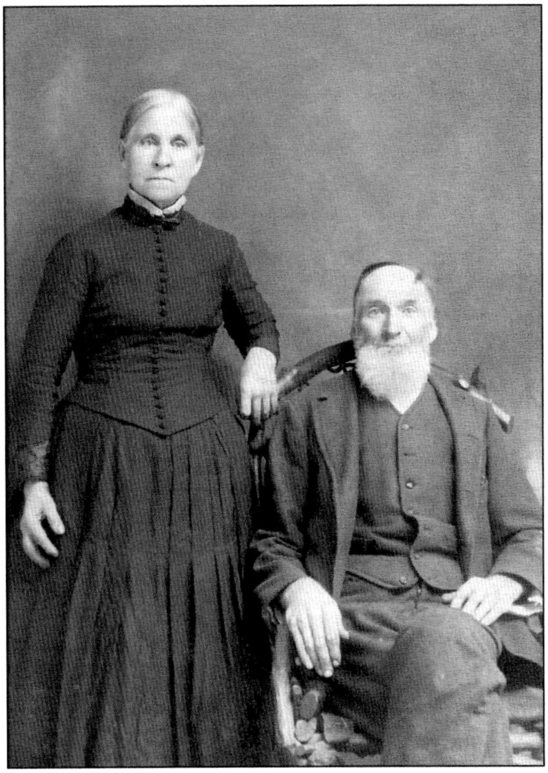

This c. 1870 photograph is of Thomas Aylor and his wife Ellen Weaver, who lived near Thoroughfare Mountain. Other members of the Aylor family acquired land near Criglersville in the early 1800s. In 1848, the Aylor family helped to found Oak Grove Methodist Church at Aylor, and a post office was established there in 1904. (Dana Smith Faulconer.)

Em Sparks, a descendant of the Capt. Andrew Carpenter family of the early 1800s, lived on the family property near Brightwood with her mother, Mag, and her Aunt Tump. Mag Sparks was widowed at an early age and in the early 1900s she and her sister and daughter Em, who never married, provided a home and family for many foster children. (John Howard Carpenter.)

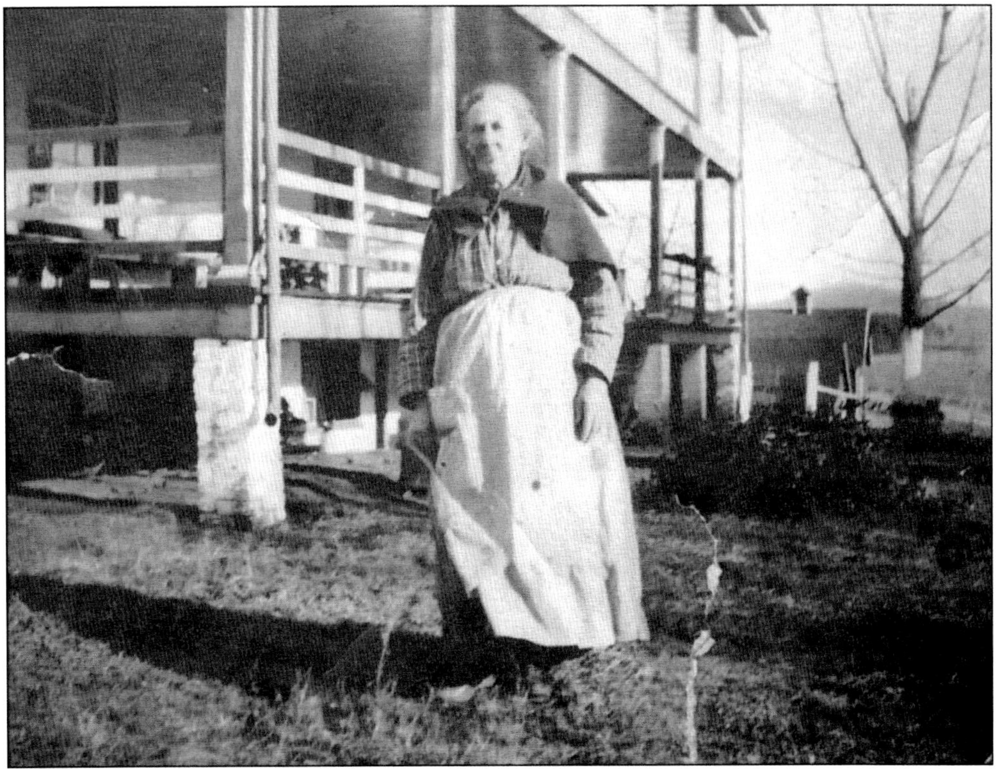

George Cumberland Carpenter, pictured here around 1920, rests at the Carpenter home place near Brightwood. He was a descendant of John Zimmerman from Germany and Barbara Kerker Zimmerman. They settled in Madison County in the 1720s. John Zimmerman's son Michael, a second-generation descendant, changed the name to Carpenter. (John Howard Carpenter.)

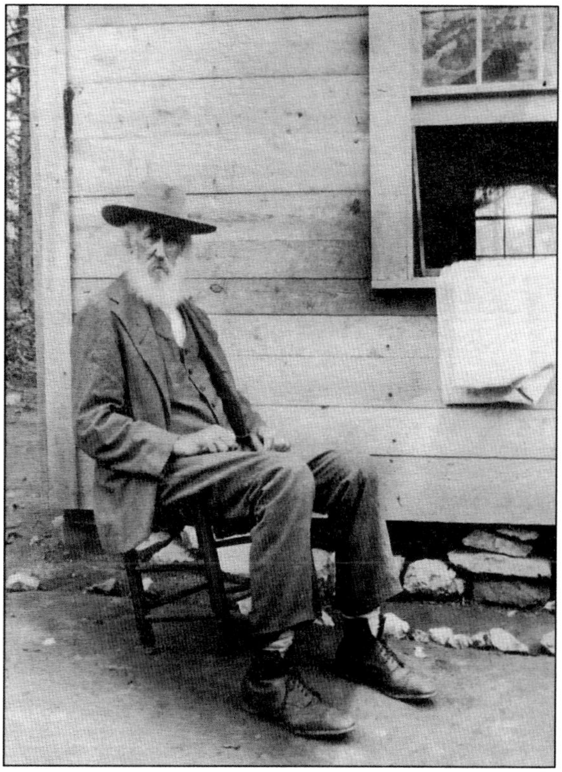

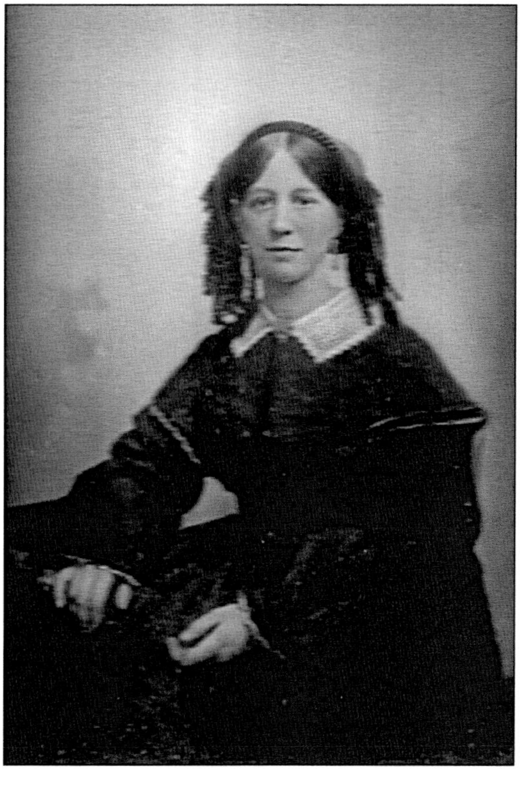

Frances Henry Hill Twyman was born in 1813. She was the daughter of Capt. Ambrose Powell Hill of "Millwood" in Culpeper County. Frances Henry Hill married Dr. William Horace Twyman in 1832 and they lived at Madison Farm, which was located between Locust Dale and Rapidan. Her brother William Alexander Hill was the first superintendent of schools in Madison County. (Frank Gray.)

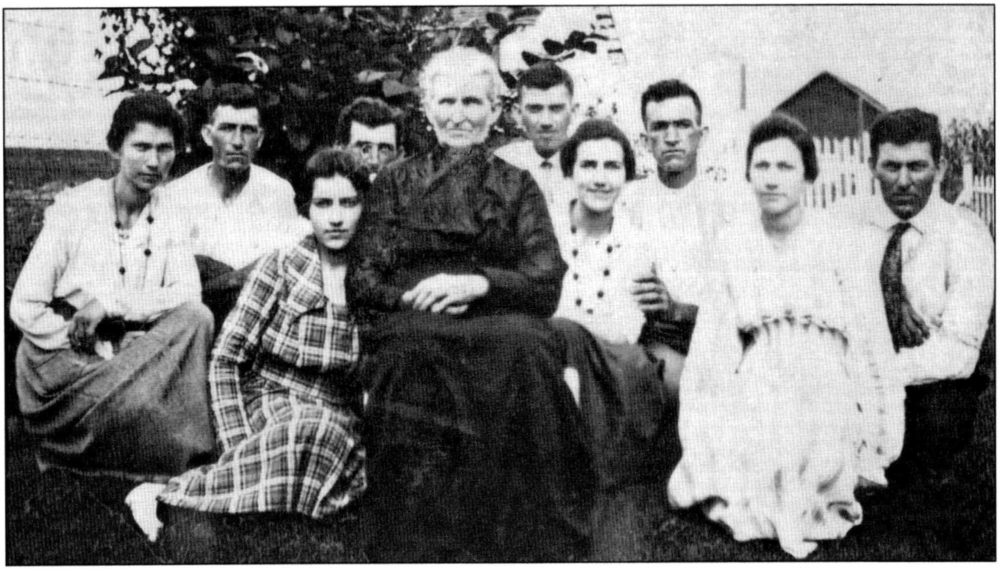

Amanda Kipps Hale (center) was the matriarch of the John William Hale family. She and her husband had a 1,000-acre farm near Pratts. They had nine children, but John William Hale died young and Amanda Hale and her children ran the farm, raising beef cattle. She was known as a strict disciplinarian and a great cook. Amanda died on the farm two weeks shy of her 100th birthday. (Jimmy Hale.)

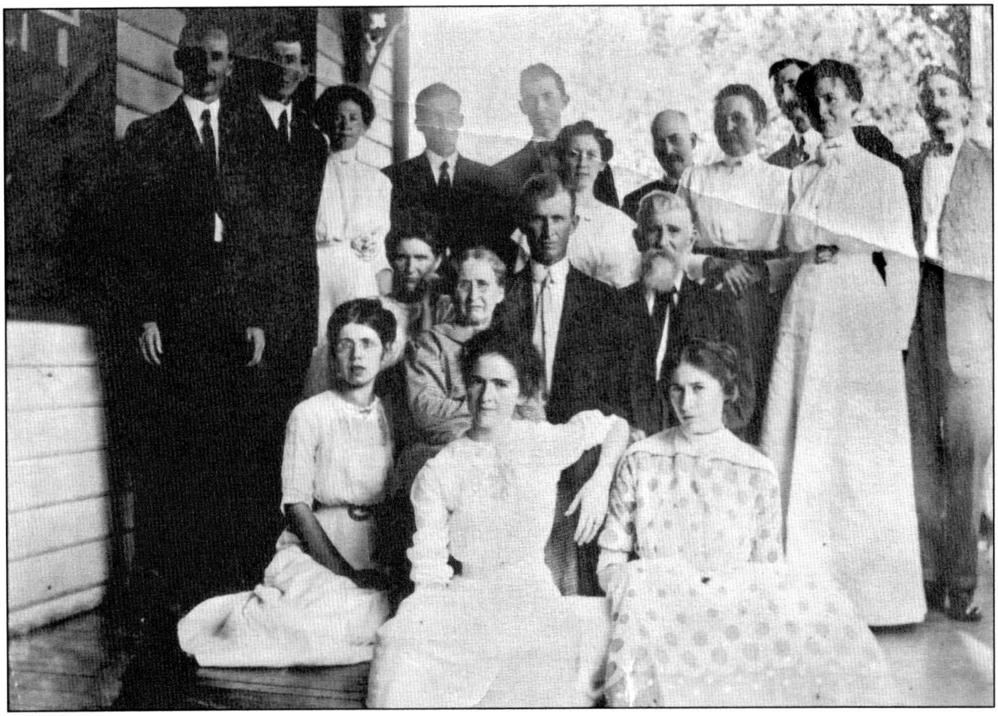

This is the Crigler family of Brightwood around 1900. Capt. Jason Cornelius Crigler, center right, served in the cavalry during the Civil War. His ancestor Jacob Crigler was one of the original German Lutheran settlers who came to Madison County in 1717. The village of Criglersville is named after him. (Dana Smith Faulconer.)

Seven

Military

Before Madison was a county, its people fought in the French and Indian War and in the American Revolution. Madison citizens also participated in the War of 1812 and in the Mexican War. During the Civil War, Confederate and Union troops passed through the county a number of times. Two battles were fought within the county, one at Jack's Shop near Rochelle and another at James City near the Culpeper border. Only two Madisonians are known to have participated in the Spanish American War, but many served in the two World Wars, Korea, Vietnam, and in other 20th century hostilities. Two cenotaphs stand on the War Memorial Building lawn in Madison. One, dedicated to the Civil War dead, bears no names but only an inscription honoring Madison's heroes; the other names 16 Madisonians who died in World War I, 24 who died in World War II, 4 who died in Korea, 5 in Vietnam, and 1 in Operation Iraqi Freedom.

On September 22, 1863, two Union cavalry divisions, one led by Brig. Gen. Judson Kilpatrick and the other by Brig. Gen. John Buford—a combined force of about 7,000 men—moved south into Madison County. Confederate Gen. J. E. B. Stuart, whose headquarters was in Orange County, commanded about 2,000 troops. At first light, Stuart's force moved toward Madison to counter the Union advance. Buford's force encountered Stuart's near Jack's Shop and the battle began with artillery fire. Stuart was attacked on three fronts by the larger Union force but by concentrating his fire on Kilpatrick's division, which he judged to be the Union's weak point, he was able to penetrate the Union line and withdraw across the Rapidan.

The James City battle was also a cavalry engagement, which developed into an artillery duel. The opposing forces bombarded each other from high ground on each side of the little town. Its few buildings were caught in the middle until the action ended with the Union withdrawal.

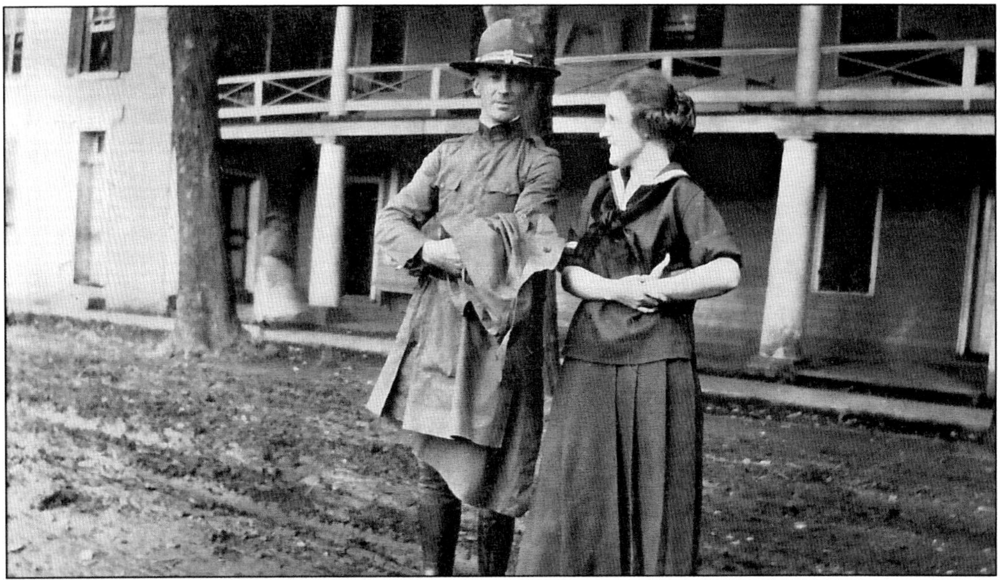

This dapper young World War I soldier is Benjamin W. Aylor. His lady friend who is posing with him is unknown. They stand in front of the Madison House Hotel on Main Street in Madison in 1917. Aylor returned from the service and took up farming in Madison County. (Virginia Aylor McGhee.)

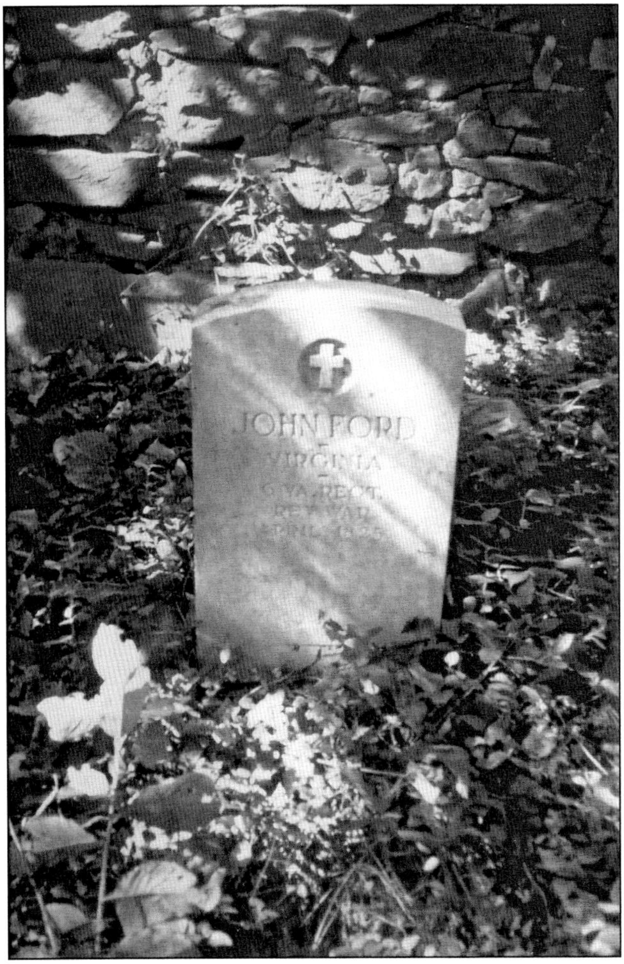

This is the gravestone of John Ford of Ford's Shop near Leon. He was a member of the Culpeper Minute Men and fought in the American Revolution. He returned from the war to run a mill on Crooked Run and resume farming. He died in 1825 and is buried at the old Ford cemetery near Leon. (Thomas Ford.)

Three of the five brothers in the Dan Washington family of Criglersville served in the military. Carl Washington, pictured at right, served in World War II, and George Louis Washington, pictured below, was in the service during the 1950s. Carl Washington spent most of his time in the service stationed in Alabama. He was 19 years old. When he returned home he married Flora Ragland in 1955 and took up farming in the Criglersville area. He had a distinguished career, serving on many agricultural boards and advisory groups. George Louis Washington served in Germany. When he returned home he worked first as an insurance agent for the Southern Life Insurance Company and then owned and operated a service station. (Both, Flora R. Washington.)

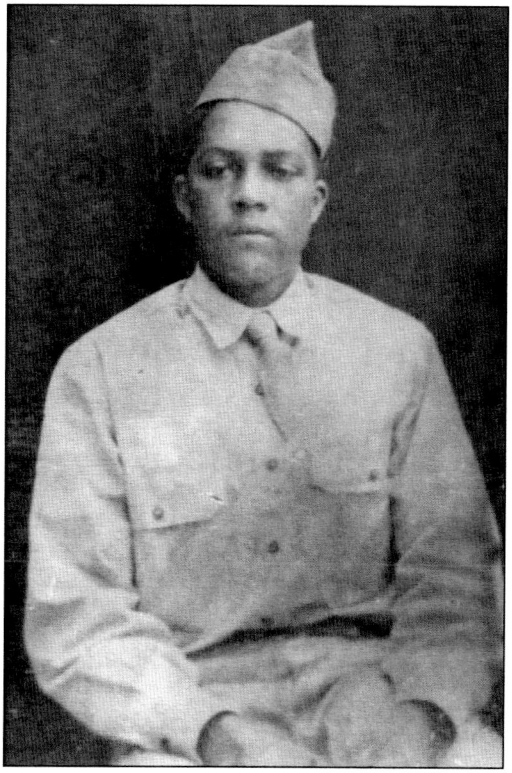

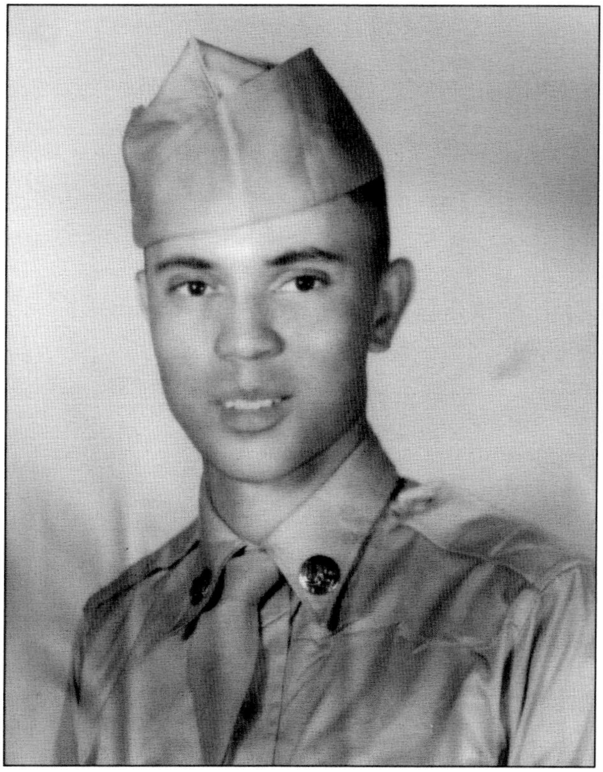

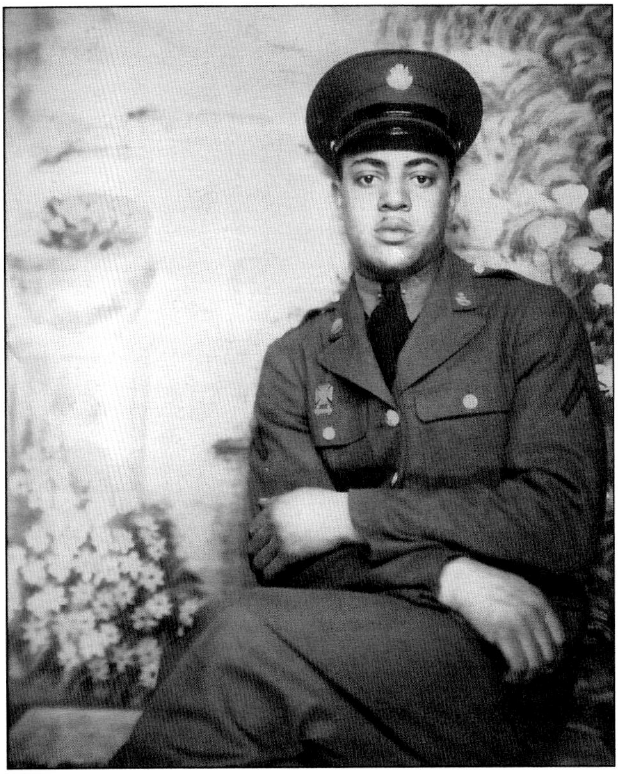

Clarence Washington was the older of the Washington brothers who served in World War II. He returned home safely and began working for the Madison County school system. He drove a school bus for many years and was much admired by the students who rode his bus. He was also a proficient house painter. (Flora R. Washington.)

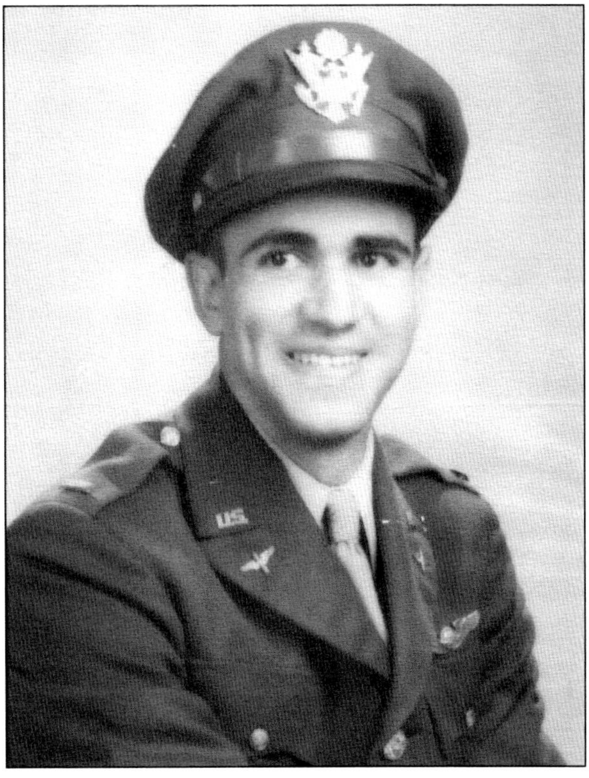

Walter Alan Arrington was born in Radiant in 1918. He was a fine athlete and attended Michigan State University on a scholarship. Arrington attended Tuskeegee Institute in 1942 and qualified as an airman navigator. He retired from the U.S. Air Force as a lieutenant colonel after 23 years. He then worked for the General Services Administration for 10 years as director of procurement. He died in 1977. (Sonya Arrington.)

Pfc. Fred Coppedge of Etlan proudly points to his newly acquired stripes in about 1942. He served in the army in World War II and then returned to Etlan to pursue life as a farmer. The Coppedge family of Etlan has farmed in the area for many generations. (Nan Coppedge.)

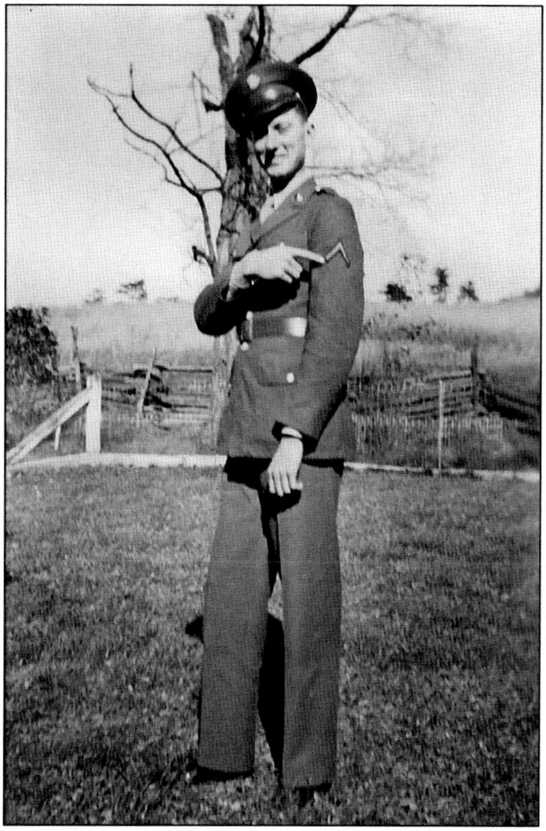

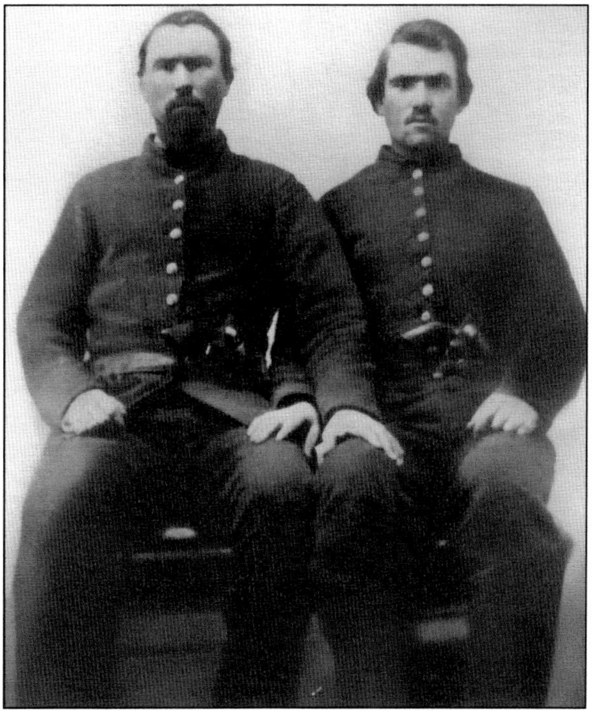

Civil War participants Fayette Henshaw, left, and Thomas Early are back home in 1865. They were both privates in Company A, 7th Virginia Infantry. Col. (and later general) James Lawson Kemper was commander of this unit when it was formed in 1861. Both men survived the war and returned to Madison County. Many years later Henshaw's son Joseph married Early's daughter Elizabeth. (Sarah Henshaw.)

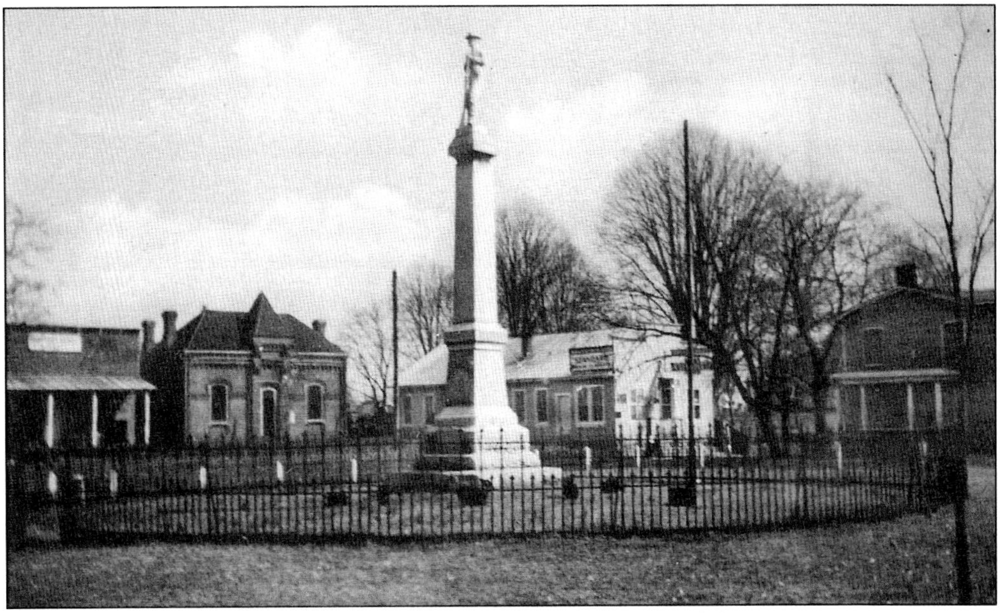

The Confederate Monument, located in front of the War Memorial Building on Main Street, was erected in 1901. It bears no names but its inscription reads in part "A hero's honors let a hero have." In this postcard view, published around 1928, the old jail, second building from the left, stands in the background. (Steve Hoffman.)

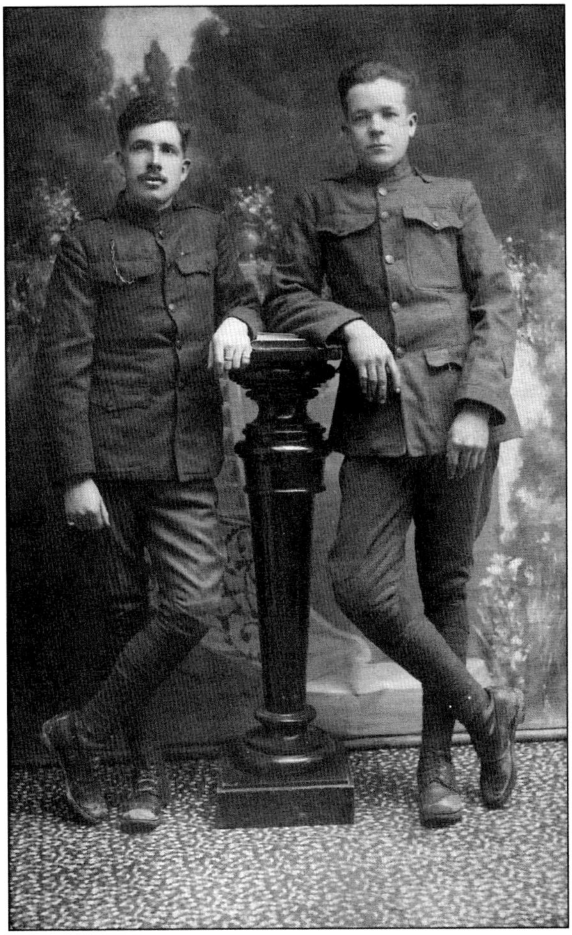

These two young men served in World War I. The soldier on the right is Lester Quesenberry. Although not from Madison County, he married Frances Clore of Madison and the couple is buried in the cemetery at Hebron Lutheran Church. The other soldier is not identified. The picture is on a postcard from a shop in Dijon, France, and appears to have been taken there. (Helen Robertson.)

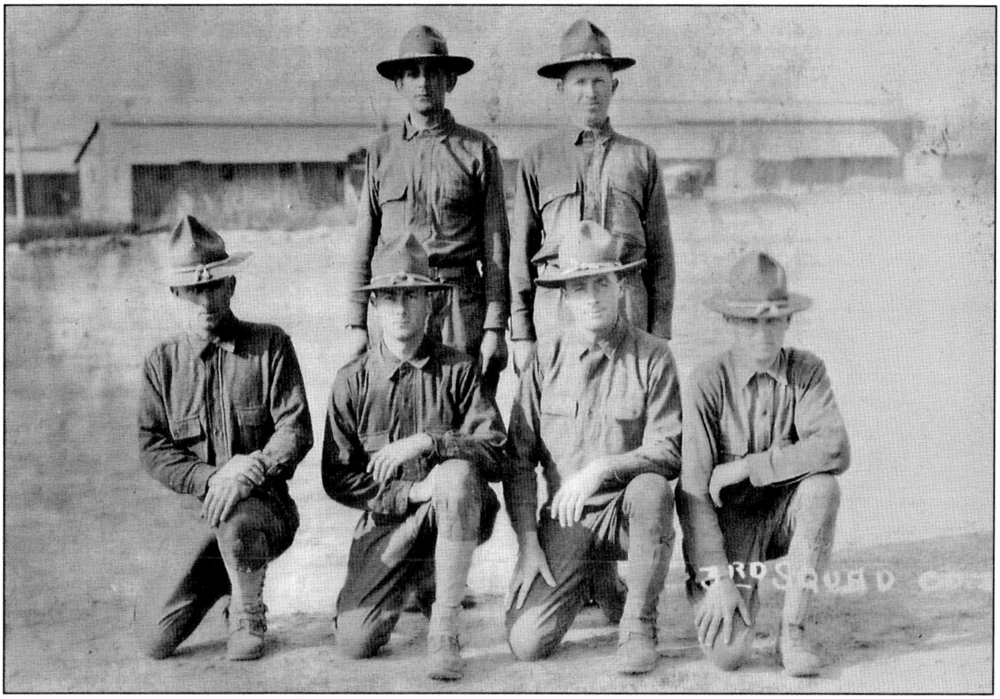

James E. Gordon of Madison County, front left, was the first man drafted for service in the U.S. Army in World War I. The draft lottery was signed into law in May 1917. In July, the secretary of war drew out the first numbers and Gordon's was the first. He was wounded fighting in France but returned and lived out his life in Syria. (Harold Woodward.)

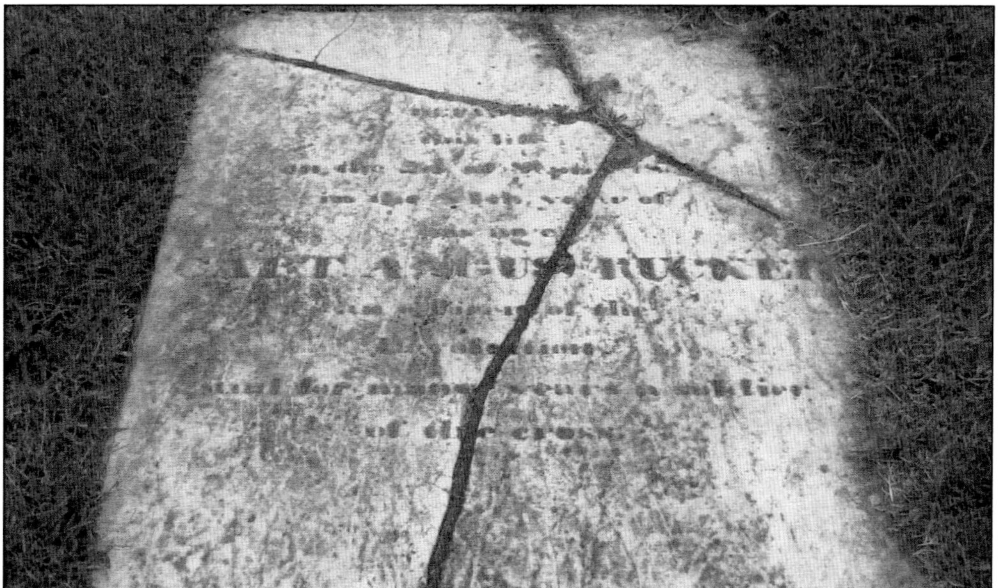

Near Wolftown is the grave of Capt. Angus Rucker, a Revolutionary War soldier born in 1743. He died September 21, 1836. A Daughters of the American Revolution marker was placed by the tombstone in 2001. Records show that a number of men who lived in what is now Madison County participated in the American Revolution. (Madison County Historical Society.)

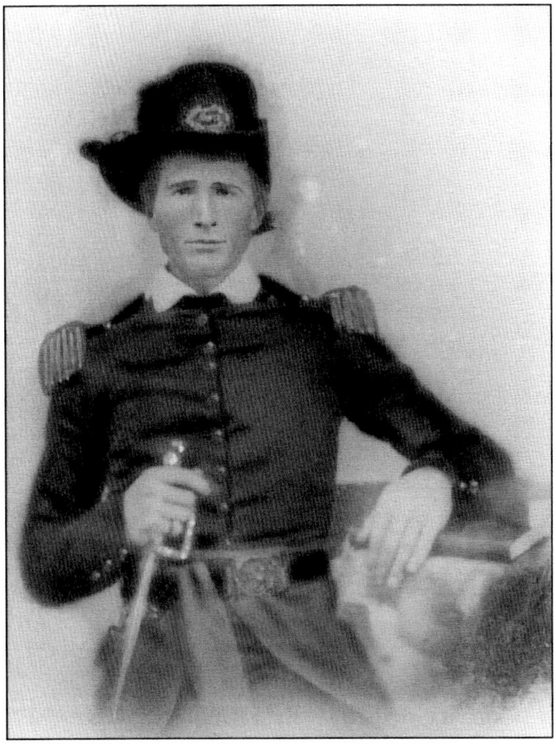

Capt. Jason Cornelius Crigler's photograph was taken around 1865 when he was a captain in Company L, 10th Virginia Infantry, a unit in which he had served since he was a second lieutenant in 1861. Company L was composed chiefly of men from Madison County. When the Civil War was over he returned home and married Mary Elizabeth Aylor. They had a large and prosperous family. (Sarah Crigler.)

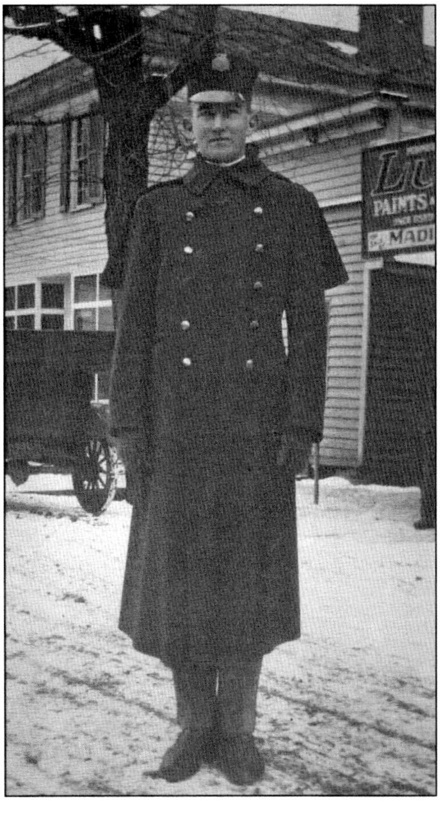

Norman Carpenter, a student at Virginia Polytechnic Institute, came home to Madison for Christmas in 1918. He was awfully proud of his uniform, as well he might have been. The name Carpenter appears 35 times in the muster rolls of Madison County for the Civil War and 20 times in the roll for World War II. (Joan Weaver.)

Eight

Town of Madison

A log courthouse was constructed in what is now the town of Madison in 1793, shortly after the county of Madison was formed from Culpeper in 1792. It stood on a ridge in the center part of the county with commanding views of both the mountains and the valleys around it. The present brick courthouse was built on the same site in 1829 and is now a Virginia Landmark. The town of Madison was laid out in 1798 but the area was not incorporated as a town until 1875. In the 1800s, a stagecoach line between Washington, D.C., and Charlottesville ran through Madison. Travelers could rest and refresh themselves at the Eagle House, which was then a tavern and inn.

The first post office in Madison County was established at Madison in 1801.The *Gazetteer*, a news magazine, described Madison in 1836 as a village with 34 dwelling houses, six mercantile stores, two taverns, two houses of public worship, two tanners and curriers, two saddlers, two boot and shoemakers, one wheelwright, three blacksmiths, one coppersmith and tin plate maker, one wagon maker, one house joiner, one cabinet and wheat fan maker, and four tailors. It had two resident attorneys and four practicing physicians, and a population of 290. Today, 174 years later, Madison's population stands at 215, although at one time in the past it was as high as 500.

Madison is a southern town where shopkeepers tell a departing customer to be sure and come back. And Madison is a patriotic town where Main Street is decked with American flags on every national holiday and where each Memorial Day a crowd gathers at the War Memorial Building to watch the Boy Scouts parade the colors and raise the flag, then lower it to half-staff; to hear the high school band play, and to hear the national anthem sung with fervor.

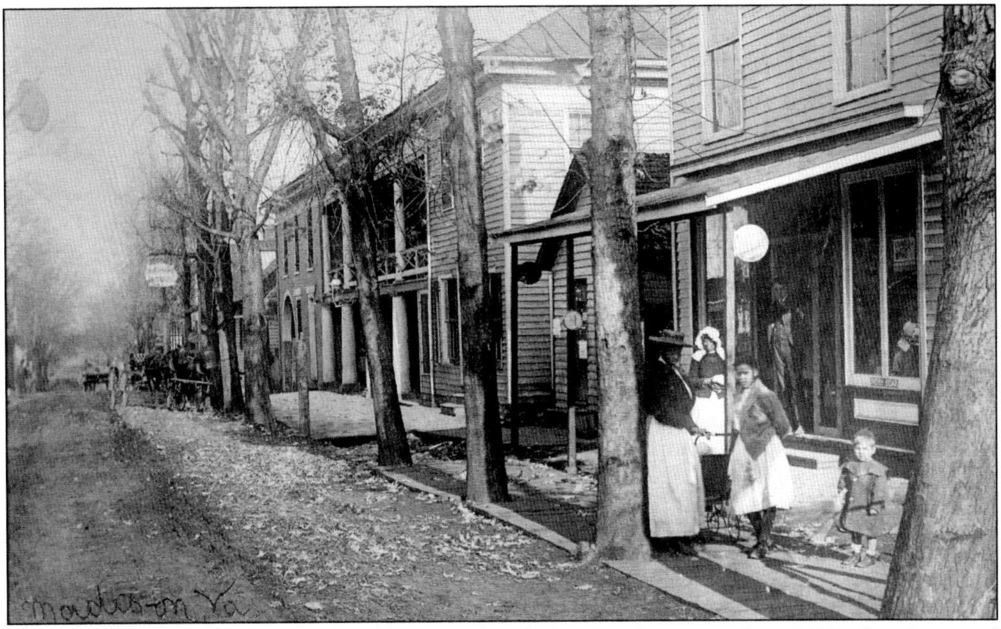

These views of Main Street in Madison were taken before the disastrous fire of 1919 that destroyed much of the east side of the street. The photograph above looks north around 1907. The first building is the drugstore and beyond is the old Madison House Hotel. In front of the drugstore are Lizzie Harrison (black hat), Aunt Louisa Beck (bonnet), pharmacy clerk Hugh Roberts (on porch), Irene Hill, (girl in jacket), and Alexander Pattie (child). The hotel was destroyed in the 1919 fire, which was stopped by the brick wall of the Arcade building attached to the north end of the hotel. The photograph below was taken in 1908 and also looks north. The building on the far left was the Banks Store (later Gibbs and Estes) and the next square brick building was built in 1838 by Dr. George N. Thrift for his office. (Vee Tull, Jim and Margie Lamar, and Steve Grayson.)

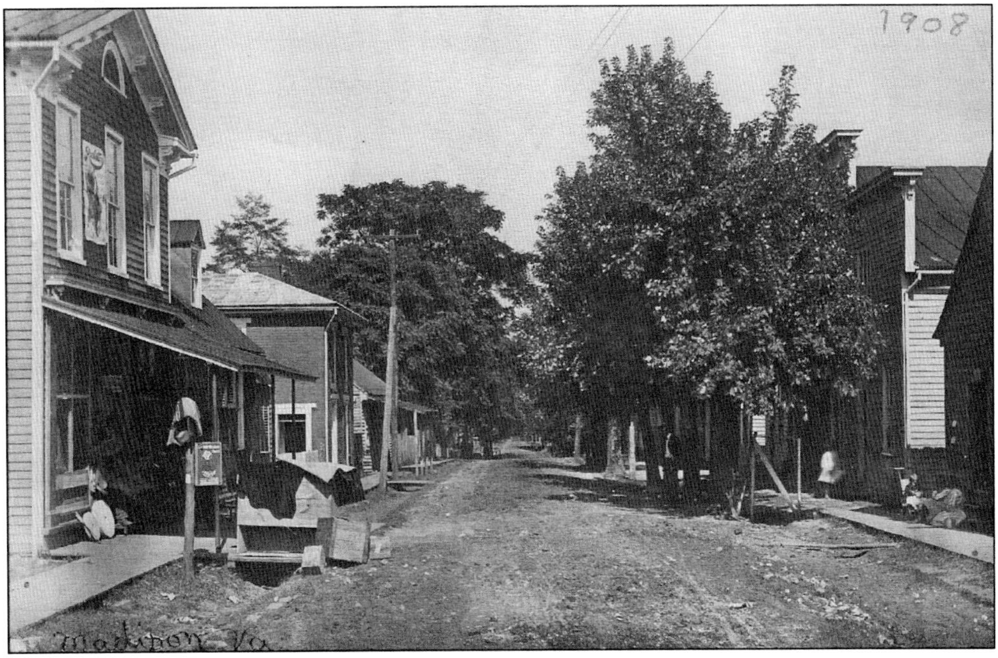

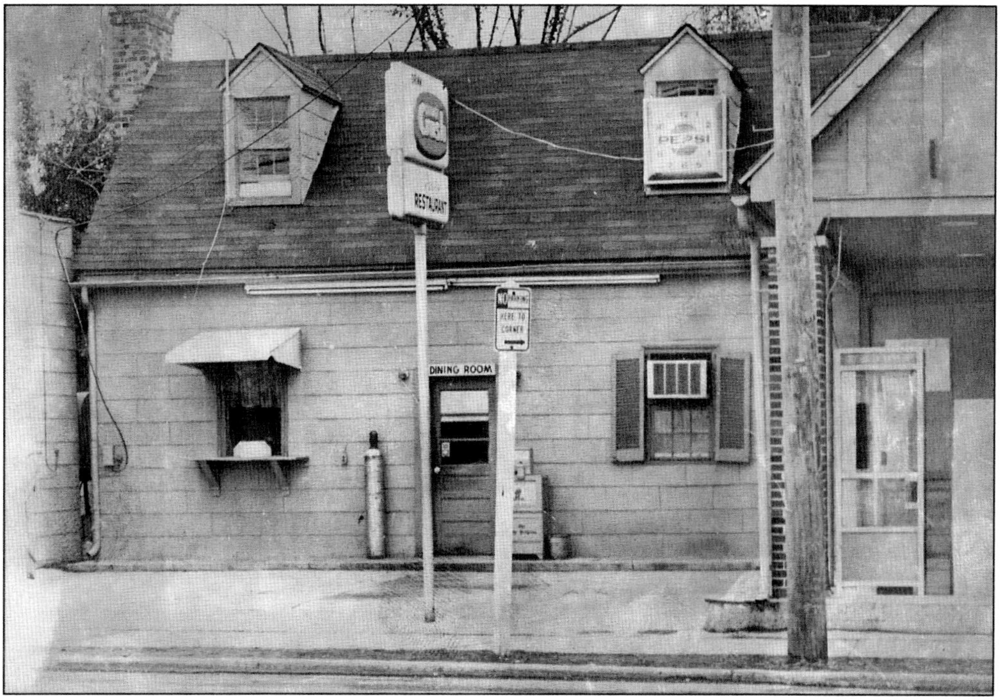

During the latter half of the 20th century, this was the only restaurant on the north end of town. It was originally called Rixey's, then it became Beulah's. When Beulah retired, a new proprietor upgraded it; it is now the Madison Inn. The eatery is at the corner of Schoolhouse Road and Main Street and has provided good country food to Madisonians for many years. (Madison County Historical Society.)

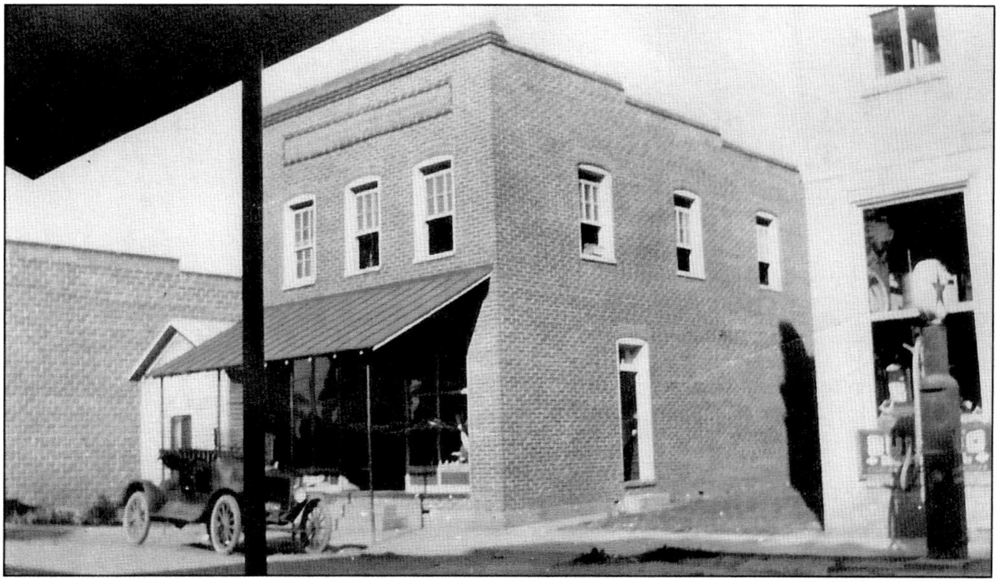

Madison's only drugstore was established in 1856. A fire destroyed the original building in 1919 and this store was built in 1922 on the same spot. The Madison Drugstore still functions in the same location today. To the left was Hobbs Barber Shop and to the right is a gas pump in front of the bank building, which is now the home of the Chamber of Commerce. (Virginia Aylor McGhee.)

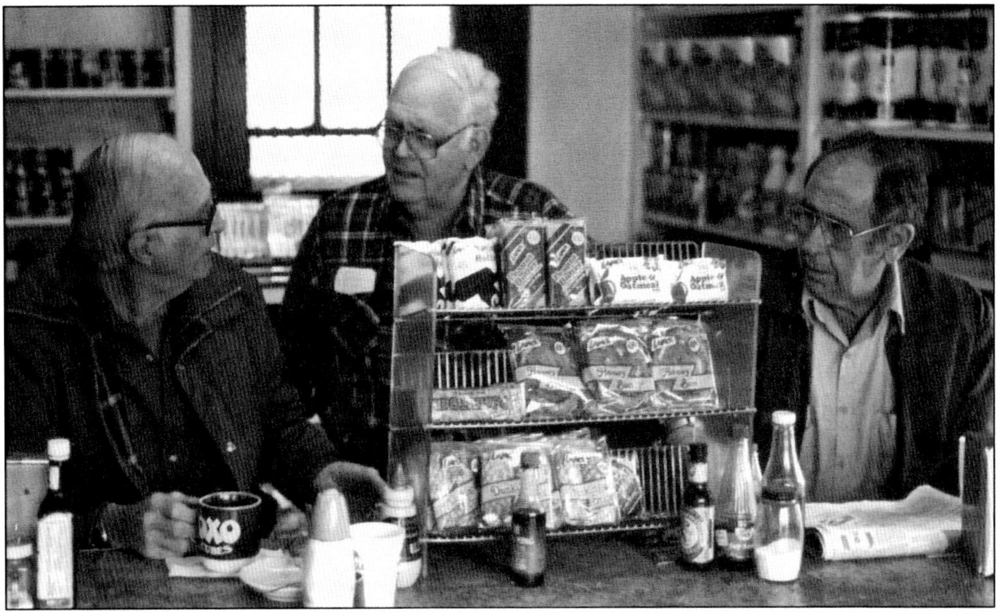

Berry's Grill, called simply "the grill" by locals, was a popular hangout through the last half of the 20th century. It was an old-fashioned lunch counter and at lunchtime all the seats were filled. Customers at the counter solved many world problems. Seen in this *c.* 1995 photograph are, from left to right, Ed DeJarnette, Thornton Berry, and Bill Hall. (Nan Coppedge.)

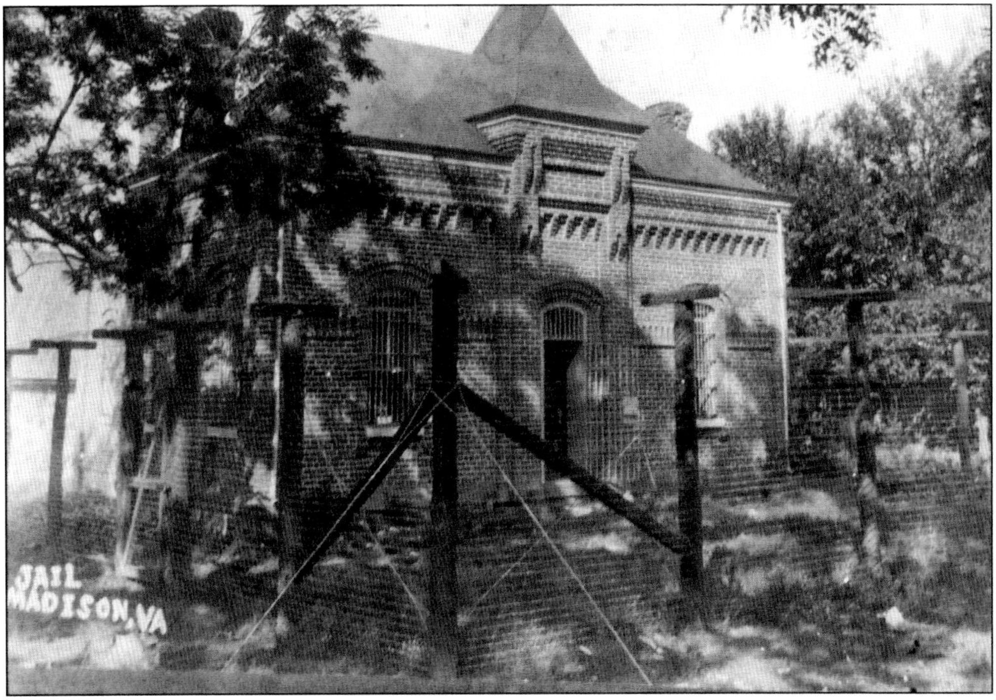

The old jail, built in 1890, was a handsome brick building. In the early days, the jailer lived in the jail, which had rooms for his accommodation. This jail was in use until the 1940s, when it was abandoned for security reasons. The first jail, a wooden one constructed in 1793, once stood on this same lot near the courthouse. (Vee Tull, Doug Graves.)

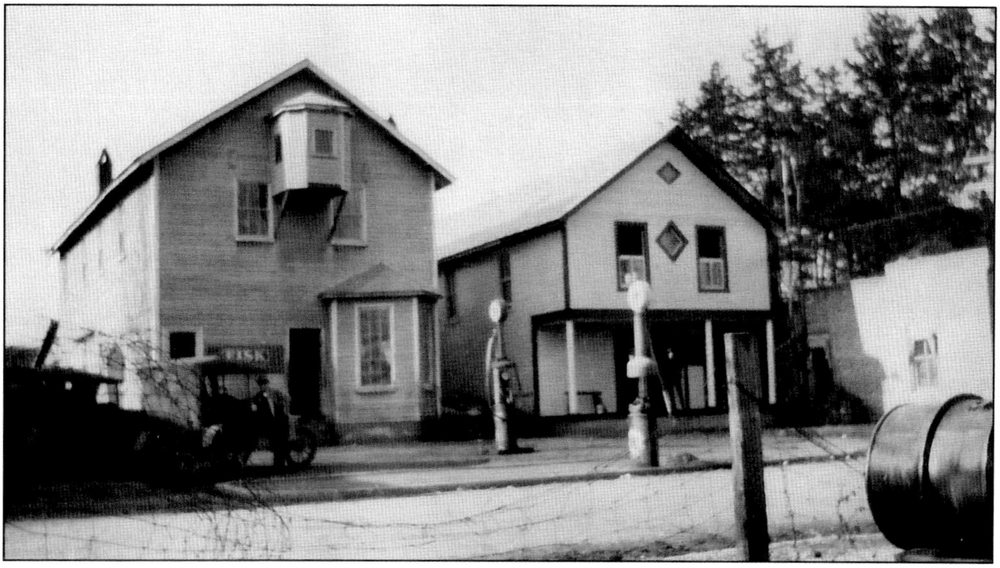

For many people, the dream of the movies was a welcomed relief from the dreary real world of the Great Depression. The old Madison Theatre, owned by T. T. Mitchell around 1920, was on the second floor of the two-story building on the left. A ticket booth stood in front of it. The lower level was a service station and later was Jack Clore's garage. By 1938, the Star Theatre was built next door and the movies were shown there. Movies were silent in Madison until 1930, when the first "sound picture machine" was installed. The Star advertised it as "new R.C.A. sound." Four days before Christmas 1938, Jane Withers in *The Rascals* blew away customers' cares for 25¢ or less. (Above, Katherine Clore Craft; below, James W. Lillard.)

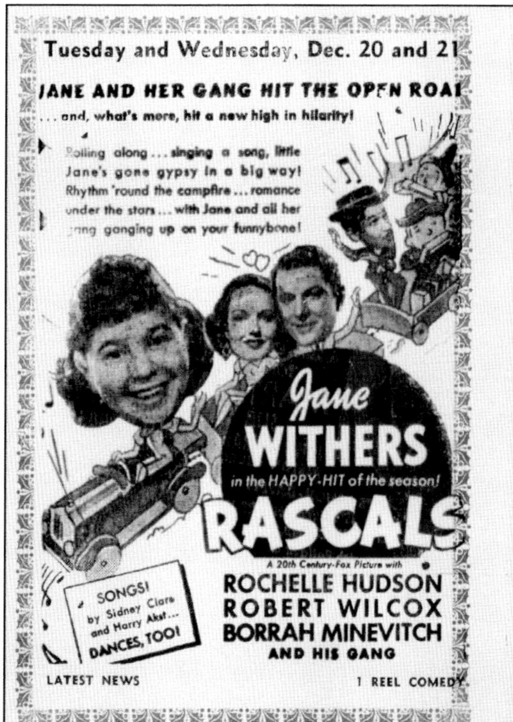

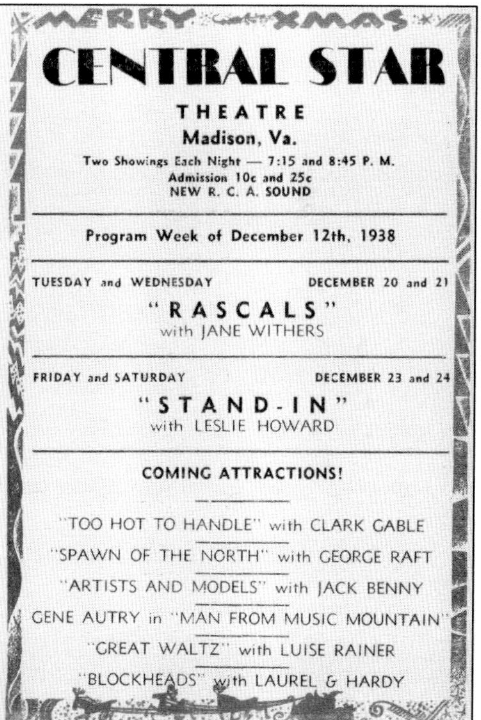

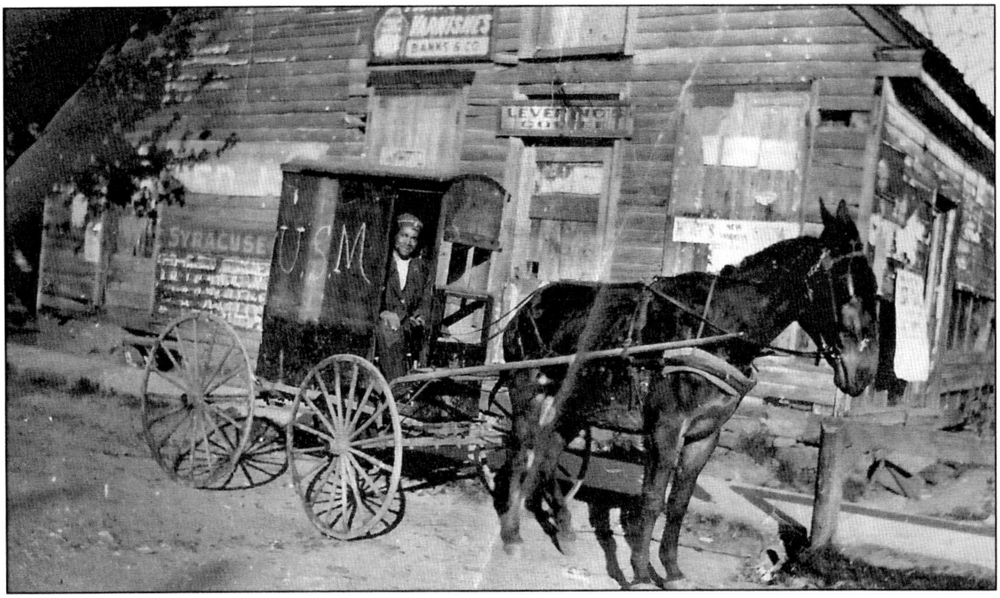

C. C. Weaver delivers the mail throughout town by horse and wagon in the early 1900s. The old Banks Store is in the background. The first post office to be established in Madison County was in the town of Madison in 1801. John M. Krider was the first postmaster. (Virginia Aylor McGhee.)

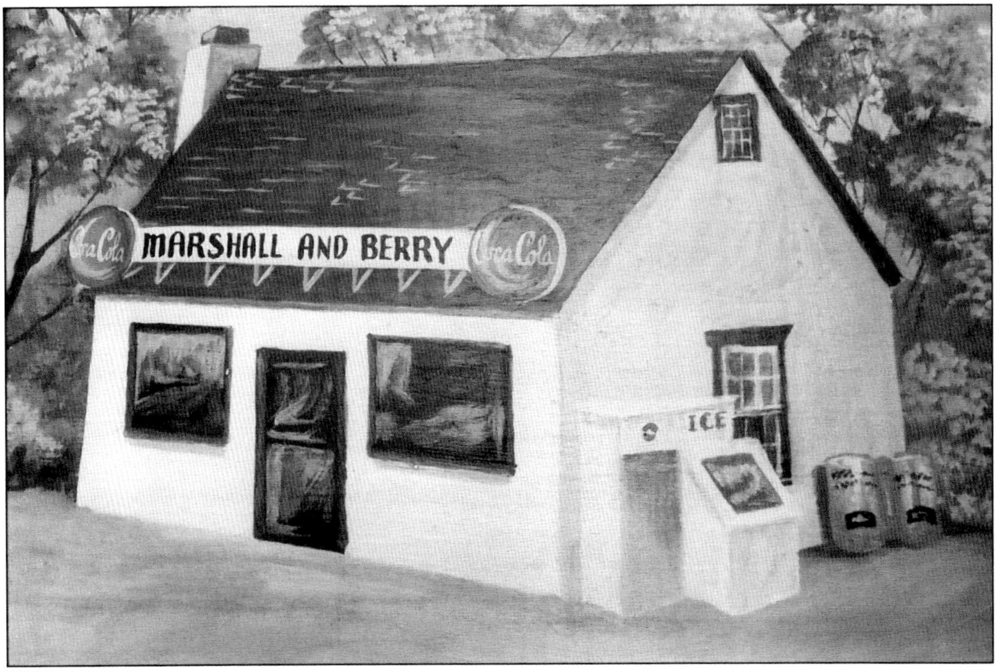

Berry's Grill on the south end of Madison was a mainstay in the town if one were looking for a tasty country lunch and some good conversation. Thornton Berry and Lawrence Marshall started serving food here in 1953. The business continued through 2000. Today the building is a gift shop and spa. (Nan Coppedge.)

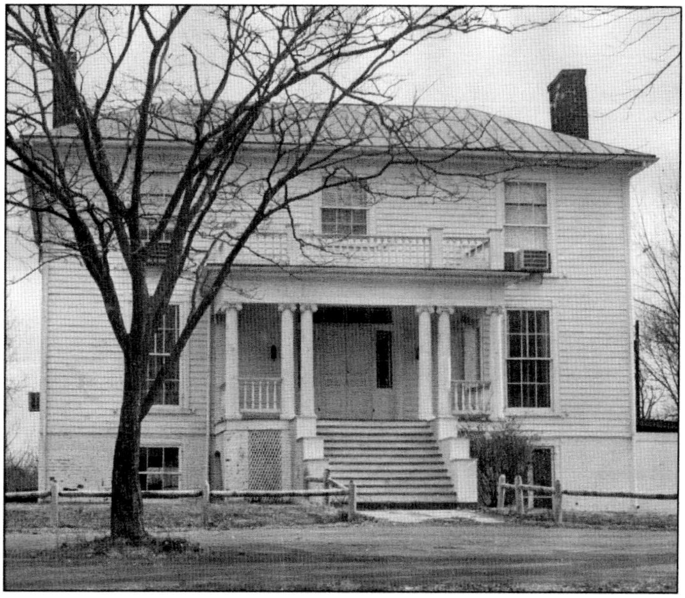

The Kemper House was built in the mid-1880s by Thomas Welch. The house was later owned by Gen. James Lawson Kemper and his wife, Cremora Conway. Kemper and his law partner, Judge Francis McMullan, maintained an office in a log building behind the house. In 1881, McMullan and his wife, Virginia Ann, founded a college preparatory school here, the Madison Female School. Kemper later became governor of Virginia. (Photograph by Vee Tull, courtesy of Madison County Historical Society.)

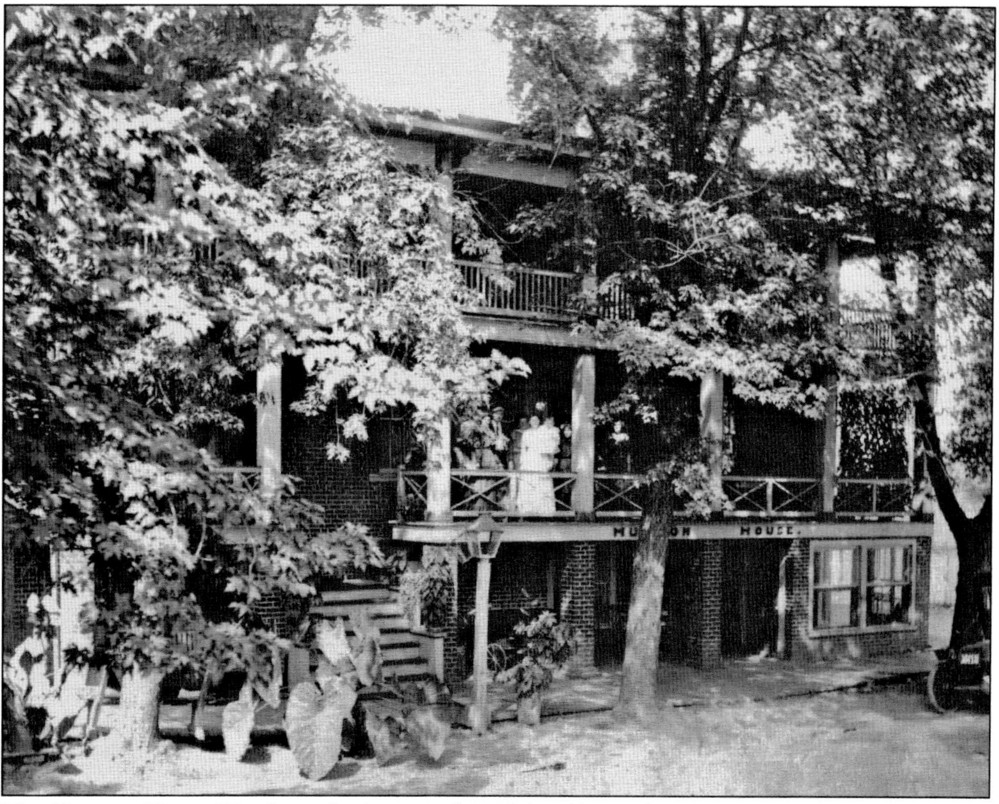

The Hunton House Hotel was built around 1800 by Alexander Hunton as a private home. In 1850, when Benjamin Carpenter acquired the property, he added the porches and opened it as a hotel. Sarah Hunton Hall assumed ownership of the property in 1900. It operated as a hotel with 30 rooms until 1953. In the late 1920s, President Hoover and his wife lodged at the hotel while building Hoover Camp. The building remains in the Hunton family today. (George M. Selby.)

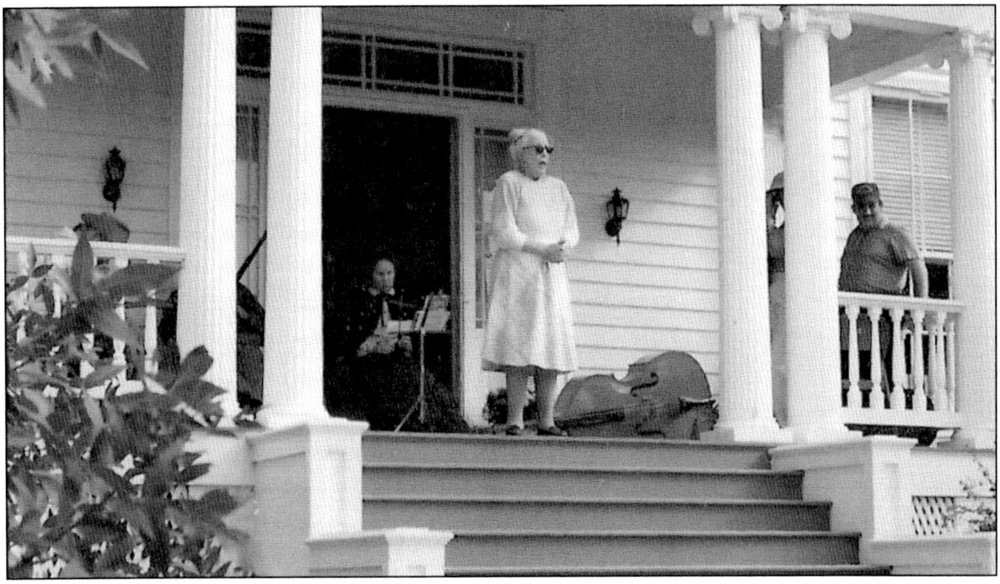

Madison town mayor Sarah Frances Johnston addresses a crowd from the steps of the Kemper House. She served as mayor through much of the late 20th century. Johnston lived on the lower floor of the old Hunton House Hotel on Main Street, which has been in her family for generations. (George M. Selby.)

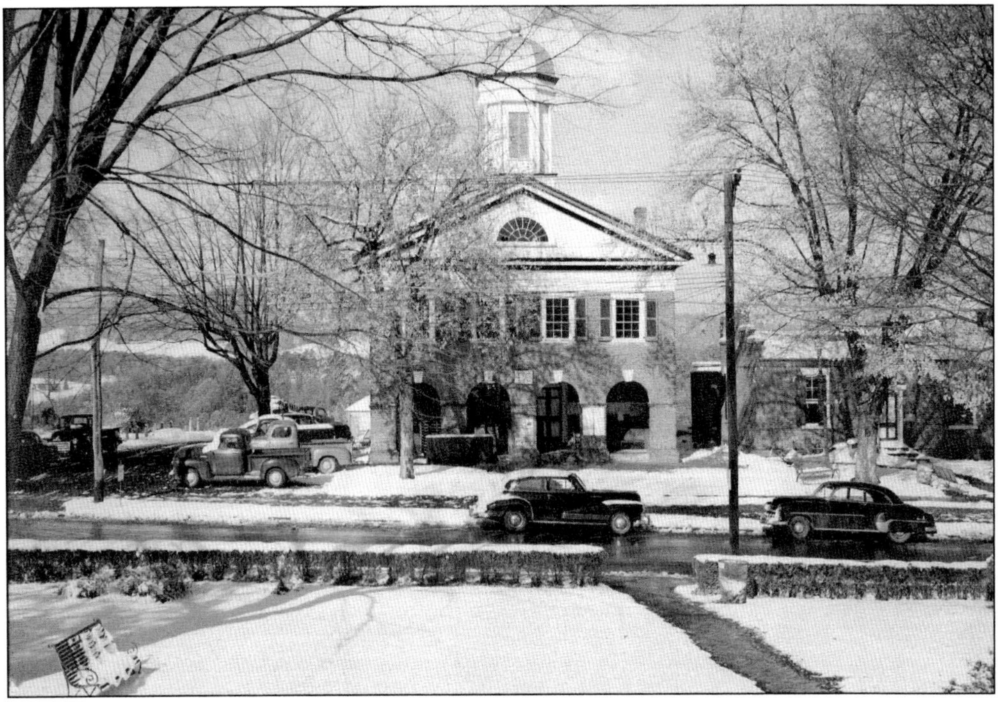

The present Madison County Courthouse was constructed in 1829 on the original site of an earlier log courthouse. It is admired for its fine period architecture and excellent brickwork. The Virginia Historic Landmark Commission has designated it a historic landmark. In 2009, Madison County began a multi-million dollar renovation of the courthouse in order to bring it up to modern standards. (Vee Tull.)

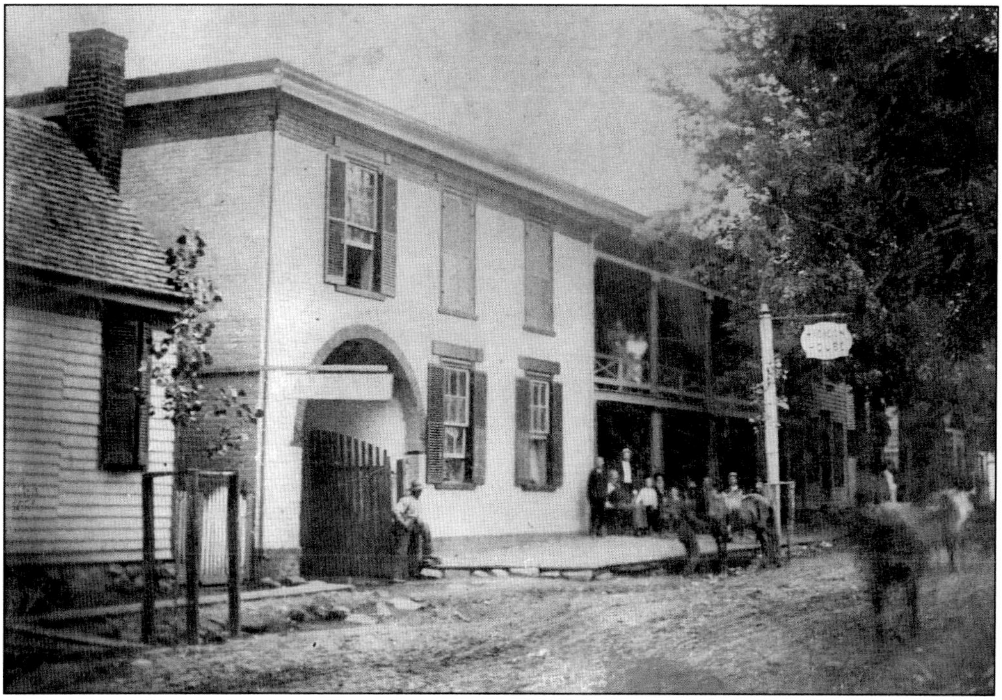

The Madison House Hotel was a wooden structure with a long porch extending across the second floor. It was built onto the brick Arcade building shown in this *c.* 1915 picture. The hotel burned in the Madison fire of 1919, but the Arcade building was credited with stopping the fire from spreading because of its brick wall. Today the Arcade building is the home of the Madison County Historical Society. (Photograph by Vee Tull, courtesy of Madison County Historical Society.)

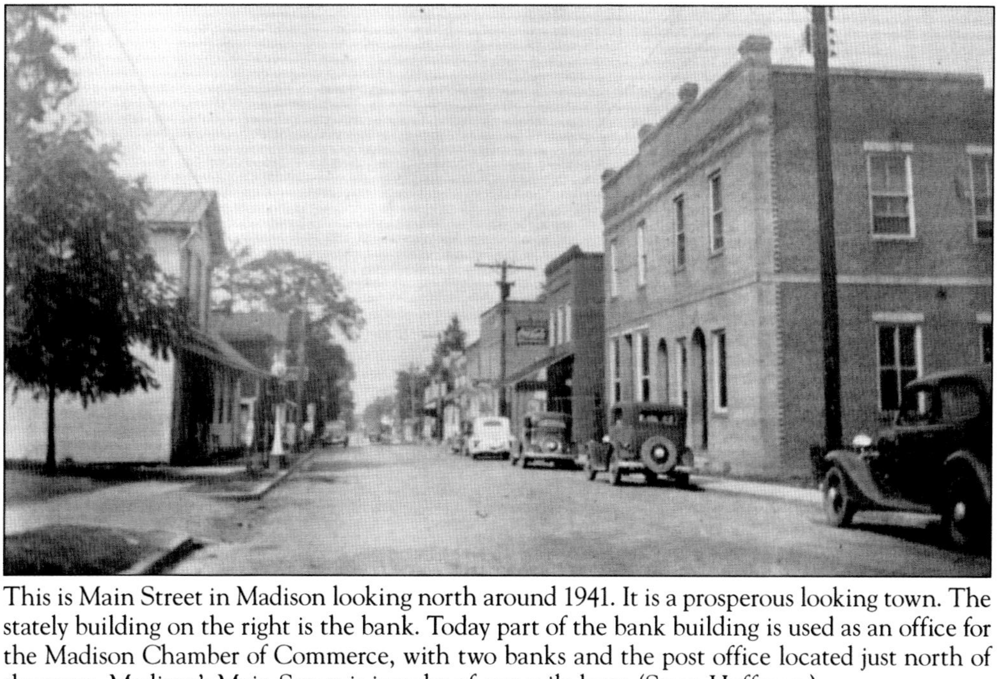

This is Main Street in Madison looking north around 1941. It is a prosperous looking town. The stately building on the right is the bank. Today part of the bank building is used as an office for the Madison Chamber of Commerce, with two banks and the post office located just north of the town. Madison's Main Street is just shy of one mile long. (Steve Hoffman.)

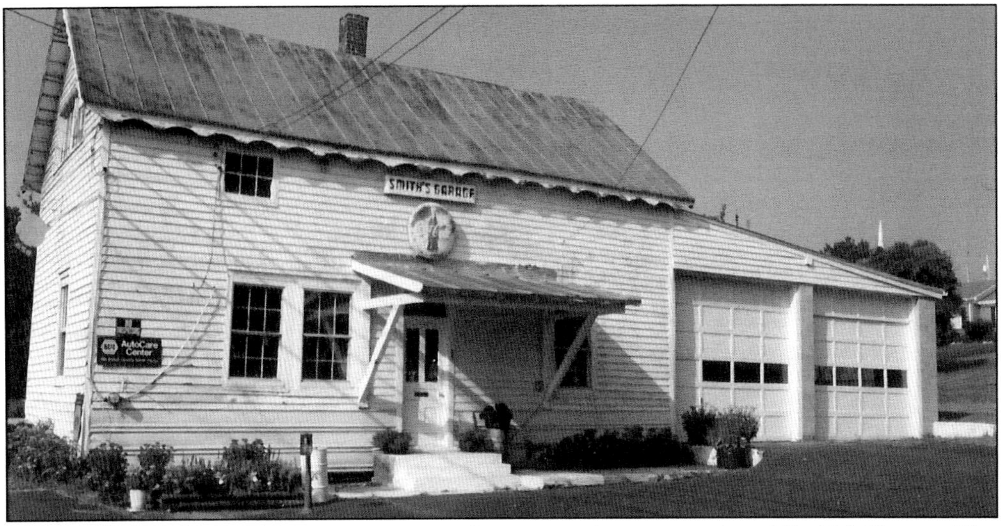

Prior to the Civil War, there was a carriage factory on the present site of Smith's Garage. The factory was run by George W. Smith, who came here from Missouri. It burned and Smith rebuilt, but with the Civil War, hard times came and carriage building ceased. Smith continued as a wheelwright and also made coffins. His grandson Jack Smith later operated an automobile garage in the same building. (Martha Cornwell.)

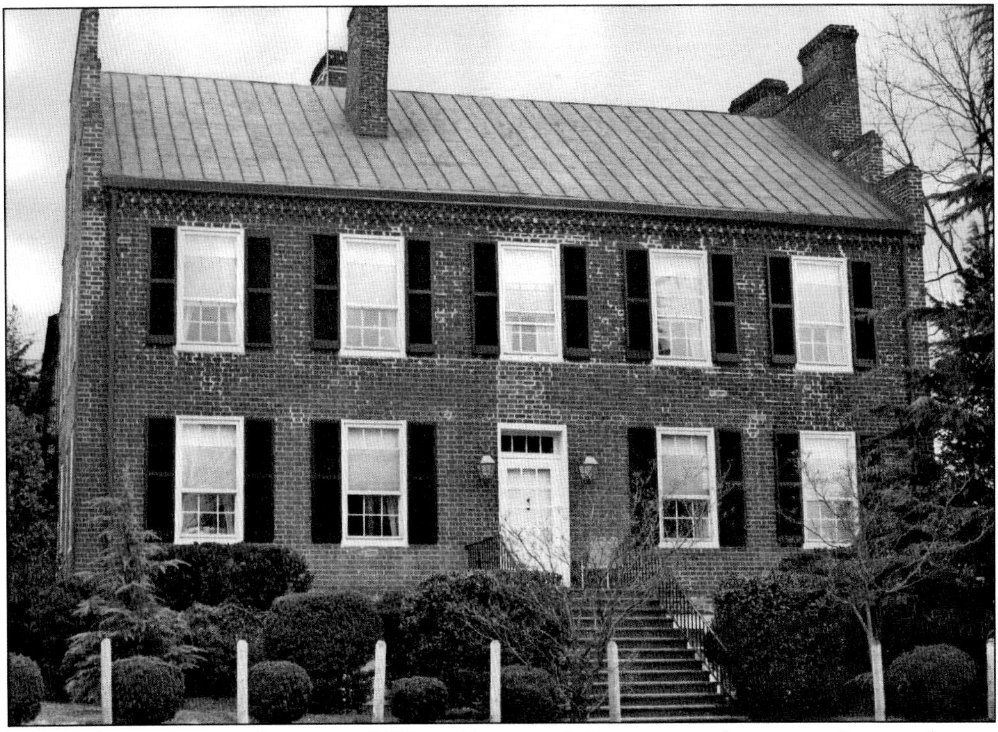

The Eagle House, once known as William Carpenter's Tavern, stands next to the courthouse. The present building was built in the 1830s but records indicate this structure was here when the county was established in 1793. At one time the *Madison Eagle* newspaper was printed in the basement of the house. It became a private residence in 1877. (Photograph by Vee Tull, courtesy of Madison County Historical Society.)

E. A. Clore is pictured here being driven by Henry Banks in the 1959 Madison Day parade. His wife Alma Clore had been named Mother of the Year. The Clores had 12 children, and E. A. wanted people to know that she did not do it alone. (David Clore.)

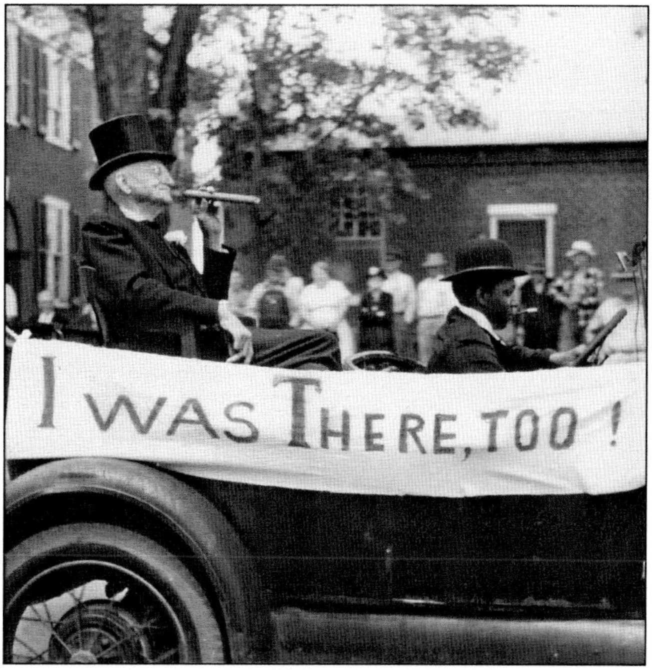

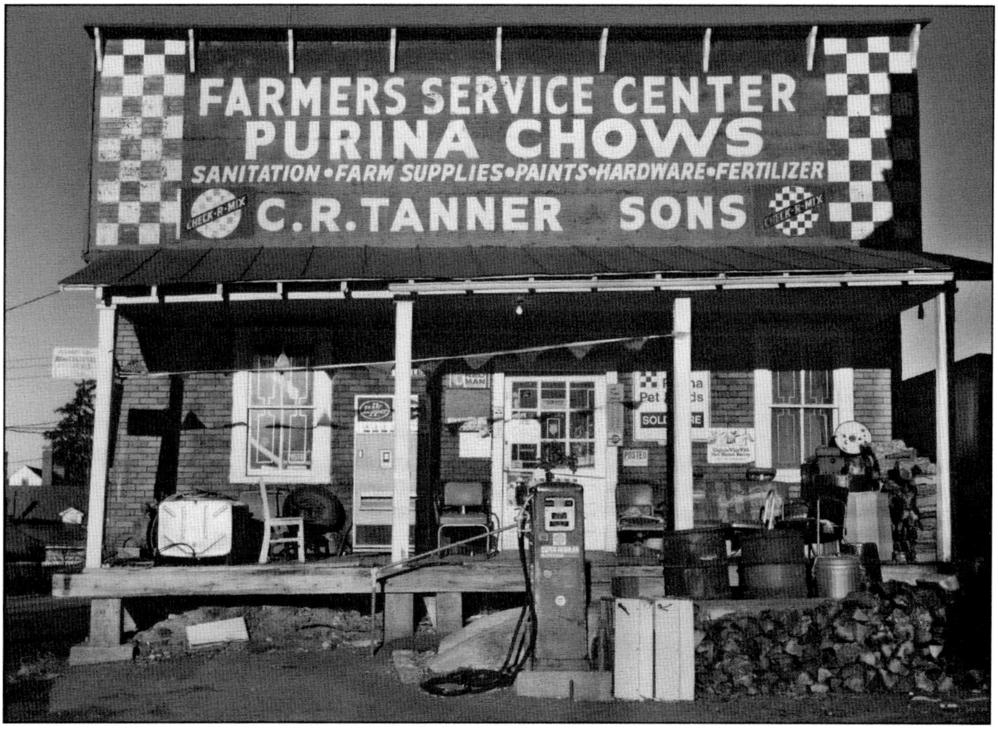

Joan and Bobby Tanner opened the Farmers Service Center in 1956. Farmers could buy feed for their livestock, as well as meal, flour, and sugar for the family. In the 1990s, Joan Tanner began bringing in collectibles to sell in the store. A pot-bellied stove in the office keeps visitors and staff warm in the winter, and a swing on the front porch offers visitors respite in warmer months. (Joan and Bobby Tanner.)

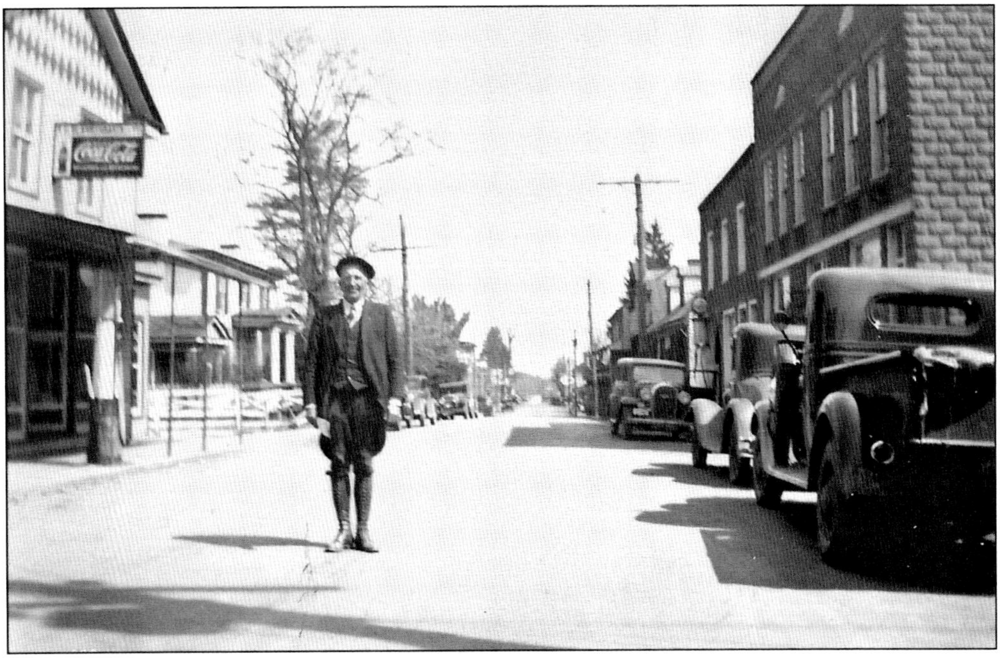

Sheriff Tom Lillard stands in the middle of Main Street around 1940. He was born in 1885 in Graves Mill. He served first as deputy sheriff, then as sheriff of Madison County for more than 30 years. Both of his sons, Carroll and Hume Lillard, also served as deputies. Carroll was elected sheriff of Madison County in 1956 and served in that capacity for nearly 20 years. (Ruth and Randall Lillard.)

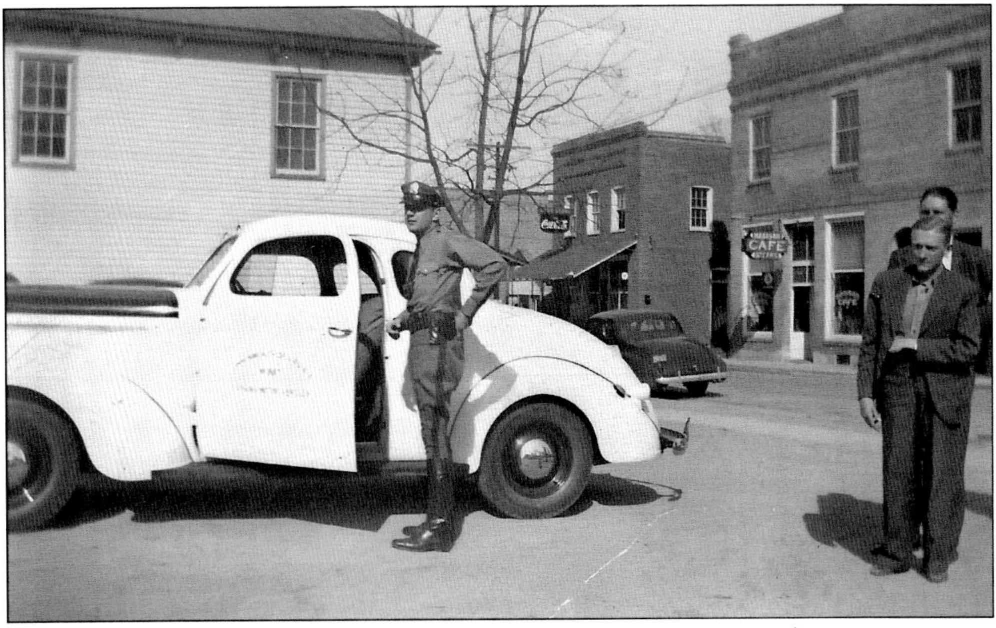

Virginia State Trooper P. W. Crews stands beside a 1939 Plymouth on Madison's Main Street. Euby Utz stands on the right. Utz was Madison County commissioner of revenue from 1959 to 1970. He followed his father, L. T. Utz, as commissioner. The senior Utz held the job for 36 years, from 1923 to 1959. (Ruth and Randall Lillard.)

Nine

FARM AND HOME

Madison County was, at its inception, an agricultural community. In the late 1700s and early 1800s, hogsheads of tobacco were sent to the Tidewater area to be sold in England. Tobacco was an excellent cash crop, but its cultivation quickly exhausted the soil. The large plantations in Virginia developed from a need to move tobacco acreage frequently from worn out land to fresh soil.

The Germans in the Hebron Valley knew how to replenish the nutrients in their fields and produced good yields annually, but the tobacco planters lacked this skill. Tobacco is no longer raised commercially in the county and good agricultural practices have become widespread. Madison County is still an agrarian county today. Many of the large farms and plantations are diminished in size, but farming remains a mainstay of the Madison County economy. There are 564 farms in the county today with an average of 224 acres each. Madison County farmers produce grains and fruit, maintain dairies, and raise beef cattle. It is said that there are more cattle than people in the county. In the 1950s, Madison County was one of the major apple producing counties in Virginia. Today many farmers produce and market their goods at farmers markets. As the demand for organically grown and chemical-free food grows, some Madisonians have formed cooperative ventures to deliver their produce directly to consumers.

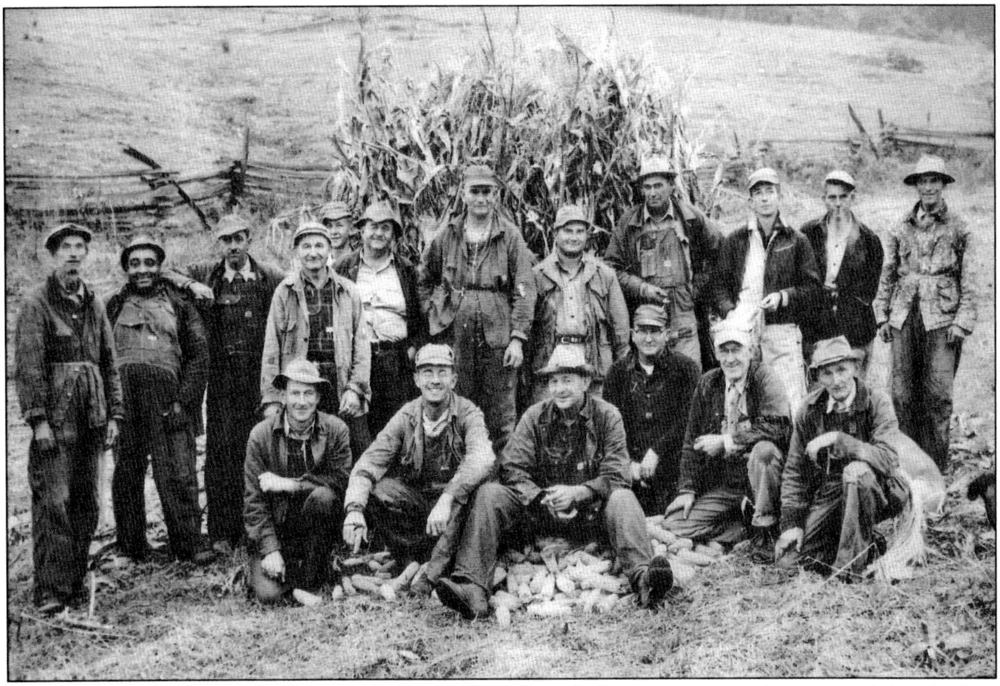

This corn shucking took place in Aylor in the 1950s. The corn had to be cut and shocked in the field to dry. The tradition was for neighbors to gather together to help one another with the harvest. During the shucking, if a red ear of corn was discovered, the lucky boy got to kiss a pretty girl. (Ann Miller.)

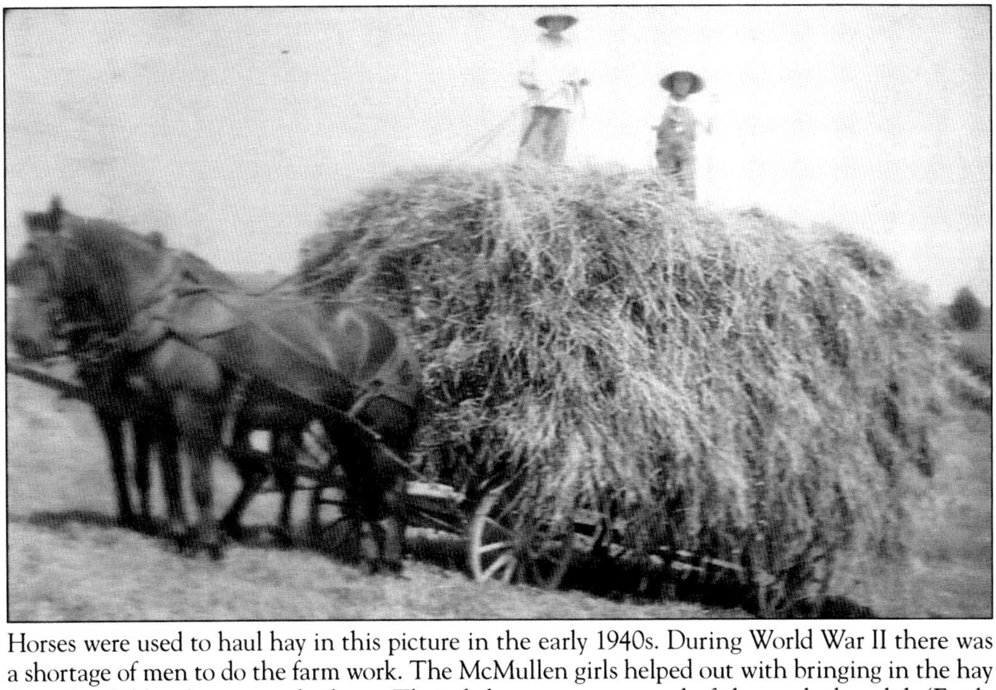

Horses were used to haul hay in this picture in the early 1940s. During World War II there was a shortage of men to do the farm work. The McMullen girls helped out with bringing in the hay from the field to be put in the barn. Their father was very proud of the work they did. (Emily McMullen Williams.)

This is the farm called Indian Trace near Locust Dale in 1907. Legend has it that Native Americans camped here on their way between the mountain hunting grounds and Virginia's Tidewater region. The house was built in 1859 of brick laid in Flemish bond. It sits on a hill overlooking the Robinson River. (Frank Gray.)

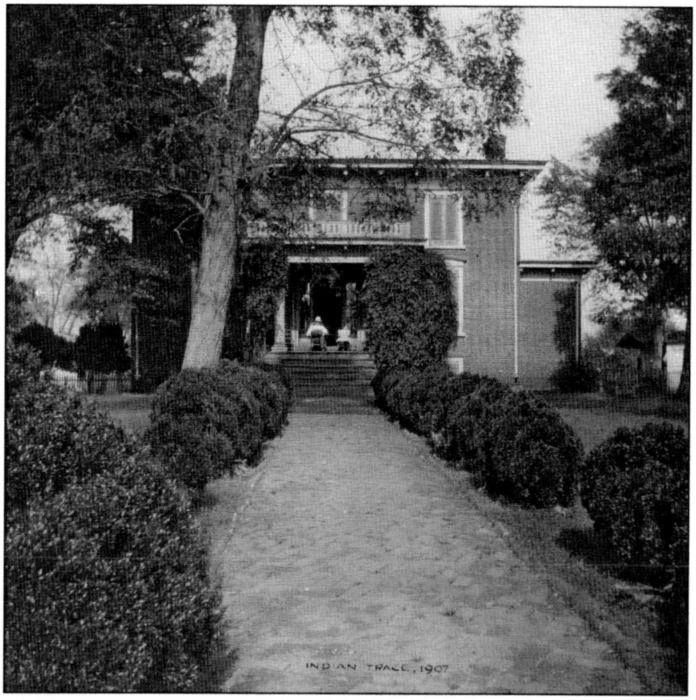

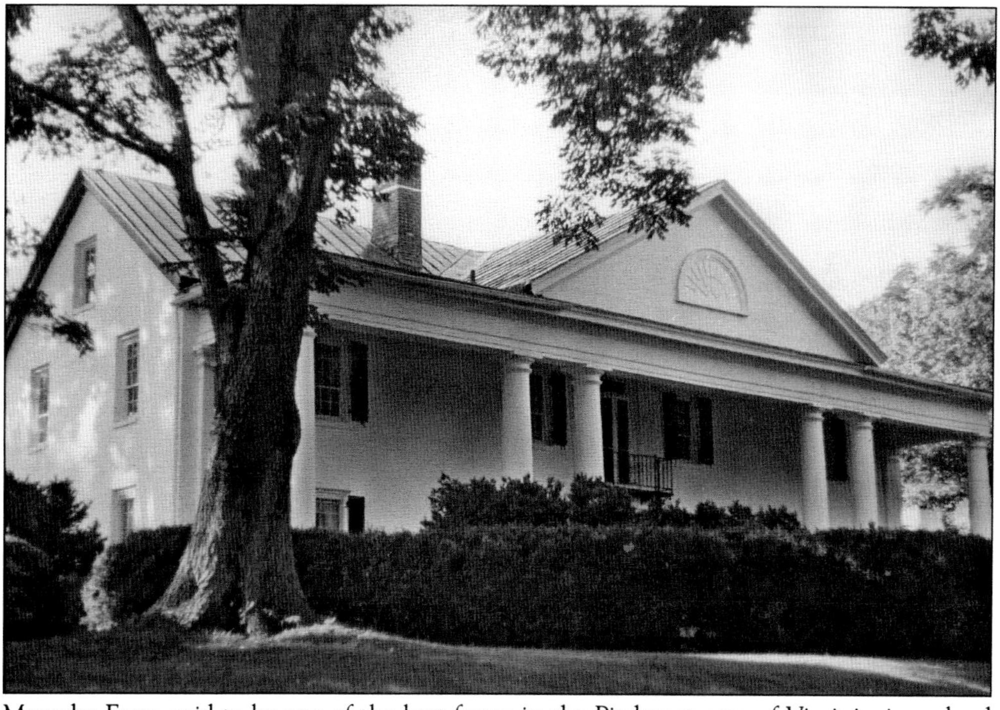

Meander Farm, said to be one of the best farms in the Piedmont area of Virginia, is on land patented by Joshua Fry in 1727. Fry, a professor at William and Mary from 1728 to 1732, owned more than 4,000 acres of land in the area but there is no proof that he ever lived on it. His son Henry Fry Sr. built a home here, Elim, in 1766. The name was changed to Meander in the 1930s. (Photograph by Vee Tull, courtesy of Madison County Historical Society.)

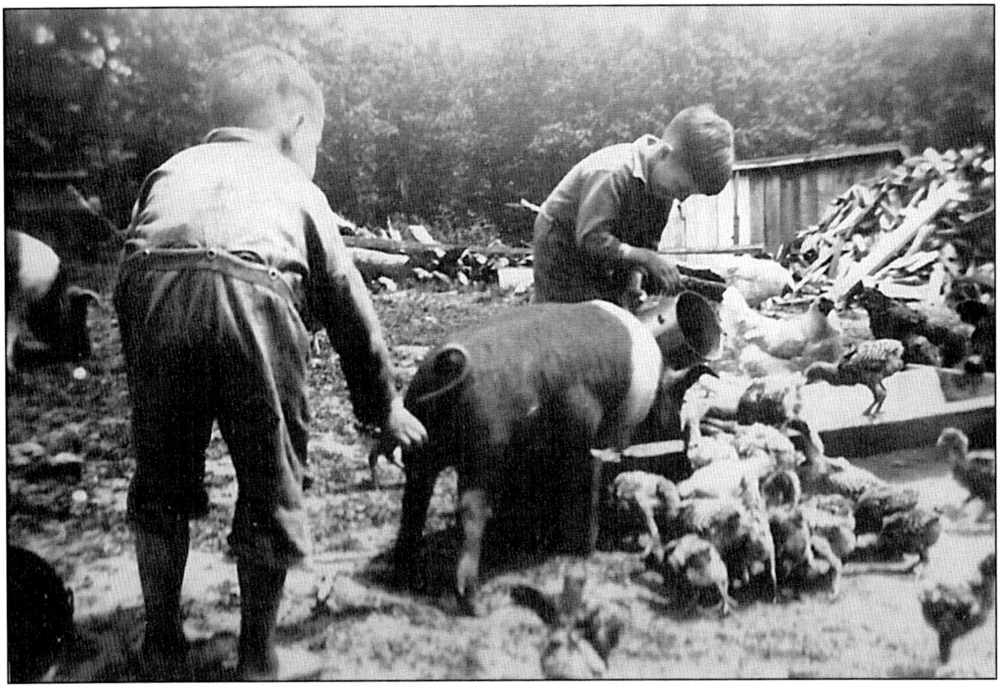

In the early 1900s, farming was very labor-intensive and required the participation of all members of a family starting at a very young age. In these two photographs, taken around 1928, the young Weaver twins, Sterling and Overton, born in 1923, feed the pigs and chickens as part of their regular farm chores. They were the sons of Gorrel and Anna Weaver and lived at Brook Falls farm in Radiant. Sterling was drafted and served in World War II. When their father died, Overton and his brother Thomas took over running the farm. Today Mrs. Overton (Ila) Weaver still lives at Brook Falls. (Both, Judith G. Mahanes.)

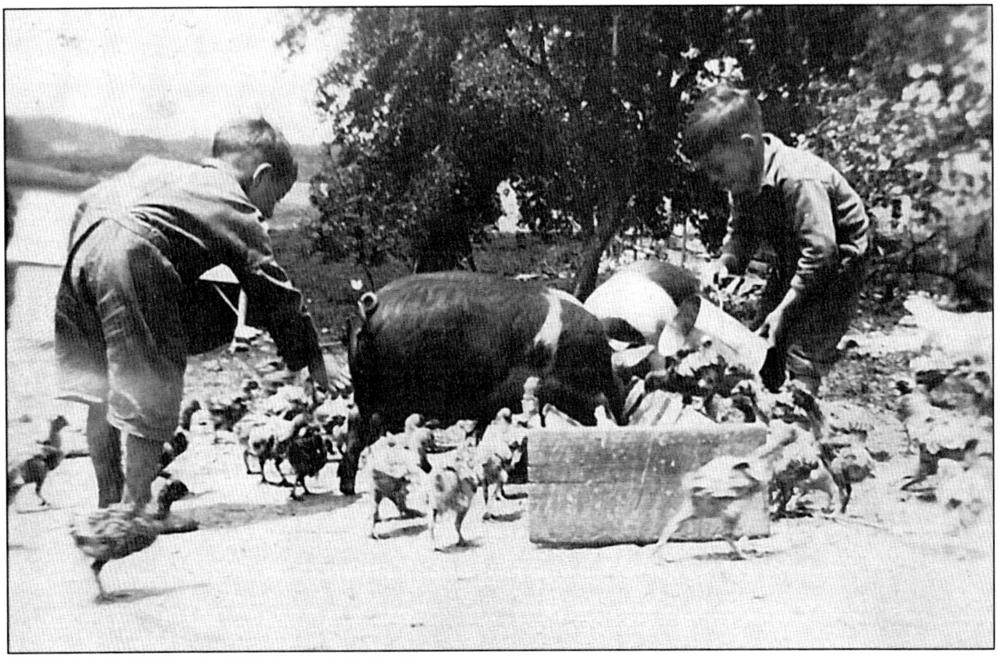

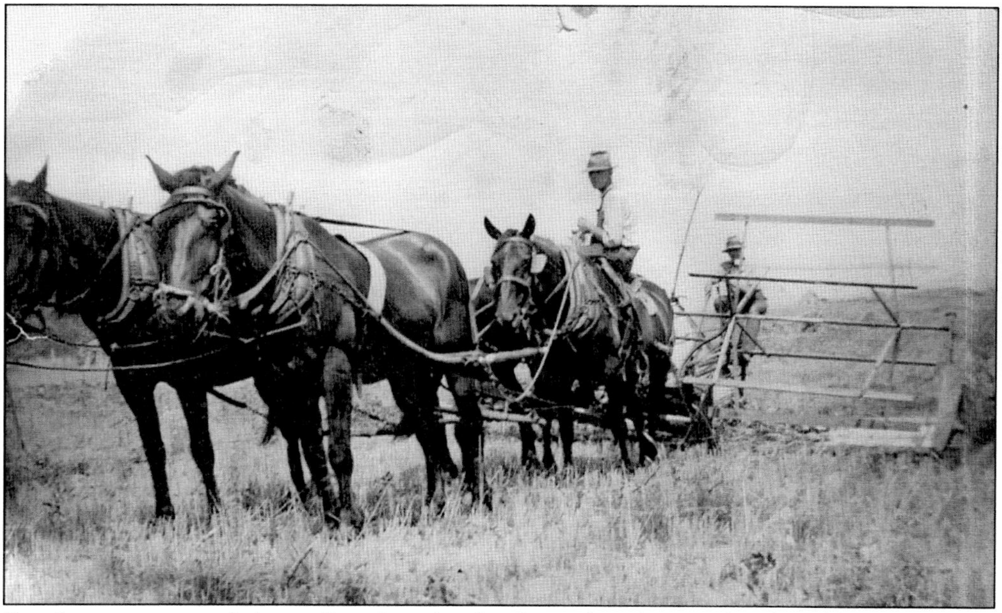

Four horses were needed to pull a wheat binder. It cut the wheat and gathered it into bundles, which were dropped in the field. Later they were picked up and put into shocks, which were gathered up and taken to the thrashing machine. The thrashing machine would go from farm to farm because not many farmers had one. (James W. Lillard.)

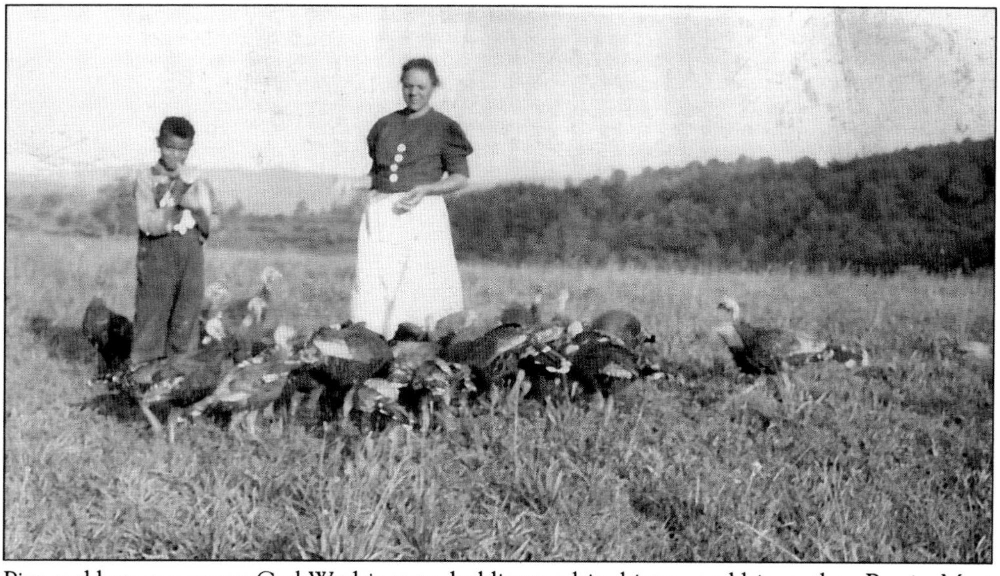

Pictured here are young Carl Washington, holding a white kitten, and his mother, Bessie. Most farm families had chickens and turkeys to provide eggs and meat for the table. Here they are tending their flock of turkeys. Dan and Bessie Washington raised six children on the family farm near Criglersville. (Flora R. Washington.)

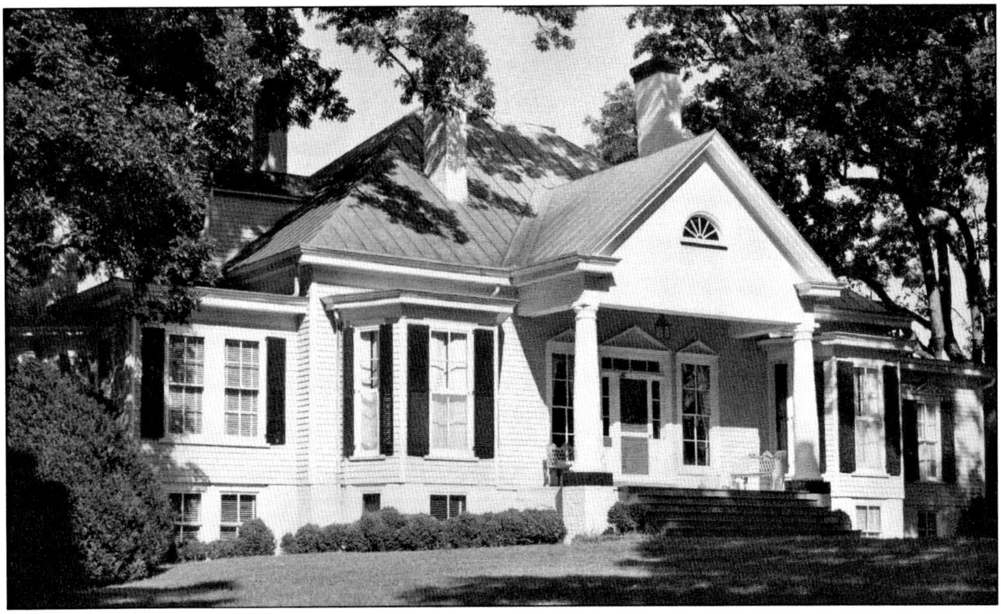

James Madison's brother William built The Residence near Madison Mills in 1793. Thomas Jefferson is credited with the design of the frame structure. In 1870, John S. Walker of Rosni purchased Woodbury (Woodberry) for his son Robert S. Walker. It is now the home of the headmaster of Woodberry Forest School, established in 1889. (Photograph by Vee Tull, courtesy of Madison County Historical Society.)

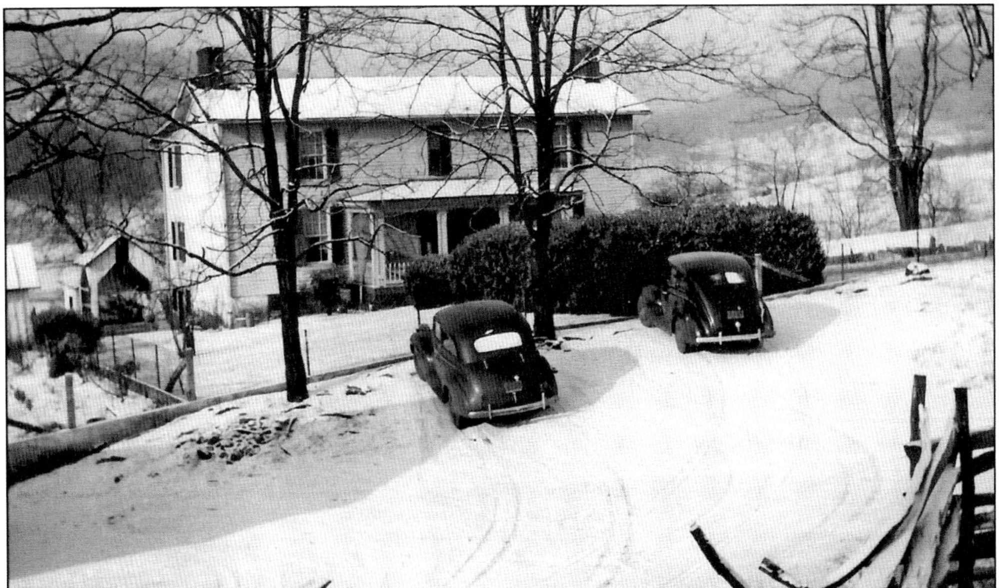

This is Thornton, the Coppedges' home near Banco. It was built by Thornton Berry in the middle to late 1800s. Construction was not complete by the time of the Civil War, so the windows and doors were boarded up and it was used as a hospital and officers' quarters by Federal troops who camped nearby. It was bought by William Wesley Coppedge and his wife, Effie Leah Leathers, in 1906. (Lillian Mitchell.)

Clifton Hill of Criglersville described farming in the 1930s and 1940s: "We took our eggs, butter, cracked walnuts, dried apples, cherries, blackberries, and chestnuts to the store and traded them for supplies. If we had some credit left over, we were given a due bill and could take it back to the store to buy more supplies. We sold our crops for money and put this in the bank." (Anna and Yancey Hill.)

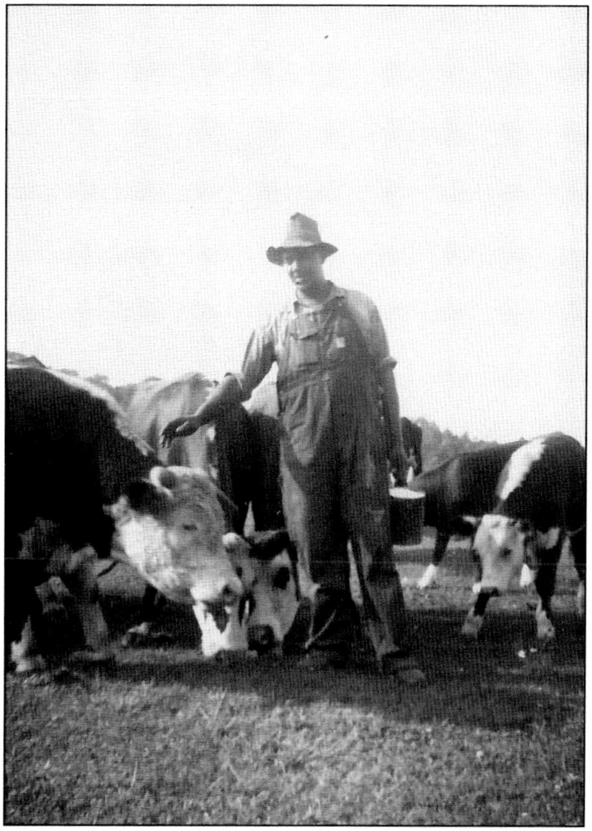

The Clifton Hill home is located about 2 miles from Oak Grove Methodist Church near Aylor. The house was built in 1840 of huge logs with the bark still on. It was mortised and put together with wooden pegs. The rock walls of the English basement are 18 inches thick. There are rock walls around the yard that were built by slaves at night after their day's work for General Banks of Rapidan. The Hills bought the home in 1942. (Anna and Yancey Hill.)

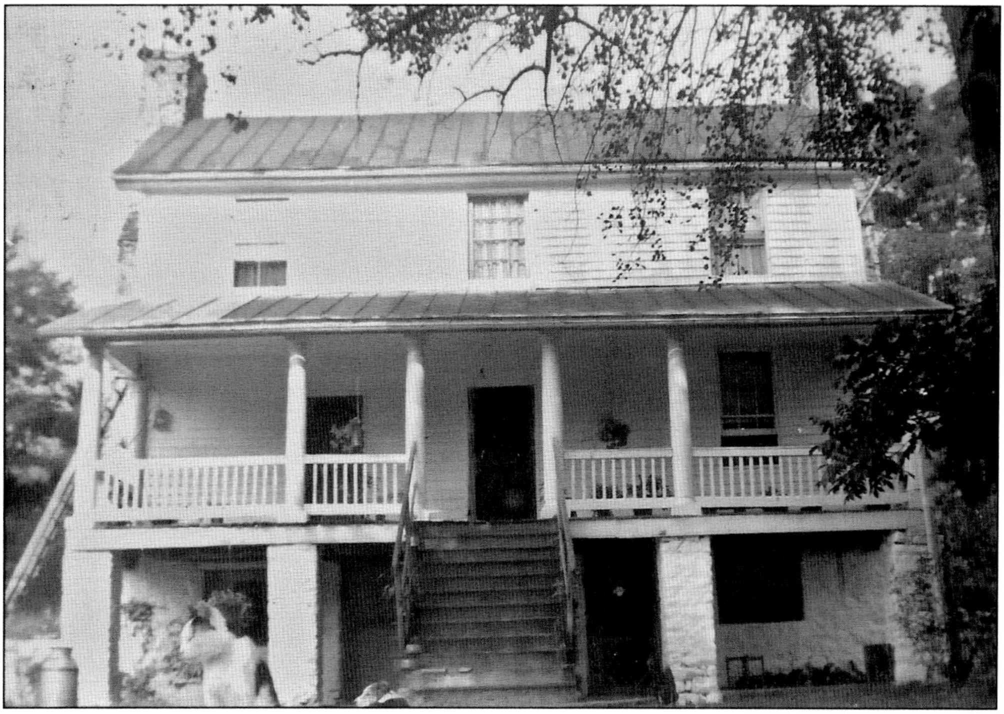

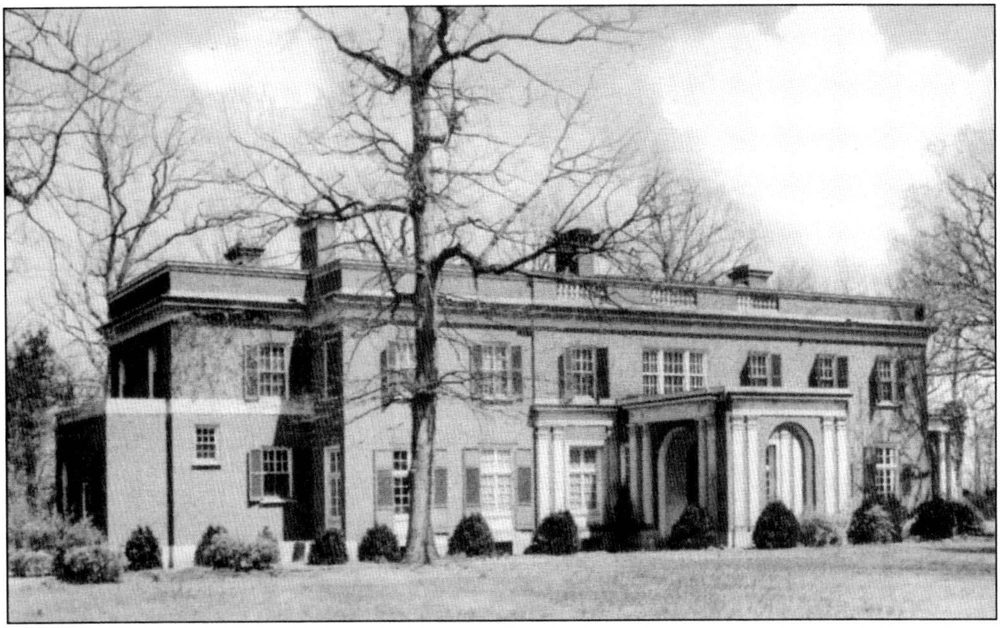

This picture of Oakland (later known as Hartland Hall and now Heartland Institute) appeared on a sales brochure. The 55-room mansion was built by Robert K. Smith and his wife, Rosa Lee. It was started in 1818 and completed in 1821. W. O. Smith, a nephew of the builder, inherited the property. (John Storey.)

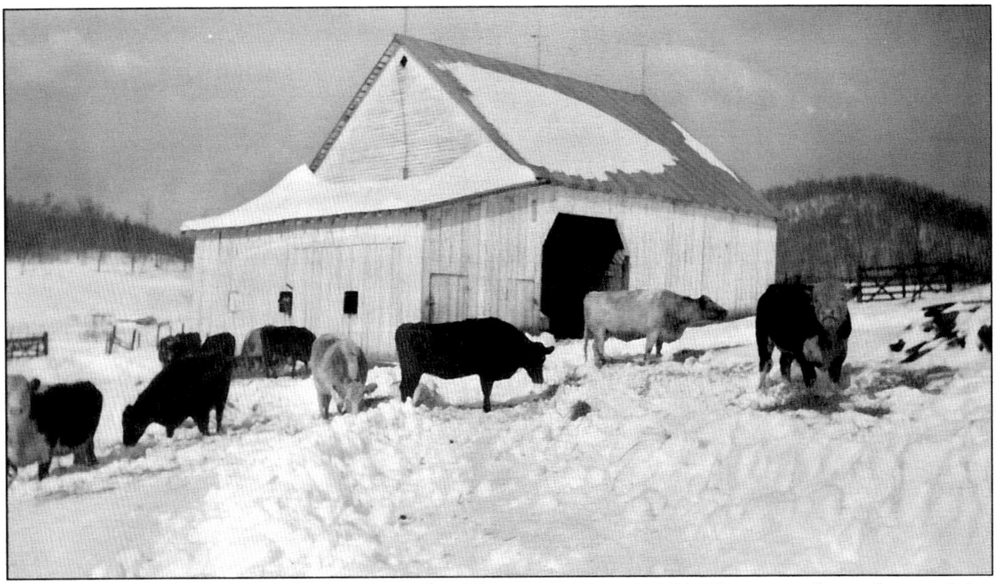

The W. W. Coppedge farm lies just north of Banco on Route 642. These cattle, in front of the Coppedge barn, are digging through new snow to find their hay. Keeping cattle is much more difficult in the winter. "Thornton," as the farm is known, is still being farmed today by a third generation of Coppedges. (Lillian Mitchell.)

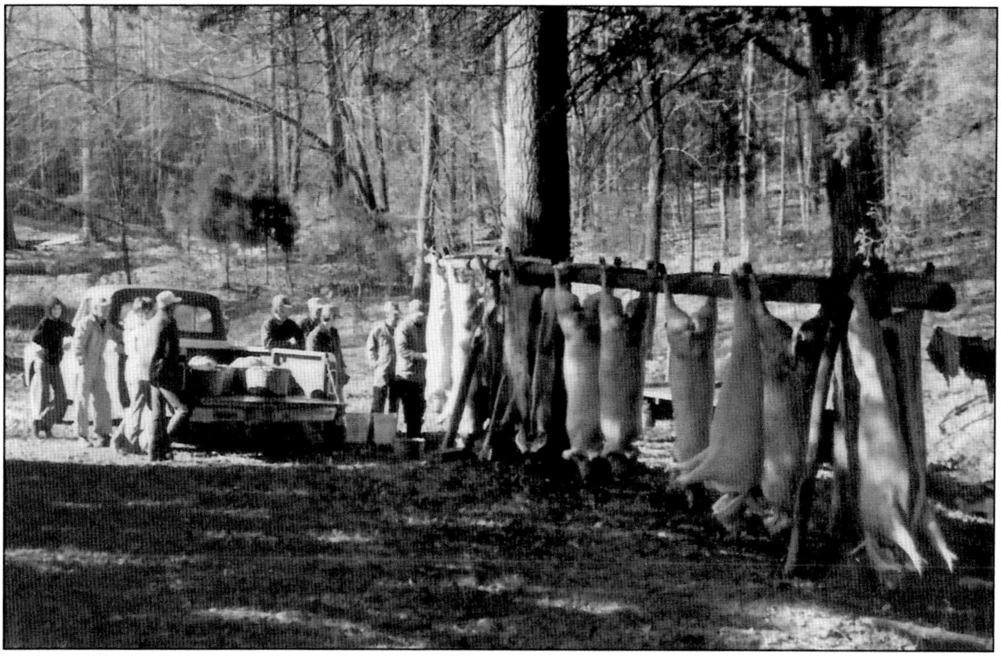

Hog killing on the Smith farm in Hood was a routine fall operation, as it was on most farms in Madison County. It took several days to process all of the meat, but everyone pitched in and this helped to feed a family of 12 in the 1930s and 1940s. (Carole Milks.)

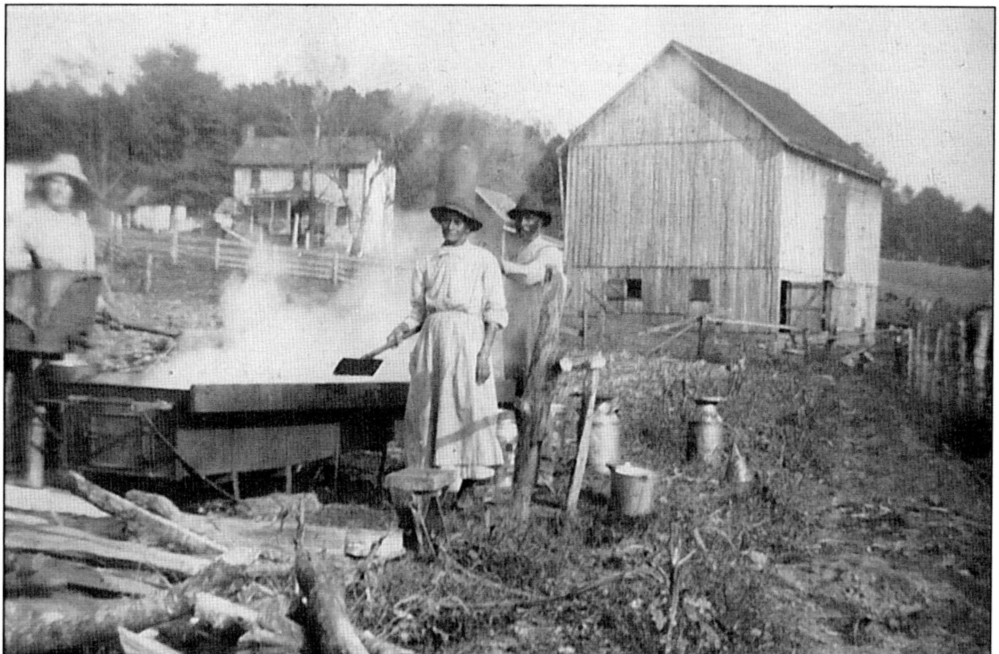

Cutting sorghum cane to make molasses was an important part of farm life in Madison County. In the early years, a horse was used to turn the cane mill and extract the juice. This juice was then slow cooked into molasses. This photograph was taken at the old Gorrell Weaver farm near Radiant around 1934. (Judith G. Mahanes.)

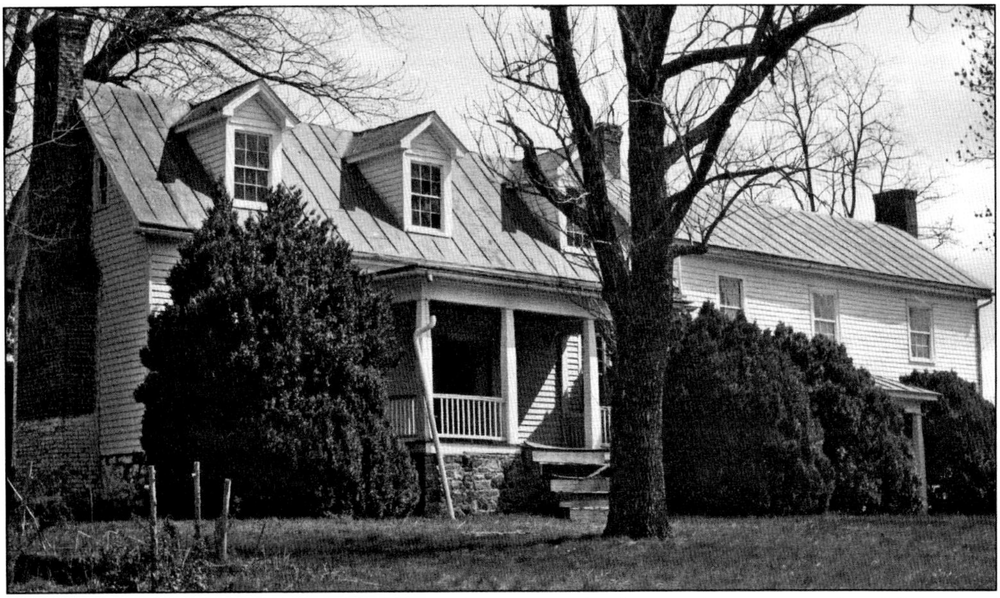

Firnew was built in 1812 by John Fitzhugh Conway and is known by many as the old Conway place. The house stands near Middle River and was part of a 10,000-acre grant made to John Conway's great-grandfather in 1732. Firnew remained in the Conway family until 1946. On the east side of the house is the family graveyard. (Photograph by Vee Tull, courtesy of Madison County Historical Society.)

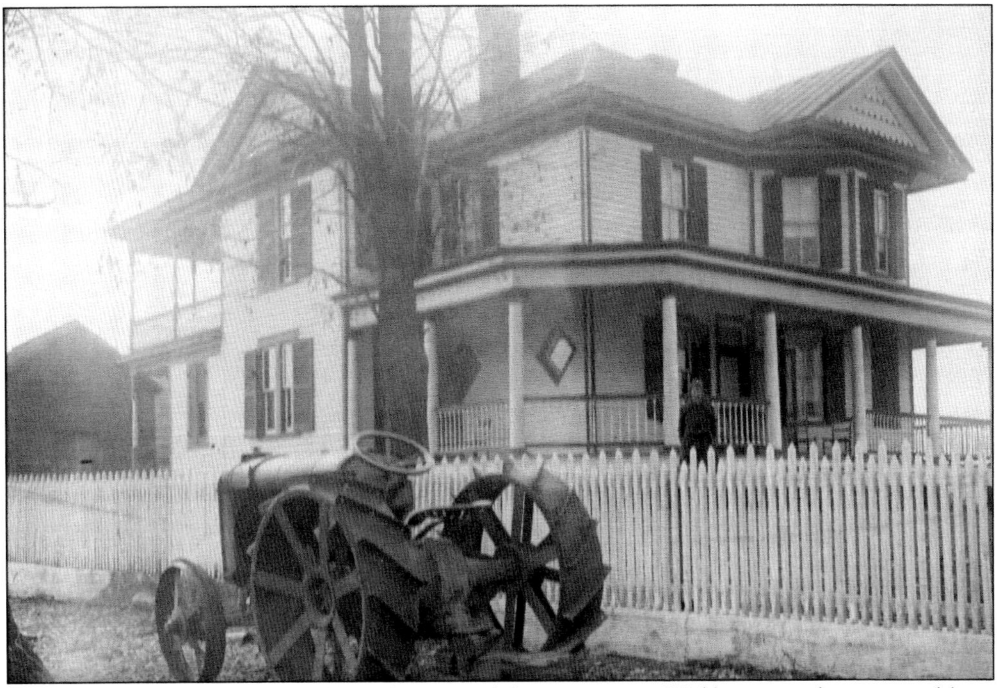

The Theodore Somerville Hoffman house and farm was near Wolftown, and is pictured here in the early 1900s. The house was built to replace the first one, which burned. This home also burned in 1941 before Madison had a fire department. An iron-wheeled tractor stands in the foreground. (Joyce Jenkins Gentry.)

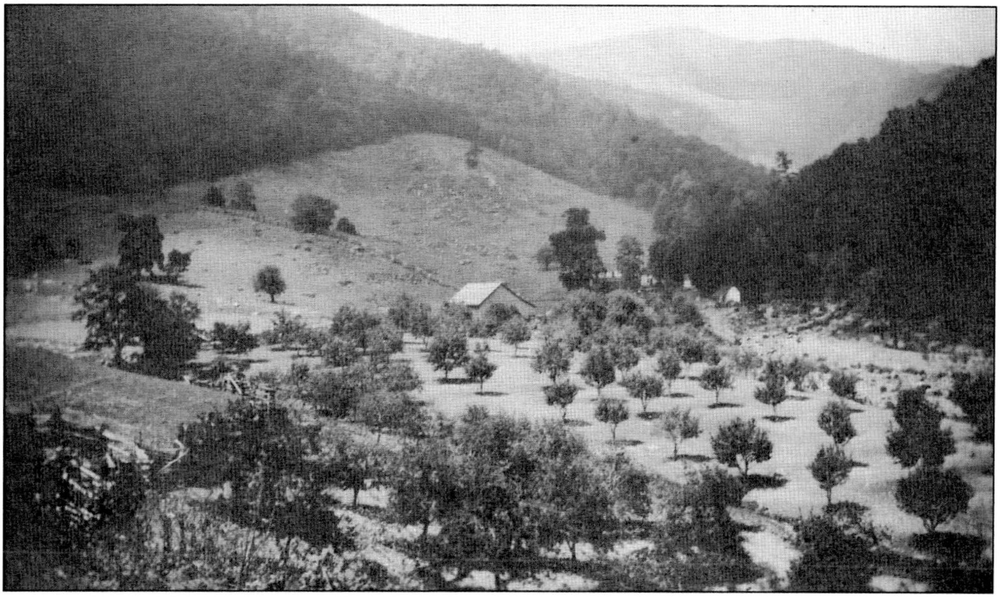

Apples were a cash crop for many Madison County farmers. The photograph above, from around 1914, is an apple orchard on the old Utz place in Rocklin, near Graves Mill. The orchard lies on the slope of the mountains. Madison County has a good climate for growing apples, as proven by the many orchards that once dotted the county. There are few signs today that Rocklin ever existed, yet it once had its own post office. The photograph below shows an apple picking crew obviously posing for the photographer. Their barrels are ready for market. The man standing on the left side of the ladder is Kemper Y. Shotwell. (Both, Ruth and Randall Lillard.)

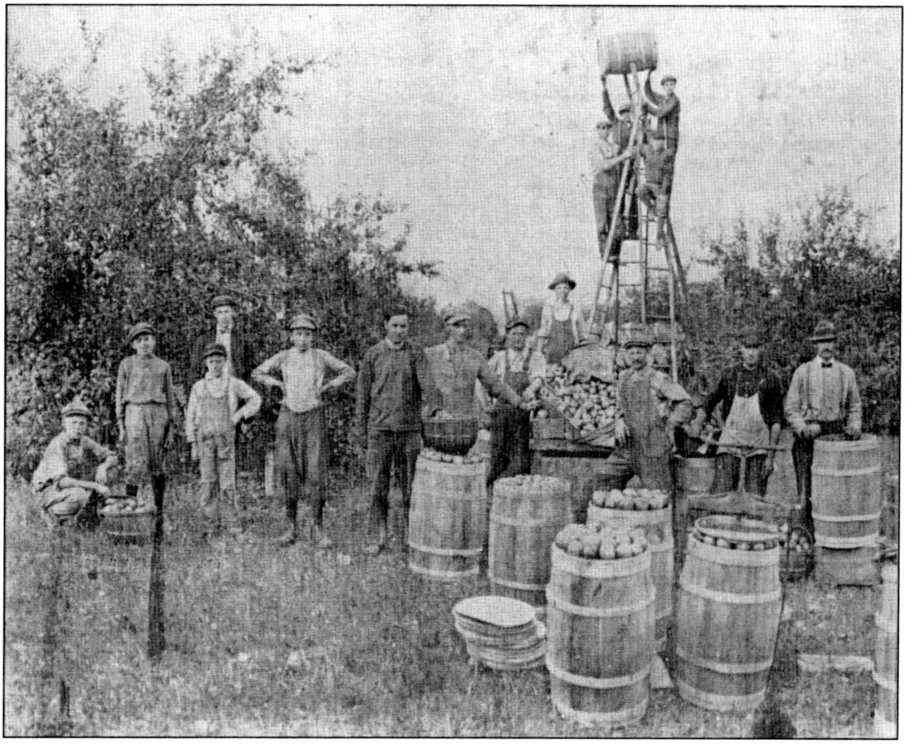

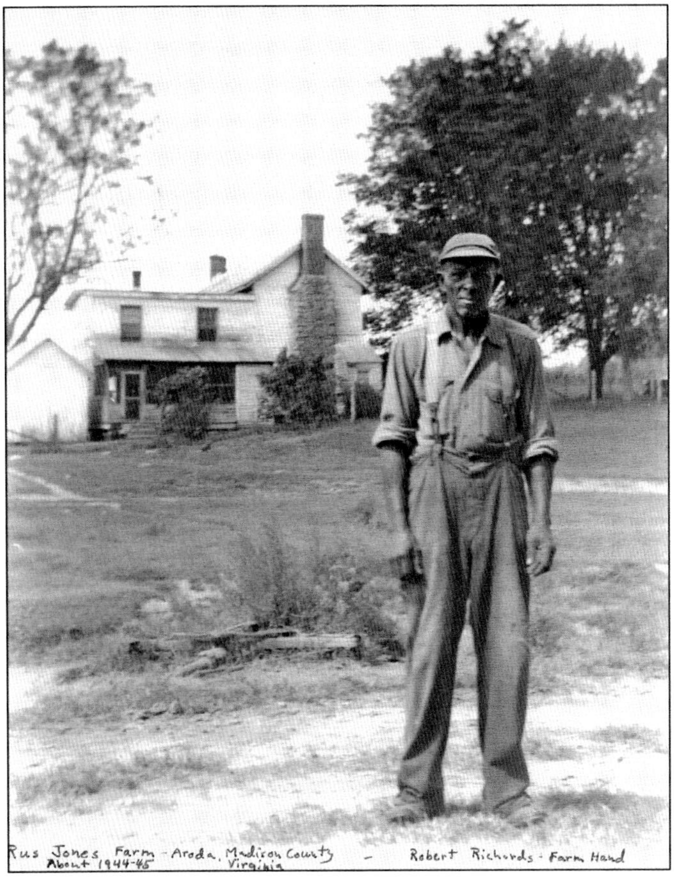

Robert Richards interrupts his work on the Jones farm in Aroda to pose for a photographer in the 1940s. Richards worked for Russ and Carlton Jones and Paul Lohr for many years. His wife, "Aunt" Millie Richards, helped in the Jones house and the Joneses took care of her in her later years. Richards was Madison supervisor James Arrington's uncle. (Photograph by Bob Humphrey, courtesy of David Jones.)

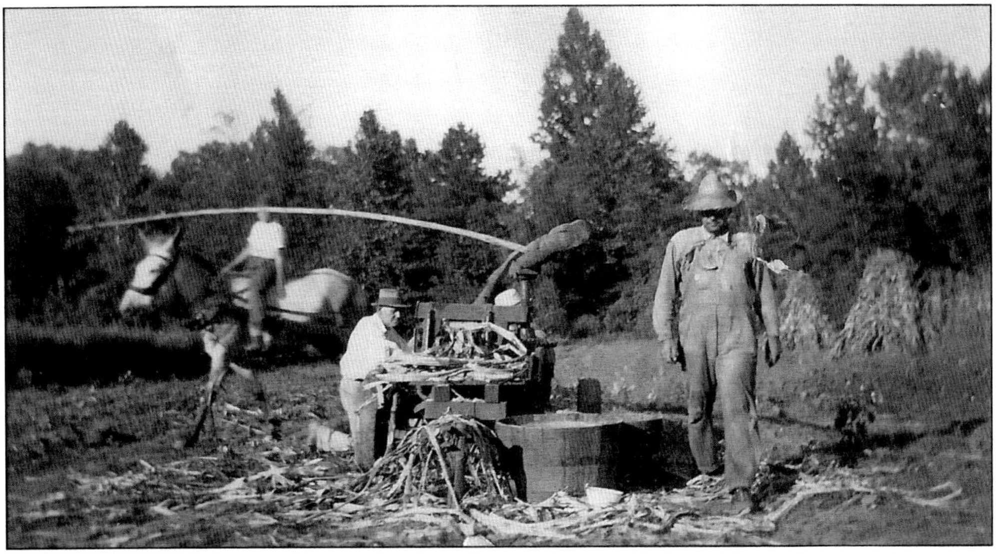

The owner of a sorghum mill moved it from farm to farm to help neighbors harvest their cane. In this c. 1942 photograph, the mill squeezes the juice from the cane as the operator, Judson Brockman, feeds it into the rollers. The mill was owned by Dewey Hoffman (right). Shirley Fishback rides the mule as it turns the mill. (Shirley S. Fishback.)

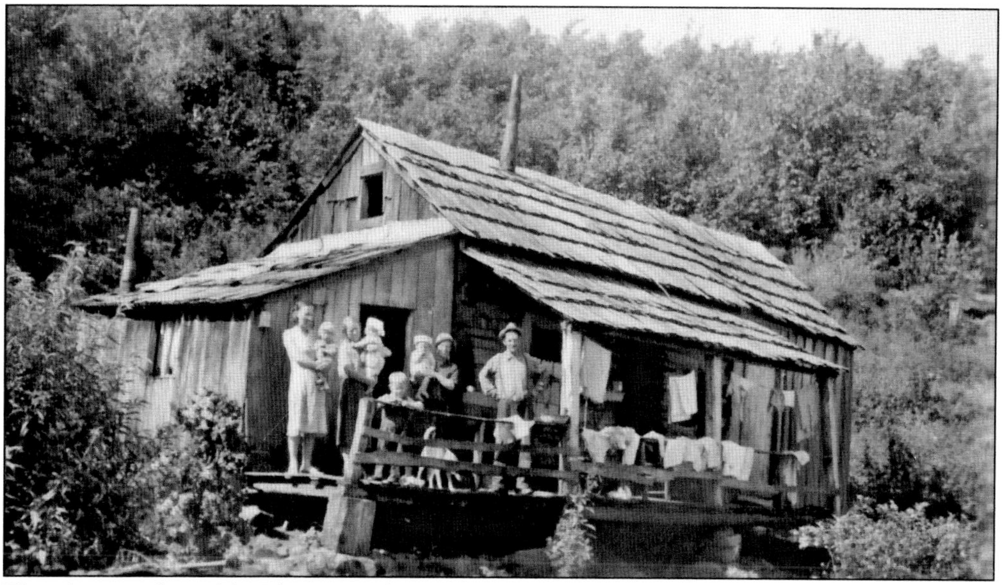

This photograph is of the Thomas Zachary Breeden family at their home in Dark Hollow. Standing on the porch are his three daughters and his grandchildren. Laundry is seen drying in the clean mountain air. This was one of the families that moved from the mountains when Shenandoah National Park was created. (Harold Woodward.)

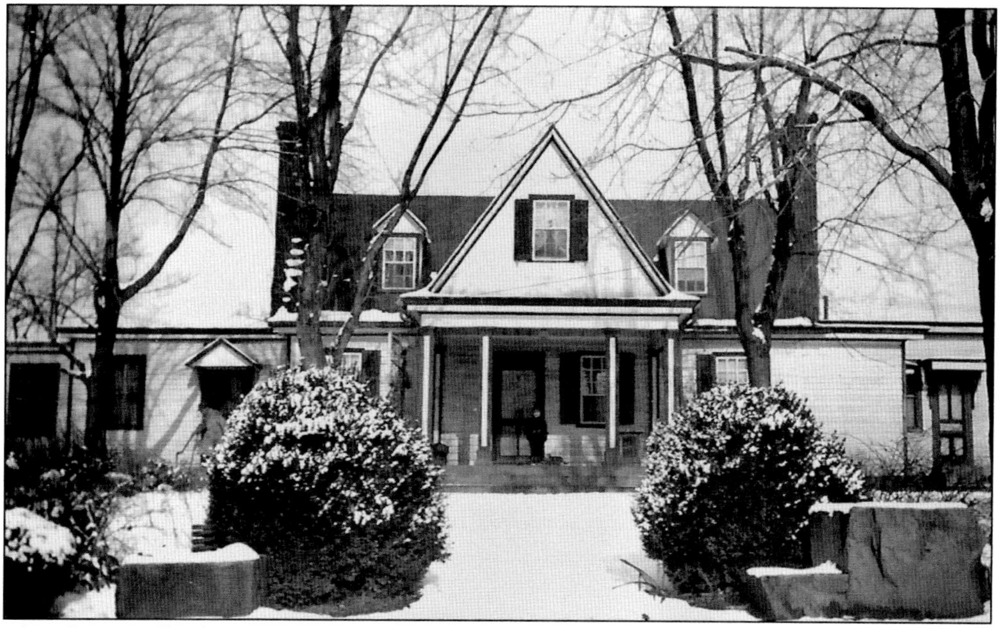

This photograph of Greenway, once called Prospect Hill, was taken in 1940. Greenway was built in the late 1700s by Francis Madison, brother of Pres. James Madison. Greenway stands near Madison Mills. The farm has been owned and worked by the descendants of Francis Madison since 1784. (Gilbert Queitzsch.)

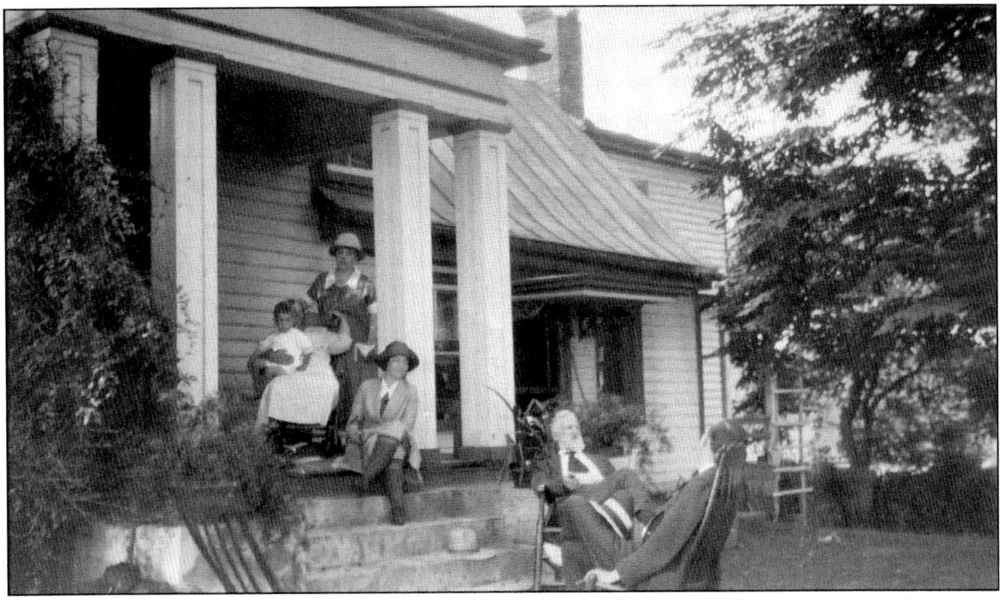

The oldest section of Belle Plaine, near Locust Dale, was built around 1760. In this *c.* 1923 picture, members of the Hill family relax on the front porch. The gentleman with the beard is Roland Flint Hill and the little boy sitting on his grandmother's lap is Roland Flint Hill III. The property has been in the Hill family since 1885. (Debbie C. Hill.)

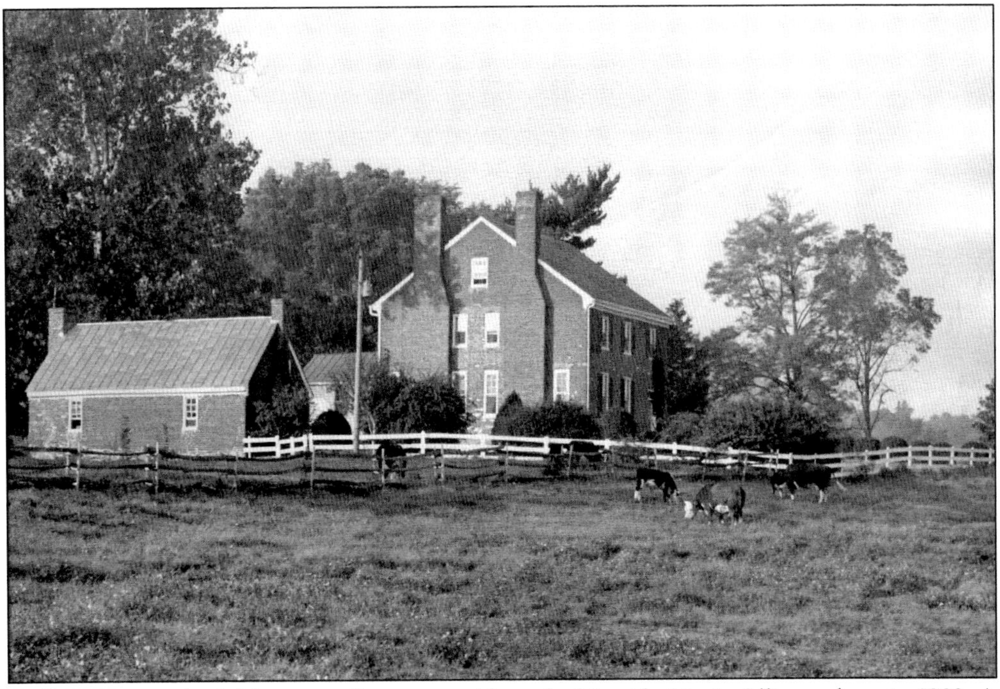

William Kemper built Mountain Prospect and brought his wife, Marie Allison, there in 1802. A brick cottage near the house was built first and was later used as the kitchen and servant quarters. At one time there were close to 1,200 acres in the property. James L. Kemper, son of William, was a general in the Confederate army and later governor of Virginia from 1874 to 1878. (Photograph by James S. C. Burke, courtesy of Madison County Historical Society.)

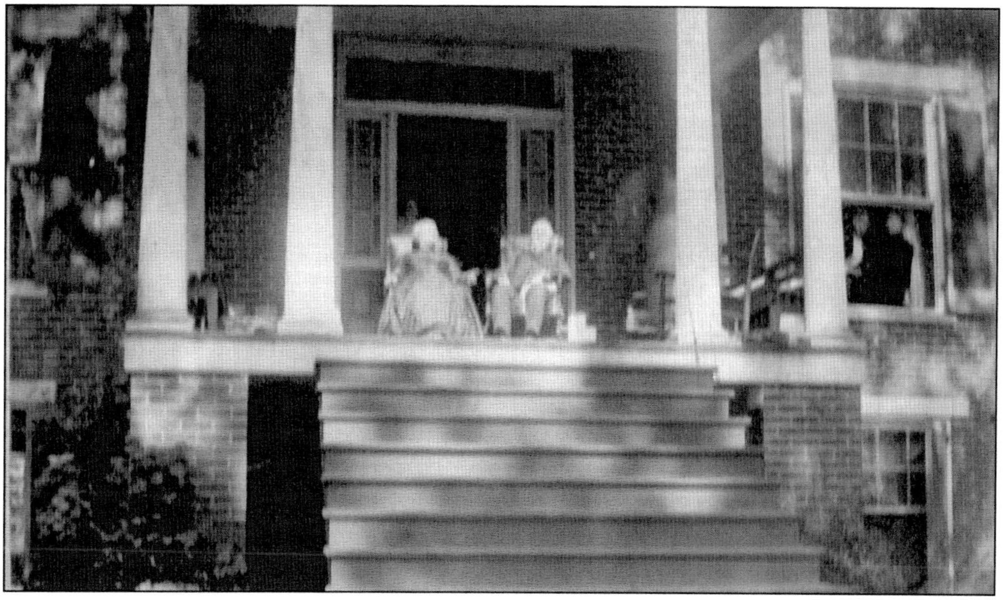

Another farm near Locust Dale is Glendalough. It was built in 1848 by Dr. William Alexander Hill of brick burned on the plantation by slave labor. Hill and his wife, Judith Booten Hill, sit on the porch at Gleandalough around 1887. In the window are Anna Lee and Julia Henry Hill. (Frank Gray.)

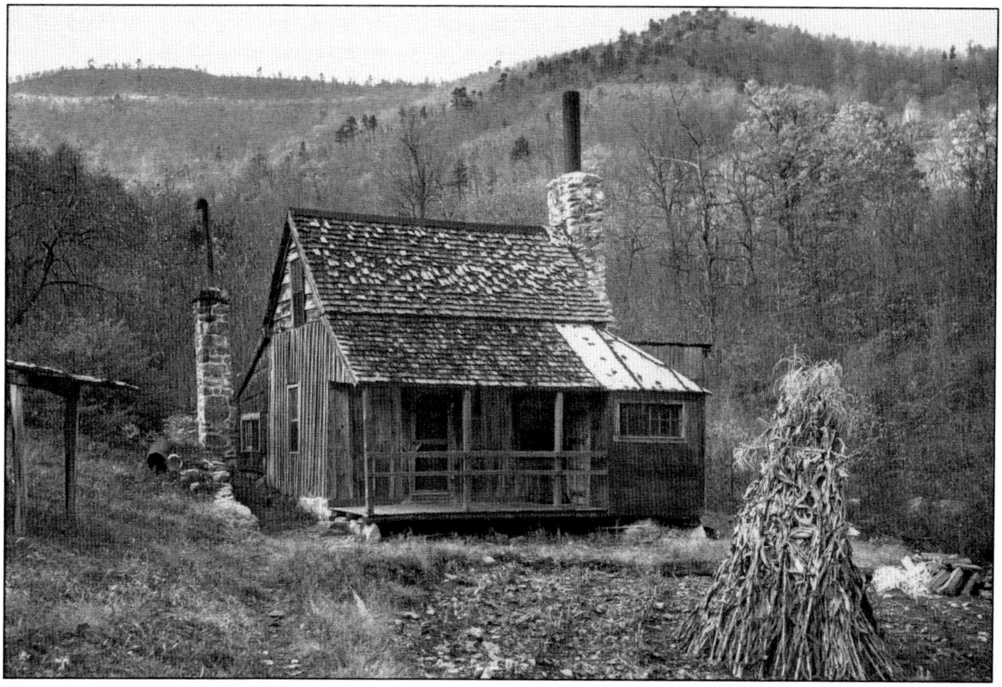

This Corbin Hollow home and farm belonged to a mountain family that had to resettle when Shenandoah National Park was established. The photograph is one of many taken for the Farm Security Administration. It appears to have been taken in the late fall with hoar frost on the tree tops on the mountain side. (Photograph by Arthur Rothstein, courtesy of Madison County Historical Society.)

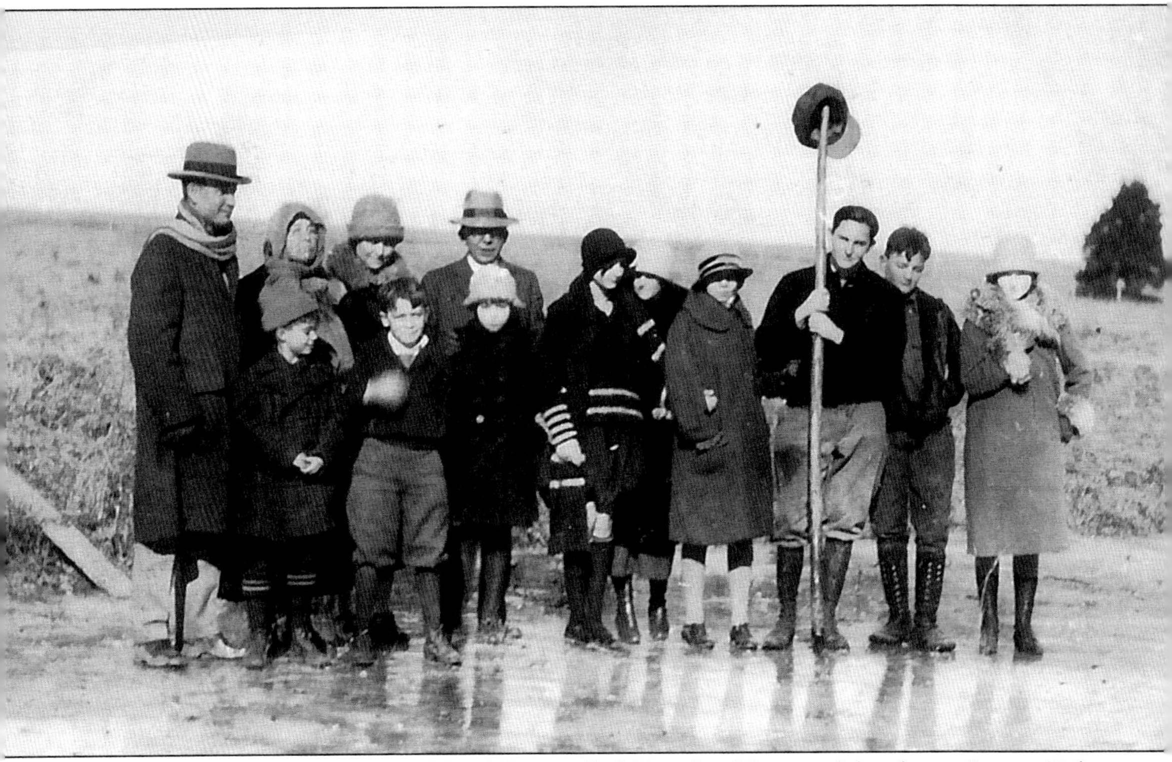

The W. O. Smith family of Oakland (now called Heartland Institute) lived near Locust Dale on the road to Rapidan. Here they gather at the ice pond in 1915 to cut ice. The ice from this shallow pond was than hauled to the ice house and used to cool milk and other perishable foods all summer long. (John Storey.)

Ten

Sports and Recreation

Madison County High School has less than 700 students, yet it fields teams in 10 sports. The school is always a contender for state recognition in any sport but it has excelled in football and basketball. In 2010, Madison County High School (MCHS) was the group A, division 1 state champion in boys basketball. Girls' teams have also been successful in basketball and soccer.

Part of the school's athletic success is almost surely due to the enthusiastic support of the community, whether from alumni or newcomer residents who become caught up in the excitement of success. On game night the stands are full. MCHS also regularly fields a strong and well-coached baseball team. Madison County residents love baseball, high school or otherwise. In the 1930s and 1950s, five Madison County players were good enough to be spotted by major league scouts and invited to join major league organizations. Their names have gone down in Madison County history—Carl Yowell, Dinwiddie Tucker, Jim Kite, Mayo Yowell, and Billy Mitchell.

In addition to organized sports, Madisonians have many other recreational activities from which to choose. The cold mountain streams offer great fly-fishing opportunities. Hunting is good, as deer and black bear are plentiful. Many mountain trails challenge both hikers and horsemen. A climb up Old Rag Mountain is an impressive and thrilling endeavor for old and young alike.

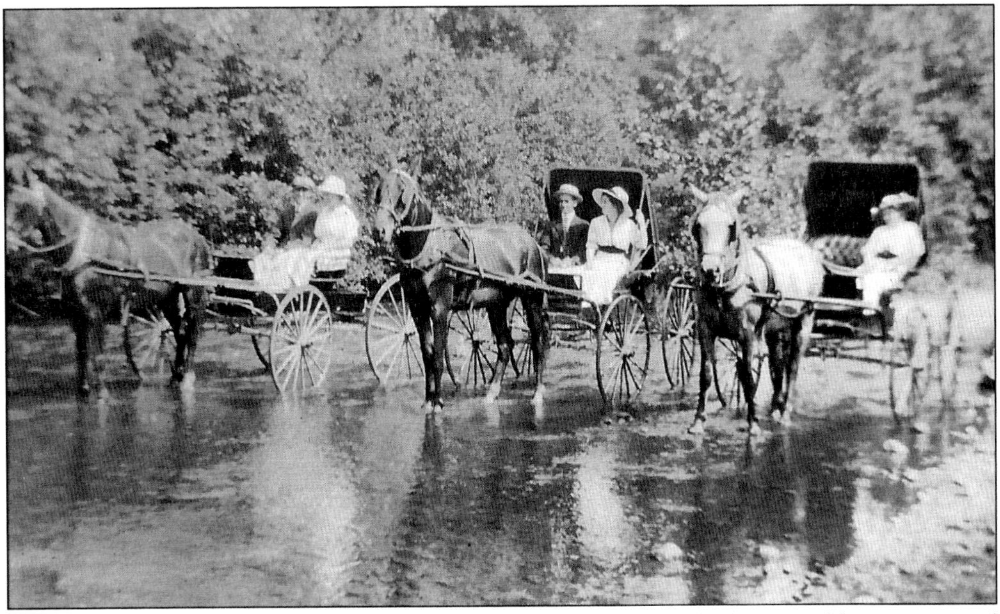

Brown Thorton, Otis Berry, and friends take their Sunday outing by horse and buggy, pictured here around 1918. It was a fine day and everyone dressed for the drive. The ladies wore big hats and the men wore straw boater hats. The gentleman driving the rig on the left has apparently waded across the run to take the picture. (Nan Coppedge.)

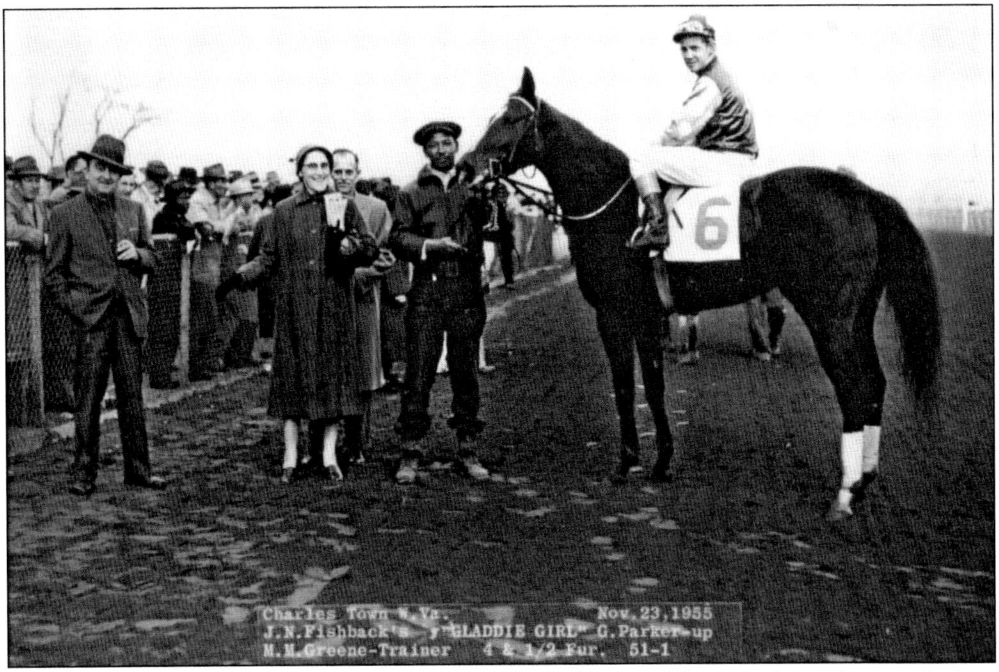

Jesse and Gladys Fishback of Madison owned and raced horses. They are shown here with their mare Gladdie Girl at the racecourse in Charles Town, West Virginia, in 1955. G. Parker is the jockey and Herbert Walker is the groom. Flat racing was uncommon in the Madison County area and one had to go a distance to find it. Steeplechase races over fences were more frequently seen. (Steve Hoffman.)

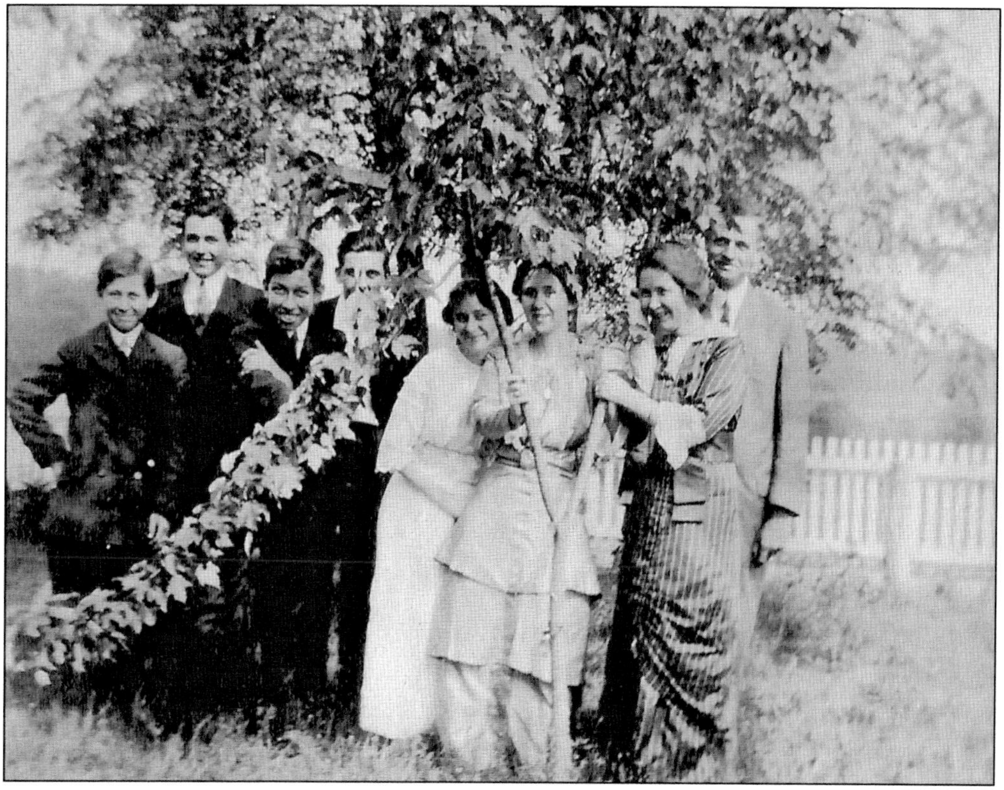

Picnics and gatherings like this May Day celebration were high moments in the social life of Madison County. Country folk learned to entertain themselves. They made up reasons for parties, created their own decorations, and supplied their own refreshments. The fashionable clothes may have been a bit restrictive, but that didn't inhibit the outdoor picnics and games. (Nan Coppedge.)

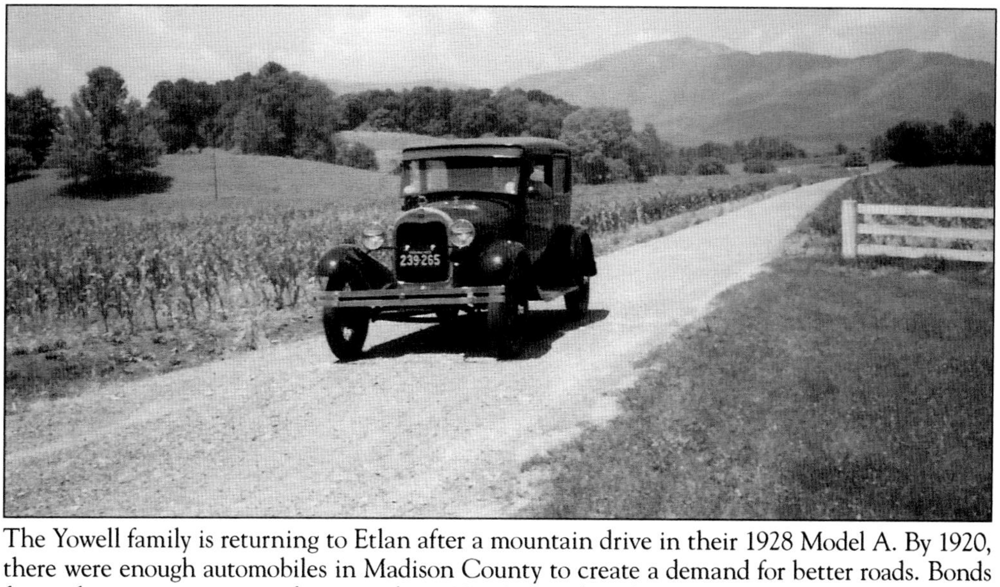

The Yowell family is returning to Etlan after a mountain drive in their 1928 Model A. By 1920, there were enough automobiles in Madison County to create a demand for better roads. Bonds for road improvement were first issued in 1921. A paved road connecting Madison and Orange was completed in 1935. (Barbara Yowell.)

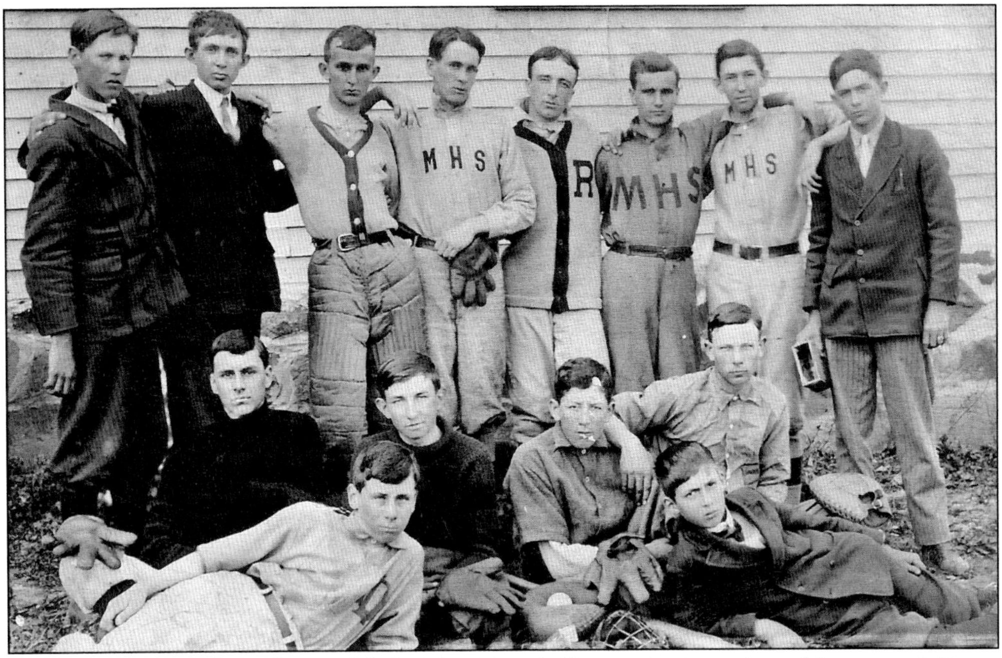

The 1910–1911 Madison County High School baseball team is pictured on this postcard. Some of those pictured, in no particular order, are catcher J. J. Fray, pitcher J. J. White, first baseman Jesse Blankenbaker, second baseman Dan Crigler, and third baseman Willie Huddle. Norman Carpenter played shortstop, Brooke Thrift right field, Max Huddle center field, and Oscar Smith left field. Carl Yowell pitched. (Sarah Henshaw.)

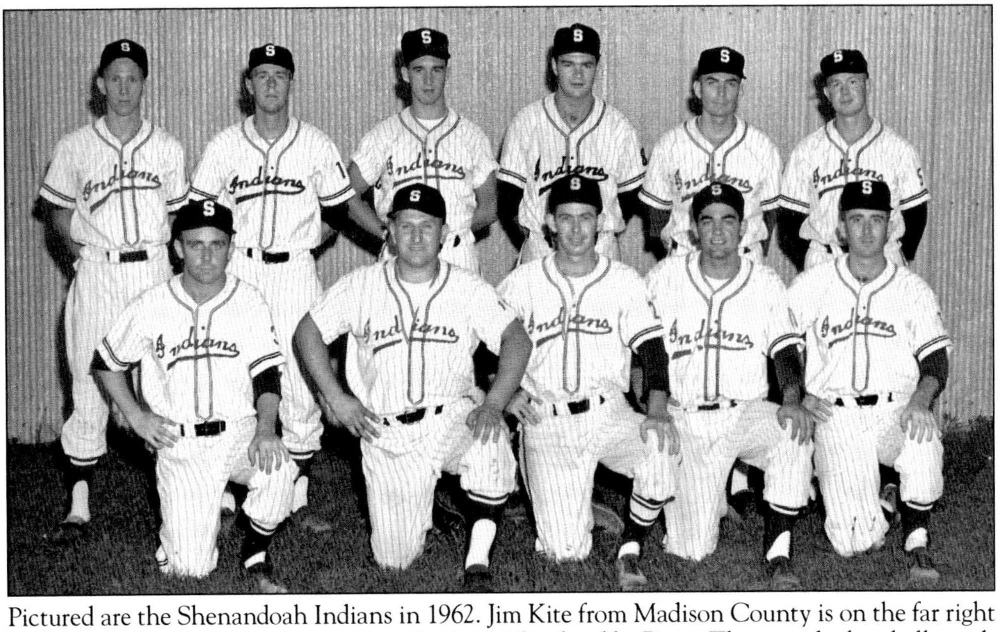

Pictured are the Shenandoah Indians in 1962. Jim Kite from Madison County is on the far right in the back row. Kite, a pitcher, was coached in high school by Rosey Thomas, the baseball coach at Fork Union Academy. He was on the way to the big leagues but chronic pain from an earlier shoulder injury forced his retirement. He then turned to a successful business selling country hams. (Shirley and James Kite.)

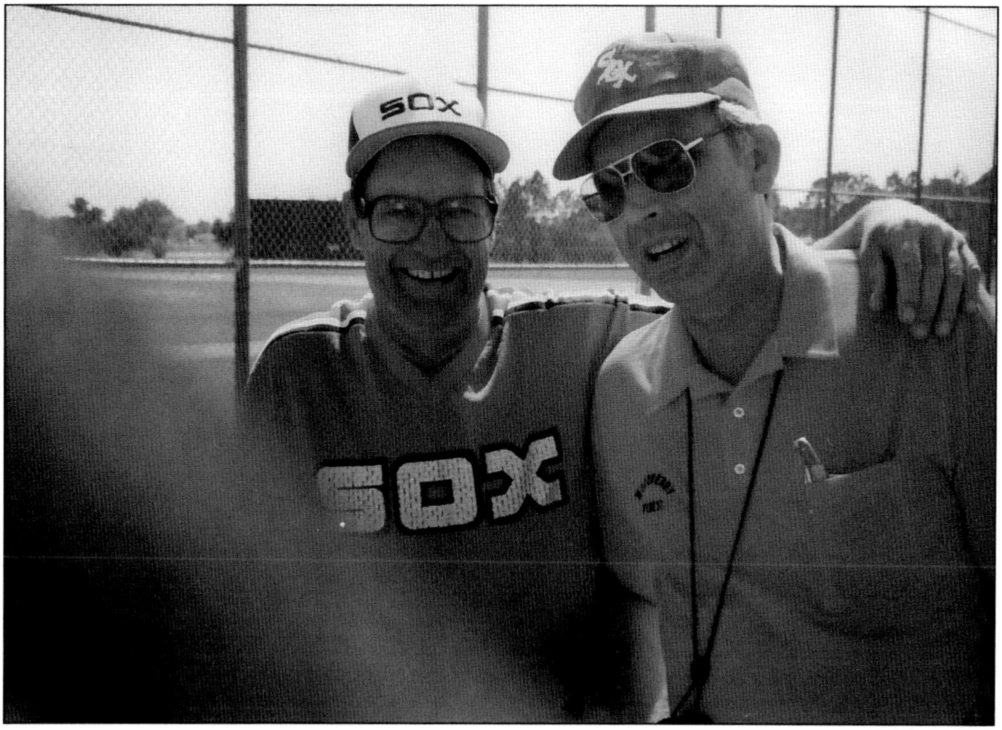

Walter Mayo Yowell (right) is pictured here with Bobby Winkles, manager of the Chicago White Sox. Yowell's great throwing arm was discovered when he played baseball for the University of Richmond in the early 1950s. He almost made it to the major leagues and he pitched on minor league teams for both the White Sox and the St. Louis Cardinals before an injury ended his career. (Mayo Yowell.)

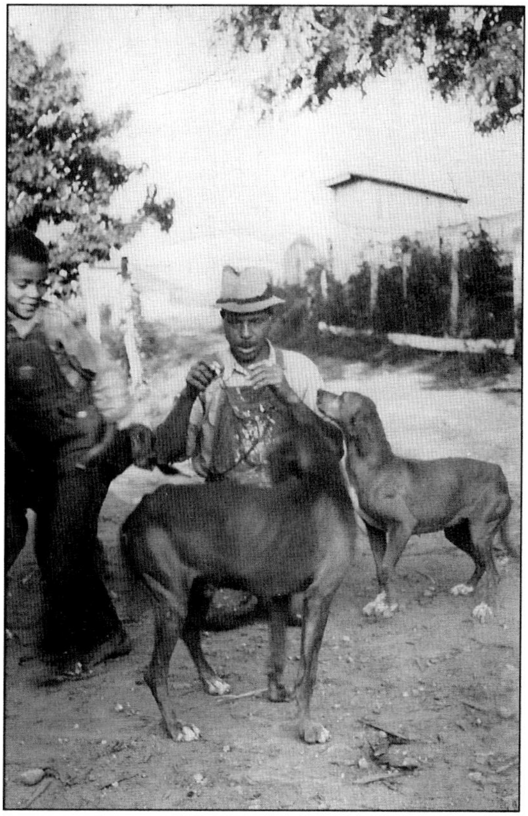

Dan Washington, who farmed near Criglersville, set great store by his Redbone hounds, known to be great raccoon hunters. Coon hunting is most often done at night with friends and a good number of dogs. Hunting is an important sport to many Madisonians, with deer and bear being the most popular. (Flora R. Washington.)

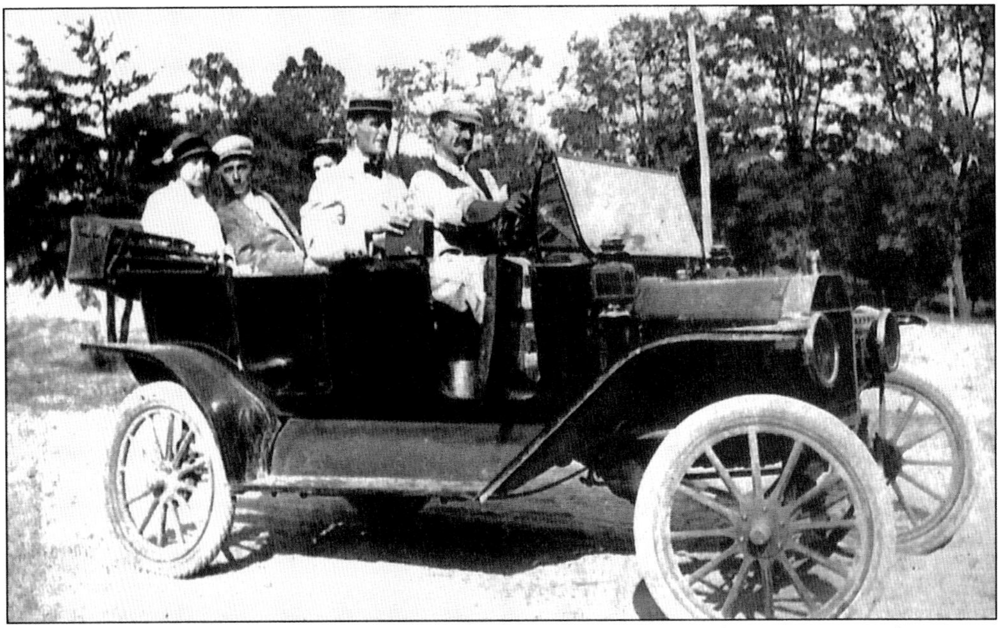

Madison roads were not very smooth in the early days, but by the time this picture was taken, some roads had been macadamized and were substantially better. These friends are returning from a trip to Luray Caverns. In the back seat, from left to right, are Elizabeth Hale, Waverly Yowell, and Florence Brown. In the front seat are Mike Kipps (left) and Turner Mitchell. (Betty Lynn Yowell.)

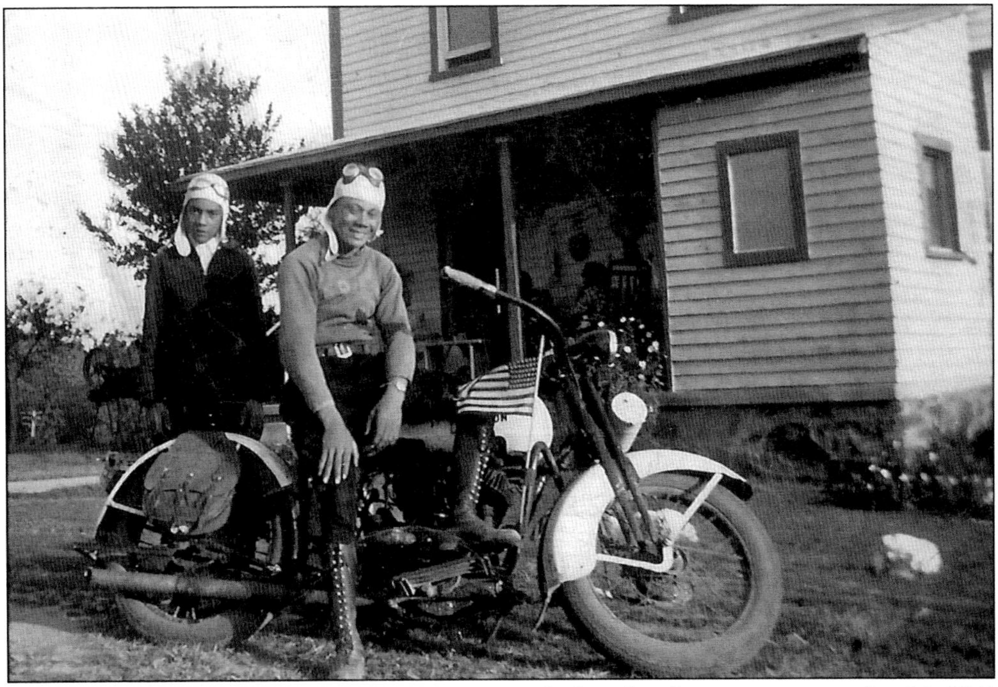

In rural Madison County, entertainment was mostly found in homegrown ways. In this 1941 photograph, James (left) and Carl Washington are getting ready to take a spin on their motorcycle. Night racing along country roads in vintage cars was another sport indulged in until the sheriff's department put an end to it. (Flora R. Washington.)

Madison County boasted a lot of fine baseball players in the 1950s. This list included Jim Kite, Billy Mitchell, Mayo Yowell, and Ernest Utz—all of whom were pitchers and all of whom were associated with major league organizations. Carl Yowell, a pitcher, and Dinwiddie Tucker, a heavy hitter, played in the 1930s. They too were placed with major league organizations. (Helen Robertson.)

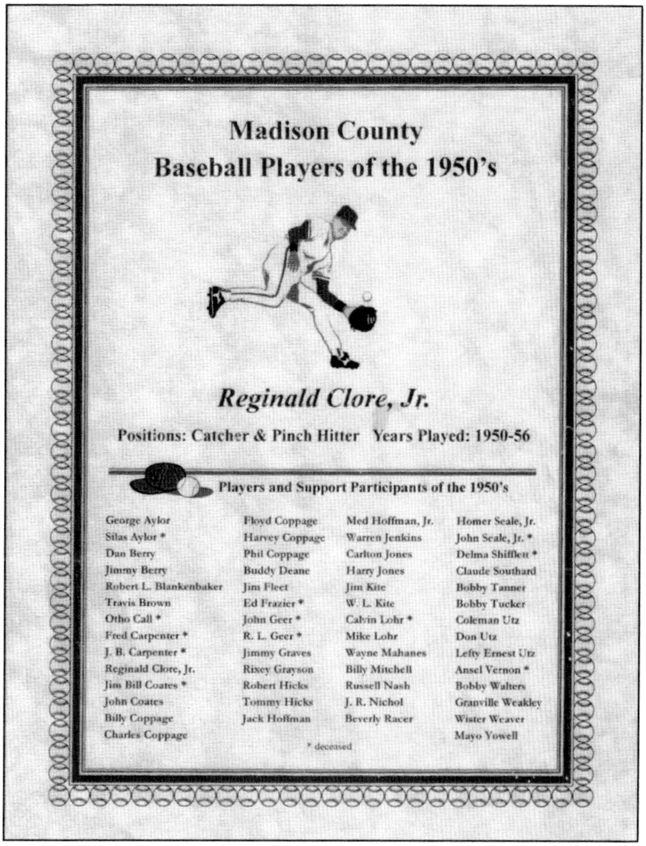

This is Madison County's Billy Mitchell warming up during spring training with the Detroit Tigers in Lakeland, Florida, in 1957. He suffered a torn rotator cuff a year later, which ended his chance for a major league career, but the injury made it possible for him to come home and be Madison County High School's revered baseball coach for many years afterward. (Bill Mitchell.)

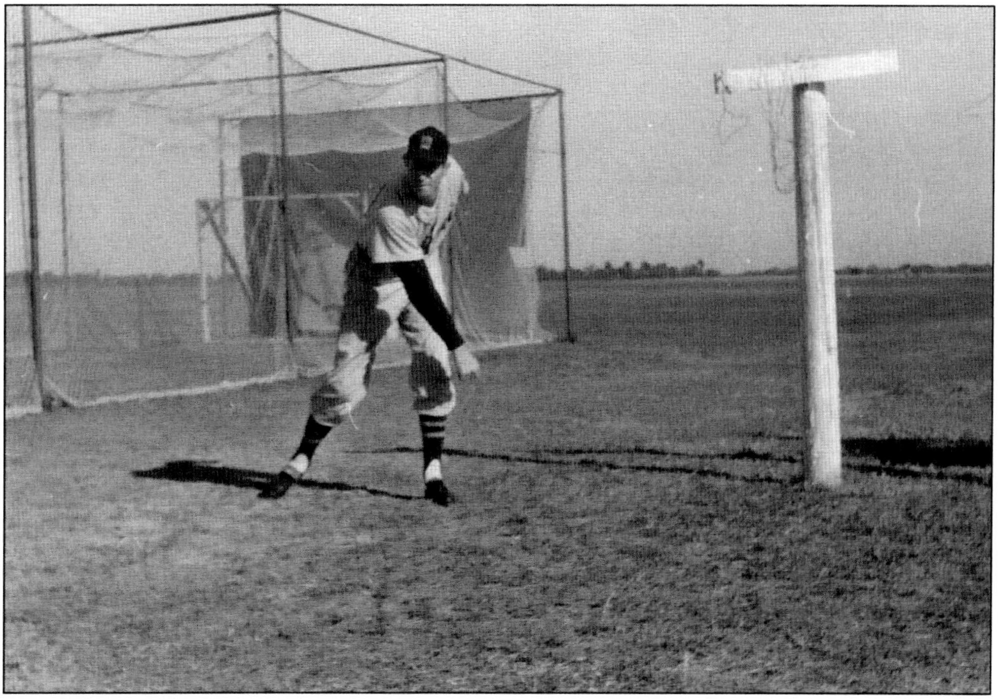

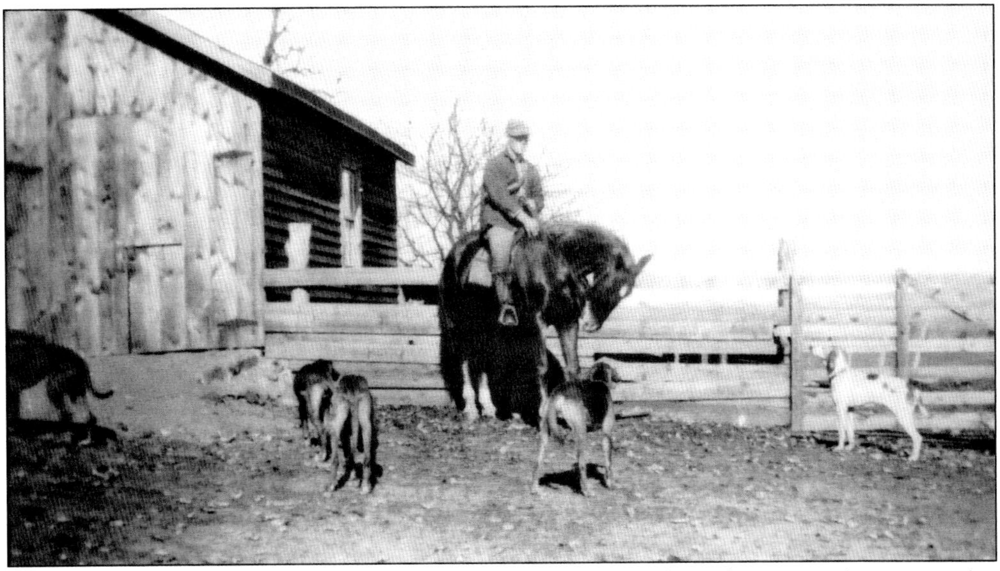

Charles Smith of Hood gathers his dogs for a fox hunt. "Riding to hounds" is a popular sport in this part of Virginia. Foxes are native and there are a few hunts not far from Madison. Charlie Smith liked riding alone. His daughter said, "He just went out with his dogs and hunted foxes." (Carole Milks.)

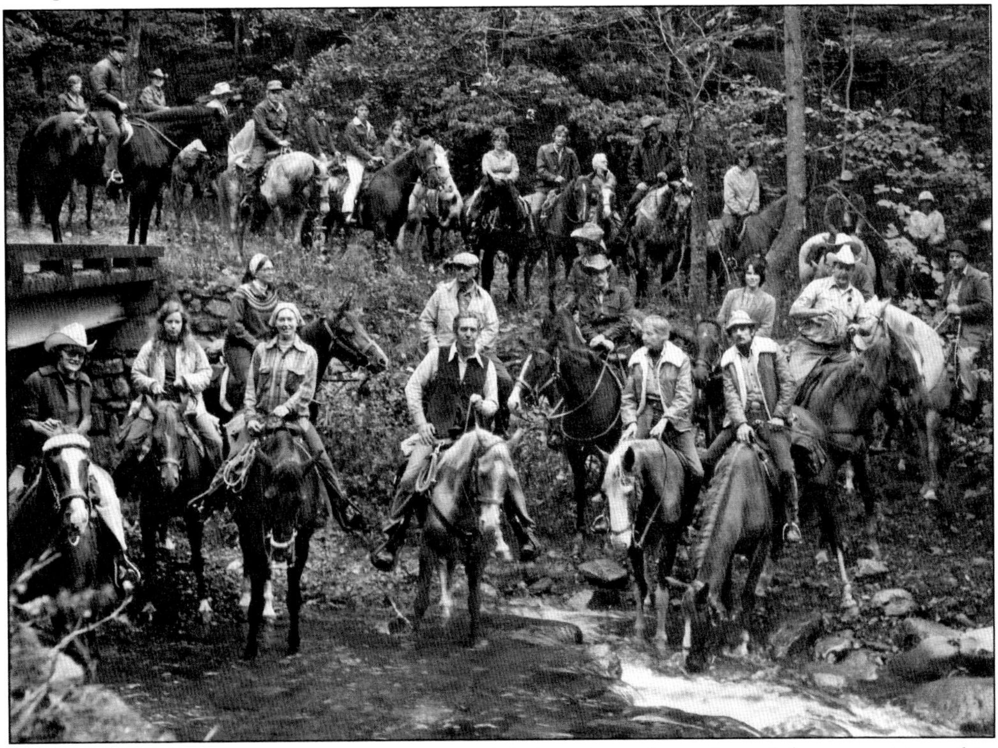

Horseback riding is a favorite activity of many Madisonians. A number of them participated in the Spotswood bicentennial memorial ride from Germanna in Orange County through Madison County to Stanley in the Shenandoah Valley in 1976, camping all along the way. Horseback riders enjoy riding the mountain trails in the park as well as over the gravel roads and trails in other parts of the county. (Jennie Hill Robinson.)

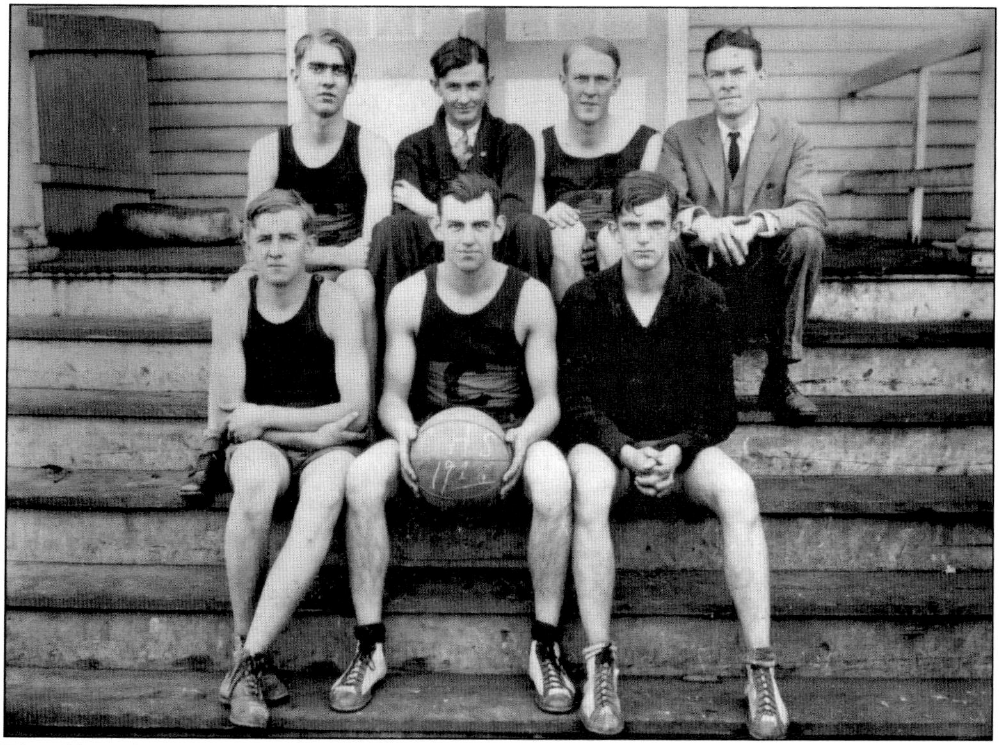

The old Criglersville High School basketball team poses for this photograph in about 1929. From left to right are (first row) John Richard Clore, Lindsey Rossen, and Thomas Clore; (second row) George Green Henshaw, Lewis Smith, Joseph Holden Henshaw, and Dr. Estes, the principal and coach. (Sarah Henshaw.)

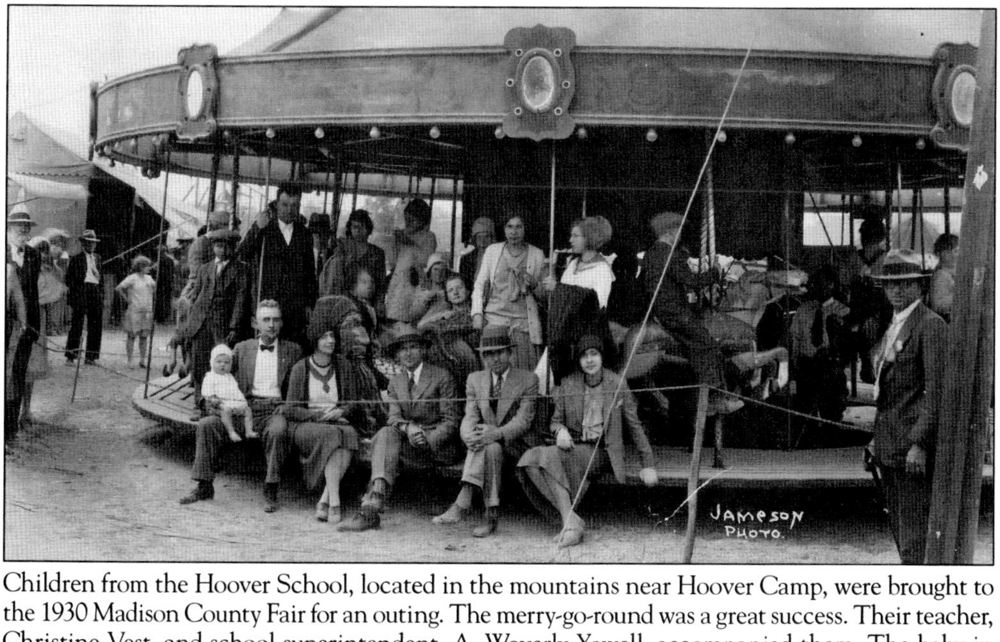

Children from the Hoover School, located in the mountains near Hoover Camp, were brought to the 1930 Madison County Fair for an outing. The merry-go-round was a great success. Their teacher, Christine Vest, and school superintendent, A. Waverly Yowell, accompanied them. The baby in Yowell's lap is Mayo Yowell. Sheriff Tom Lillard stands by the pole at the right. (Barbara Yowell.)